SERGEANT NIBLEY PhD

SERGEANT NIBLEY PhD

MEMORIES OF AN UNLIKELY
SCREAMING EAGLE

HUGH NIBLEY AND ALEX NIBLEY

SHADOW
MOUNTAIN

For the Swedish widow's daughter,

who made it all possible.

Photographs on the pages listed are from the following sources:
Nibley family collection: 1, 3, 6, 8, 15, 23, 33, 37, 47, 57, 263, 301, 322, 323, 330, 338; Utah State University Special Collections: 7; Paul E. Springer collection: 11, 35, 320; Theda Lucille Bassett collection: 18; Marguerite Goldschmidt collection: 65; Jack Gieck: 74; Alex Nibley: 122, 209, 316, 332, 336; Boyd Peterson (original painting owned by Nadine Nibley): 199. All other photographs courtesy the National Archive.

Visit us at shadowmountain.com

Library of Congress Cataloging-in-Publication Data
Nibley, Hugh, 1910–
   Sergeant Nibley, Ph. D. / [edited by] Alex Nibley.
       p.   cm.
   Includes bibliographical references and index.
   ISBN-10 1-57345-845-7 (alk. paper)
   ISBN-13 978-1-57345-845-0 (alk. paper)
   1. Nibley, Hugh, 1910–   2. United States. Army. Airborne Division, 101st.
3. World War, 1939–1945—Military intelligence—United States.   4. World War, 1939–1945—Campaigns—Western Front.   5. World War, 1939–1945—Personal narratives, American.   6. Intelligence officers—United States—Biography.
7. Mormons—United States—Biography.   I. Nibley, Alex.   II. Title.
D769.346101st .N53 2006
940.54'8673092—dc22   2005036505

Printed in the United States of America
Publishers Printing, Salt Lake City, UT

10 9 8 7 6 5 4 3 2 1

CONTENTS

INTRODUCTION

Hugh Nibley did not want to write his memoirs. We—his children, his wife and his colleagues—advised, begged, cajoled, threatened, and employed various other verbs of persuasion and compulsion to get him to write them. It had no effect.

"Dad," I said on several occasions, "you have made a long career out of mining the historical accounts left by others. You owe your professional life to those who wrote down what they saw over the centuries. Now you have lived through ninety percent of the twentieth century during which you had a front row seat to the most cataclysmic events in all human history. It would be nothing short of criminal for you leave no record behind of what you witnessed. At least write down your memories of the war." He would nod and shrug and say he might get to it once his other, more important, work was done. He was close to ninety and had been working for well over a decade on a project with no end in sight. I didn't have much hope.

"If you won't do it," I said, "I will. I have the interviews we shot on 16 mm in '83, I have the conversations we recorded on Utah Beach in '84, if you will sit down in front of a camera and talk to me some more, I will record your memories and edit them together and write your memoirs for you." Hugh Nibley enjoyed intellectual sparring, but personal confrontations like this made him uncomfortable, and he realized I wasn't going to give up. He agreed to talk to me in front of a camera.

I recorded several sessions with him, starting in 1998 and continuing up to a few months before his death in 2005. Like other veterans I've heard of, the older he got the more willing he was to talk about the war. The problem was that he almost never gave me any of his stories in anything like a complete form. He would tell small snippets of anecdotes, switching from one place and time to another, flitting from this story to that like a hummingbird. I got an incident here and a detail there, but in the end I was left with a huge jigsaw puzzle with lots of pieces missing.

I began to read about the war. This was also a problem because there is just so much written about World War II that I could spend a lifetime studying and they would just keep publishing more books faster than I could ever read them. I am not a historian (or any other kind of scholar for that matter) and I wasn't trying to write a definitive historical work on the war, I just wanted to record my father's experience to understand what he had experienced in order to know him better. But what I got from him was so fragmented I had to somehow find a way to stitch it together into something that made some sort of sense.

When I met with Shadow Mountain and they agreed to publish the memoirs, Sheri Dew, the head of Shadow Mountain, asked me how much time I would need to finish the manuscript. Six months, I said with a confident nod. Truth is, at that point I was thinking of adding extra material in the margins such as photographs, maps, and poems partly because I felt they made the war experience more accessible, but also because I wasn't sure I had enough memoir to make a respectable volume of text. Six months and five years later I staggered back to Shadow Mountain with a manuscript and a few hundred photos and we began to discuss how to keep the book from getting too big.

As I said before, I am not a historian nor, for that matter, a writer of books. My training is in film and I followed my cinematic instincts and pieced this book together like a documentary film. The problem of the fragmented stories I approached by piecing together composites of several partial tellings of the story I got in various interviews combined with accounts that sometimes appeared in his letters. Since Dad always underplayed the violence and drama of the situations he was in, I have borrowed from the memoirs of others to supply the kind of visceral detail that didn't play a big part in Dad's recollections. While making a documentary about Dad in 1983–84, I had interviewed his friends Paul Springer and Lucien Goldschmidt, and those interviews provided some pieces of the puzzle. The memoirs of other friends he knew in the military, George Bailey, George Allen, and Max Oppenheimer were also very useful. It wasn't all the pieces of the puzzle, but I thought it might be enough that a picture might begin to emerge from the jumble. When I began reading my father's letters written in the late thirties and early forties, I found things I hadn't wanted to find. My immediate reaction was: I can never publish this! The next reaction was less instinctive: If it makes me feel that strongly, I have to publish it, like it or not.

After he was confined to his bed in 2003, I began reading Dad chapters of his memoirs. He was disturbed to hear the chapter on his pre-war letters, as I had been when I wrote it. He lost sleep over it. After I had read him the first several chapters there was a pause of a few weeks during which I continued to write but didn't go to read to him. One day I got a phone call. My mother was on the line.

"Your father wants to talk to you."

Dad didn't make phone calls very often. I had received few enough to count them on the fingers of one hand. Now, confined to bed, he had to get Mom to dial for him. He came on the line.

"I don't want you to publish this book."

"Okay, Dad, I'm not going to put your name on something that embarrasses you. If you say don't publish, I won't publish." Meanwhile I'm thinking, it's going on five years I've been bleeding for this manuscript, I started doing interviews twenty years ago, I've got thousands of hours invested in it and now he's telling me not to publish it? There was an uncomfortable pause.

"I have a new chapter," I said. "It's the Holland invasion. Want me to come read it to you?"

"Well, yes, that would be nice."

It was not in Hugh Nibley's nature to call his son and say, "You haven't been around lately, I want to hear more of what you're writing about me. Please come read to me, I'm tired of sitting in this bed watching CNN." But that's what he really wanted.

He was still very uneasy about all the letters. He was sickened by the arrogance of what he had written when he was young. Another thing that bothered him was the anger he had expressed at the Germans at the end of the war. It was my mother who persuaded him that, pretty or not, these were parts of history and the formative process that made him who he eventually became. With her support he agreed to have these less than admirable parts of himself exposed to the public. To me, knowing him as I do, that was an act of courage on a par with those that win medals in battle.

Hugh Nibley listened to me read a complete manuscript of this book and agreed to have it published under both our names. Since the draft I read to him I have made some changes and included some extra marginalia and deleted of some repetitive material. The book as it appears here is essentially what he approved with two exceptions: the last chapter, which I wrote after he died, and the chapter on his pre-war letters. In the earlier draft I had included more of my own criticism of his letters, and I was quite harsh, which is one of the reasons that chapter bothered him so much. At the gentle suggestion of Emily Watts, a wise and gracious editor at Shadow Mountain, I reexamined that chapter and decided to tone down my preaching and left the readers to make more of their own judgments. So the only substantial difference between the draft Hugh Nibley approved and the final version is that he gave his go-ahead for a book that was more critical of him.

Hugh Nibley was not a military type of person. But then, neither were most of the men who fought World War II. He enlisted as a private at the age of thirty-two, even though he had several years of ROTC training. He became a master-sergeant in Intelligence where he was assigned to an elite Order of Battle team. He thought this would keep him in an intellectual capacity analyzing information far from the battlefront, but instead he was attached to the 101st Airborne Division and found himself with the now famous "Screaming Eagle" patch on his shoulder. He was with the 101st through their baptism by fire in Normandy, where the division was tasked with some of the toughest fighting including the capture of Carentan, the first French town to be liberated in the invasion. After a brief break in England, the 101st were sent into Holland for what was intended to be a lightening-quick operation that would get the Allies across the Rhine in a few short days. But after seventy-two days of steady combat, the 101st were replaced, and the operation never achieved its original objective. The day the 101st set out for their historic defense of Bastogne in the Battle of the Bulge, Hugh Nibley was sent to help British Intelligence track down Germans infiltrating Allied lines in American uniforms. The two men who replaced him in the 101st both died there in Bastogne, where the commander of the division gave his famous reply to the German surrender demand: "Nuts!"

I have been told by some who have read the manuscript for this book that it is not for the squeamish. I'm not sure if that is a criticism or a compliment. War is the most hideous of all human creations and this is a book about war. During my research I spent several days in the National Archives looking at thousands of photographs from the war. Even for someone who has a fascination with World War II, as I do, it is not *a cheerful experience. In one single day I spent over ten hours looking at hundreds of images from concentration camps and battlefields. I left exhausted and drained, and that was after less than a full day and without the sounds, the smells, the hunger, cold, heat, and terror that photographs can never convey but are very much a part of the real war experience. This book is about war. I have not sought to sensationalize the war, but any book that gets anywhere near the reality of war must include some material that is not comfortable to read. I think it is a good thing not to be comfortable with some things. And I think it is essential that we not forget them to the point that we can become comfortable with repeating them.*

Racism is usually a part of war, and it was a big part of World War II. Racism and anti-Semitism was very strong in pre-war America. In the case of those races whose countries we were fighting in the war, the country worked hard to fan the flames of hatred as part of the war effort. I should also point out that this book deals only with the European war, and with only a part of that. But this was a worldwide war and American racism was much stronger against the Japanese than against the Germans. As Hugh Nibley lived among the Germans before the war, I lived in Japan after the war and listened to my friends tell how their families died from bombs dropped by the fathers of other friends of mine. I saw the son of a commando who was tortured by the Japanese baptize a man who had been trained to be a Kamikaze pilot. So I was shocked, in doing my research, to see the virulence of hatred against the Japanese that not only existed, but was actively promoted by our government in its campaign to dehumanize the Japanese. The publishers of this book expressed strong reservations that some of the examples of racism I wanted to include could be more offensive than enlightening. They were concerned that including racist elements would do violence to the belief that all human beings are children of God, equally deserving of love and respect. I agree that there is a fine balance to be struck between exploiting past racist attitudes in a way that sensationalizes them and, at the other extreme, trying to revise history to make it more palatable. We have tried to find that balance by including some samples of the racist propaganda that was so prevalent before and during World War II without dwelling on it to the point of exploitation. In reality it was much worse than it appears in this book.

A standard disclaimer in a war memoir is that memory is a tricky thing. What I have recorded here is World War II as Hugh Nibley remembered it, supplemented by the memories and historical research of others. And memories are often inaccurate. Even historical research often yields inaccuracies. As a researcher and a writer, Hugh Nibley was meticulous in backing up his work with masses of evidence and I think this is one of the reasons he balked at the idea of memoir writing. In my research I discovered many errors in his memories of the events of six decades earlier. Certain characters were assigned the wrong ranks or jobs, I would find a story he told as having happened in Normandy would have had to have taken place in Holland, and so forth. Most of the errors I found I have corrected, as Hugh Nibley would have done himself. In other cases I have added footnotes to explain that his memory is inconsistent with other accounts. There were also instances where his various versions of stories disagreed with each other in detail—for example, what was a .75 mm shell in one telling would be an .88 in another, and so forth. In these cases I have used either the most often used version or the one that made the most sense to me based on my research. Some of these details are certainly erroneous, but I hope that will not detract from the essence of the stories.

The world is full of people who know much more than I (or Hugh Nibley) about World War II and who are sure to find other errors and who may disagree with this portrayal of the events. I apologize in advance for those errors I have not detected and remind the reader that this is not necessarily the war exactly as it was, but as Hugh Nibley remembered it. The essence of memoir is what the person remembered, and what our minds choose to hold on to says a lot about us. In the end, the memoir may tell us more about the person who remembers than it does about the remembered events.

1

THE SEEDS OF WAR

The story begins long before the young professor signed the papers and took the oath that made him a soldier. It starts before Pearl Harbor slapped America awake, before Winston Churchill became prime minister of Great Britain, and before Roosevelt's election to the presidency. It starts way back, more than a decade before the German armies crashed into Poland and the war officially began. This war story begins in the late 1920s with two zealous young preachers in the southern regions of Germany. In many ways they were quite similar; in other ways they could not have been more different. Their names were Adolf Hitler and Hugh Nibley.

Hitler was an obscure politician, a failed artist preaching the doctrine of National Socialism in beer halls, parlors, wherever he could get anyone to listen. Nibley was a budding teenage intellectual, a poet and nature lover full of Emerson and Thoreau, preaching the gospel of Jesus Christ as defined by The Church of Jesus Christ of Latter-day Saints, which had sent him to Germany as a missionary at the age of seventeen. He too was teaching in parlors and on street corners, wherever he could get anyone to listen. Neither of them was born in Germany, but both believed the German model of culture, education, philosophy, science, and art was superior to all others. They both considered the work of Goethe, Schiller, Bach, Beethoven, and Brahms to be the examples the rest of

Hugh Nibley's passport photograph, age 17

Adolf Hitler, far left, as a corporal in the Great War

the world should follow. Both believed fervently in the doctrines they taught and worked hard at their proselytizing.

Hitler's preaching led to a national fervor that united, energized, and ultimately destroyed his country, killing scores of millions and laying waste to much of the world. Nibley's preaching gained a smattering of converts but mostly annoyed people. Adolf Hitler became a name known all over the world, a name that will always be identified with war and killing on a massive scale. Hugh Nibley became a name known mostly to people in the Mormon Church who read obscure books. He never got as much press as Hitler, and he is known among the Mormons who follow his work as a scholar and career curmudgeon who every now and then said startling things about life, culture, religion, and war.

Hitler's impact on Nibley's life was extreme—it drew him into a war that changed his life forever. Nibley's impact on Hitler? It's hard to say. Probably not much, at least directly. But if you think of Hugh Nibley as just one of several million who put their lives on the shelf and went to stop Hitler's rush for power, one of the many quirky individuals who never dreamed of soldiering but went out anyway and joined together to bring Hitler down, then maybe you can think of the Hugh Nibleys of the world as the ants that helped dismantle the great dragon of Nazism and reduce it to dust and memory.

HUGH NIBLEY: When I arrived in Germany in 1927 things weren't going so merry. They'd lost the Great War, and the French were occupying the Saar, and there were all sorts of pressure and worry. President Tadje, our mission president, was a marvelous man and in the first meeting we missionaries had with him he said, "You know, I won't be surprised to see all you boys in uniform in another five years."

Hugh Nibley, center rear, in Germany, circa 1928

"A SAD STORY OF COMPLICATED IDIOCY"

The Treaty of Versailles, June 28, 1919, was the official end of the World War I, the Great War, the "war to end all wars."

WINSTON CHURCHILL: When Marshal Foch heard of the signing of the Peace Treaty of Versailles he observed with singular accuracy: "This is not a peace. It is an Armistice for twenty years."

The economic clauses of the Treaty were malignant and silly to an extent that made them obviously futile. Germany was condemned to pay reparations on a fabulous scale. These dictates gave expression to the anger of the victors, and to the failure of their peoples to understand that no defeated nation or community can ever pay tribute on a scale which would meet the cost of modern war.

The multitudes remained plunged in ignorance of the simplest economic facts, and their leaders, seeking their votes, did not dare to undeceive them. The newspapers, after their fashion, reflected and emphasised the prevailing opinions. . . . No one in great authority had the wit, ascendancy, or detachment from public folly to declare these fundamental, brutal facts to the electorates; nor would anyone have been believed if he had. The triumphant Allies continued to assert that they would squeeze Germany "till the pips squeaked." All this had a potent bearing on the prosperity of the world and the mood of the German race. . . .

History will characterise all these transactions as insane. They helped to breed both the martial curse and the "economic blizzard." . . . All this is a sad story of complicated idiocy in the making of which much toil and virtue was consumed. . . .

The victors imposed upon the Germans all the long-sought ideals of the liberal nations of the West. They were relieved from the burden of compulsory military service and from the need of keeping up heavy armaments. The enormous American loans were presently pressed upon them, though they had no credit. A democratic constitution, in accordance with all the latest improvements, was established at Weimar. Emperors having been driven out, nonentities were elected. Beneath this flimsy fabric raged the passions of the mighty, defeated, but substantially uninjured German nation.[1]

He could see it, because the Treaty of Versailles was so unsatisfactory for the Germans they were going to raise hell.

It is possible that the two preachers crossed paths as they went through southern Germany distributing their tracts and conducting their lessons in cottages and on street corners.

HUGH NIBLEY: Once I was in a building where they were holding a political meeting. I had gone in there to go the restroom, but there was someone already in there, so I waited, and after a minute a man came bustling out, and I think it was Hitler. He just ignored me, but I think it was him in that restroom. I thought I recognized him, but it could have been somebody else. You see, the Germans call the restroom the *"Wozelbest der Kaiser muss,"* "the place even the Kaiser must go."

Perhaps the main difference between these two men is that Hitler thought of nothing but power—how to get it and how to use it—while Nibley's mind was interested only in learning. Here are samples of what these two young men were thinking in the 1920s. First from Hitler's Mein Kampf, *written in 1924:*

Hitler at a Nazi rally, 1928

ADOLF HITLER: Leadership itself requires not only will but also ability, and a greater importance must be attached to will and energy than to intelligence as such, and most valuable of all is a combination of ability, determination, and perseverance. The future of a movement is conditioned by the fanaticism, yes, the intolerance, with which its adherents uphold it as the sole correct movement, and push it past other formations of a similar sort.[2]

And here is what was going on in Hugh Nibley's mind:

DIARY ENTRY, MARCH 9, 1929: My recently adopted method of learning is proving itself the only thing. I give lectures—good, plain, orderly treatises on various subjects—to the atmosphere. In Medford[a] I used to work myself into a teary enthusiasm over religious discussions held in bed. My thoughts, reactions, motives, and interests are exactly the same today as they were then. At seven years Hugh Nibley was Hugh Nibley, just as conscious of the world and spirit and with the same ideals which he sports today—a notable improvement indeed!

Young Hugh Nibley

MARCH 16, 1929: Read my blessing.[b] Must it always be the same old story? Hindered by physical and moral weaknesses—Can one hour of Greek a day be playing the devil with my mission?

The Mormons have a wonderful oxymoron in referring to the young missionaries the Church sends out as "elders." These lads, mostly in their teens when they are ordained to the office of elder and sent off to preach the gospel, are expected to leave worldly concerns like girls and school behind and concentrate fully on the Lord's work for the duration of their time in the mission field. It's not unusual for young missionaries to feel sharp pangs of guilt when the

---

[a] Hugh Nibley lived in Medford, Oregon, as a child.

[b] *Patriarchal blessing:* The Church believes in continuing revelation, that people can get messages directly from God now, just as they could in Old Testament times. Each Mormon can receive a patriarchal blessing, which is essentially his or her own personal chapter of scripture. Among other things, it identifies which of the Tribes of Israel the person belongs to—an important part of Mormon doctrine. It generally also contains advice and prophecies about the person's life and his or her strengths and weaknesses.

enticements of the flesh distract them from their commitment, so Hugh Nibley's comments are not atypical. What is unusual is for a young elder to get his guilty conscience from breaking mission rules to study classical Greek. But Greek was a real temptation for Hugh Nibley, especially in the intellectual climate of Heidelberg, the center of German (and therefore, in his mind, civilized) learning.

A group of Mormons somewhere in Oregon, circa 1910. Second from left is Melvin J. Ballard, fourth from left is LDS Church President Joseph F. Smith. Right of President Smith are Agnes Sloan (Sloanie) Nibley and Alex Nibley, Hugh's parents. Eighth from left, with beard, is Charles W. Nibley, Hugh's grandfather. Identities of others are unknown.

DIARY ENTRY, APRIL 15, 1929: Since visiting Heidelberg I haven't got the school idea out of my head. . . . I am not humble—I haven't even faith enough to trust my education to the Lord.

HUGH NIBLEY: I was set apart[a] by Melvin J. Ballard,[b] and he told us at that time to warn the people that they would be destroyed by fire if they didn't repent and accept the gospel. President Tadje, the leader of the German mission, was very indulgent and let me do things my own way. All along the Rhine in those villages on the Rhine Plain I took my trusty bicycle to go out and tract[c] all alone. It was hard. It was grim. The Calvinist villages were the toughest. The Catholics were next. The Lutherans were rather kind, but it was rough. Toward the end of my

---

[a] *Set apart:* Made an official missionary and representative of the Church through a ceremony where a Church official lays his hands on the subject's head, "sets him apart" as a missionary, and pronounces blessings as inspired. These blessings are often considered prophetic like those in a patriarchal blessing.

[b] Melvin J. Ballard (1873–1939) was an Apostle, one of the leaders of The Church of Jesus Christ of Latter-day Saints.

[c] *Tract:* To go from door to door to preach the gospel. Mormon missionaries use tracting to try to find potential converts.

mission I threw away the tracts and everything else and just started crying repentance, telling them they would be destroyed by fire.

DIARY ENTRY, MARCH 25, 1929: . . . These people really have had a chance. These many testy attempts to dismiss the subject entirely are plainly the workings of a guilty conscience, then former enthusiasm is in nearly all cases proportionate to present testiness. . . .

MARCH 27, 1929: . . . Never has the joyless self-satisfaction of the people so seemed like blindness. They didn't know it—the ninnies! dunces! The joke was all on them and I enjoyed [the tracting] thoroughly.

Map Hugh used on his mission, marked with red and blue pencil

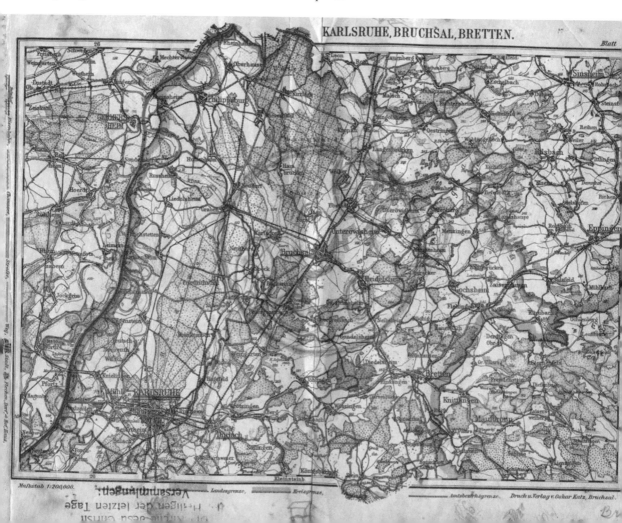

Nibley wrote to his grandmother:

Dear Grandma,

Nobody [here in Germany] believes in a God. The strongest Catholics in Frankenthal are professed atheists. And the suddenness of the thing is unbelievable. One feels a strange spirit like a cloud—a real thing that makes the people every *week* more testy and intolerant. You feel the spirit closing in on the people; something mean & unpleasant seems to inhabit the average house. Not a spirit of uncertainty but of settled, determined indifference. I often wondered where the wickedness was that the Lord accuses the world of—I suppose it is simply indifference, nobody seems to be really bad—but who has a right to be satisfied? . . . So I must again issue forth to a few hours of intense persuading, decoying, tempting—well nigh bullying. We are supposed to invite & recommend but nearly all the people are past that stage. I am becoming quite artful.

HUGH NIBLEY: During a conference in Karlsruhe I went and tracted right by a big church on the main street where it forks and leads out to the Odenwald forest. There was a butcher shop there, and I went to it and started giving my voice of warning. On impulse I said what Brother Ballard told me, that the people would be destroyed by fire from heaven, and a gigantic Hessian woman had a fit. She ran to the back of the shop and came out waving a huge meat cleaver and said, "Don't you tell me we'll be destroyed by fire from heaven!" So I moved on.

Nibley wasn't the only one who found the smug indifference of the German people disconcerting. The other preacher, Hitler, was having trouble as well, as William L. Shirer points out in The Rise and Fall of the Third Reich:

> **WILLIAM L. SHIRER:** The years from 1925 until the coming of the depression in 1929 were lean years for Adolf Hitler and the Nazi movement, but . . . he had the patience to wait and the shrewdness to realize that the climate of material prosperity and of a feeling of relaxation which settled over Germany in those years was not propitious for his purposes. . . . One scarcely heard of Hitler or Nazis except as the butt of jokes.[3]

Nibley's sermons didn't convert much of Germany to Mormonism, and in the 1928 election the Nazis got only 2½ percent of the vote. But both men, ardent and zealous as they were, kept at their proselytizing, even when the odds seemed impossible. Hitler, like Nibley, used strong language in his preaching.

ADOLF HITLER: The greatness of every mighty organization embodying an idea in this world lies in the religious fanaticism and intolerance with which, fanatically convinced of its own right, it intolerably imposes its will against all others. If an idea in itself is sound and, thus armed, takes up a struggle on this earth, it is unconquerable and every persecution will only add to its inner strength.[4]

Hugh's mission ended, and by the time he arrived home in Los Angeles the American stock market had crashed and the Great Depression settled over the world like a toxic fog. With the depression came the economic and social turmoil that gave Hitler the opportunity he would so masterfully exploit to raise himself to leadership of the German people—people like the woman in the Karlsruhe butcher shop who chased away the young missionary when he warned her of destruction by fire. Hugh went home and entered UCLA. When he was in his junior year Hitler was granted German citizenship. By the time Hugh graduated and went to Berkeley for graduate school, Hitler was chancellor of Germany and the Nazis had, among other things, broken the Treaty of Versailles by starting to rearm Germany, outlawed kosher butchering, revoked the German citizenship of Jews, and opened what they called a "school for good citizenship" at a little village called Dachau in the region where Hugh Nibley had recently been riding his trusty bicycle and preaching repentance.

In 1934 Hugh Nibley entered the doctoral program in history at the University of California at Berkeley, where he met another young intellectual.

PAUL SPRINGER: Hugh of course was a walking jigsaw puzzle. He was then a grad student, and I met him because he was the only other student in the university dumb enough to take [classical] Arabic. We became very close friends, and then prior to World War II we made a number of trips to the canyons in Utah—Capitol Reef, The Arches, of course Zion, Bryce—and on those long walks we had many,

many interesting discussions. We usually disagreed, which is of course the thing that made it interesting.

HUGH NIBLEY: Oh, was Springer Prussian! Was he militarist! Oh, he was one hundred percent German, always proud of being a German; we clashed on that. I knew that he was a Junker[a] and a red hot Prussian and he knew I wasn't, so that was that. He was very violently anti-Roosevelt and I was for him.

Paul Springer

[a] *Junker* (yun'ker): "A young German noble; as a term of reproach, a narrow-minded, over-bearing (younger) member of the aristocracy of Prussia, etc.; *spec.* a member of the reactionary party of the aristocracy whose aim it is to maintain the exclusive social and political privileges of their class" (*Oxford English Dictionary*).

One of the themes running through the Book of Mormon (which the Latter-day Saints consider scripture as authentic as the Bible) is a people repeatedly given the choice between some form of self-rule or government by despotism. Their unfortunate tendency is almost always toward the strong leader rather than the confusing discussions and compromises that characterize democracy. Despots are dangerous, but they are never as dangerous in themselves as the popular attitudes that put them in power. Hitler was hungry for power and Germany was hungry for a strong leader. When the German president Hindenberg died, Hitler seized the opportunity to become Führer and commander in chief of the armed forces. Soon thereafter he repudiated the Treaty of Versailles by ordering the creation of an air force and expansion of the German army and navy. He then engineered the return of the Saar and Rhineland regions, then under French occupation, to German control. Meanwhile, civil war broke out in Spain, and Germany joined in on the side of the fascists.

HUGH NIBLEY: Springer and I talked all the time about the Spanish War.[b] We had friends who were in that war, and we thought a larger war would have to come because Hitler was planning to conquer the world. He was already taking over

[b] The Spanish Civil War (1934–39) served in many ways as a rehearsal for World War II. It pitted a coalition of right-wing forces backed and supplied by the Axis Powers of Germany and Italy against another coalition made up of left-wing interests that got its support from the Soviet Union. Many idealistic young people from all over the world were drawn to join the fight on both sides. The conflict became a major testing ground not only for ideologies, but also for the military hardware and tactics that would be used in the coming global conflict.

everything, and he didn't intend to stop until the Nazis had all of Europe under their fingers. I was finishing my degree in 1937–38, and the subject I wanted to use for my thesis was the phenomenon of the mob in ancient Rome, but the committee rejected it because they said it wasn't relevant. Things like that didn't happen anymore, they said, so I had to change my subject.

About the time the history department at Berkeley declared the subject of mob violence irrelevant to the modern world, Germany experienced "Kristallnacht," the "Night of Broken Glass." It was a carefully organized "spontaneous uprising" of young Nazis who rampaged through Jewish neighborhoods shattering windows, burning more than a hundred synagogues and 7,500 Jewish businesses, killing 91 Jews, beating hundreds more, and sending 26,000 Jews to concentration camps.

Springer left Berkeley before Nibley did, and their arguments were continued in a series of letters that eventually spanned more than forty years.

HUGH NIBLEY: After Springer left Berkeley we would write these long letters to each other—long, eloquent, literary letters so full of scatology that I wouldn't let them see the light of day.

But Springer saved those letters and now they have seen the light of day. The letters from Nibley to Springer are useful in understanding the prewar thinking not just of Hugh Nibley but of much of America in general.

Undated letter, late 1938

Suh:

Here we are—all pounding down the home-stretch in the triumphant finish. The unremitting toil of years is about to be laid at the feet of an enraptured committee. We can't stop; we can't breathe. . . . I want to finish this damn thing before they have me reviewing German grammar on the inside of a Cyclone Super-charged Fence at the instance of one N. Chamberlain.[a]

"Gott strafe Englande,"[b]

Hugh

[a] Neville Chamberlain (1869–1940) was prime minister of Great Britain from 1937 to 1940. In September of 1938 he flew to Munich where he met with Hitler and agreed to allow him to take over a large part of Czechoslovakia in exchange for an agreement that the Germans would then leave the rest of the country alone. Chamberlain proudly waved the agreement to cheering crowds and declared he had achieved "peace for our time." Six months later Hitler broke his pact and took the rest of Czechoslovakia by force. The abandonment of Czechoslovakia came to be known as one of the greatest betrayals in history and Chamberlain's name is forever linked with "appeasement" of ambitious dictators.

[b] *Gott strafe Englande:* God punish England. A curse that was fulfilled with the blitz of 1940–41.

P.S. A long controversy has been settled by the latest excavation at Ur: 1) the Swastika is taken from the Edinnu sign, better known as the Seal of Solomon, Star of David, Shield of Israel: 2) the salute with the open hand and outstretched arm was taken by the Romans from Syria, where it was derived from the "Hand of God" greeting of the Ancient Hebrews. Please forward this information to my dear friend and colleague, Goebbels (you may have heard of him), who has been eagerly awaiting this substantiation of A. (Izzy) Rosenberg's*" beautiful faith.

*"Alfred Rosenberg (1893–1946) was the chief author of the Nazi racist doctrine. Nibley gives him a Jewish nickname (Izzy) to go with his surname which, ironically, is a popular Jewish name.

GUSTAVE GILBERT: A document by Hitler's adjutant Schmundt recorded Hitler's outright decision for aggressive war in another secret meeting on May 23, 1939. . . . The document goes on to quote Hitler: "The national-political unity of the Germans has been achieved, apart from minor exceptions. . . . Further successes cannot be obtained without the shedding of blood. . . . There is therefore no question of sparing Poland, and we are left with the decision: to attack Poland at the first suitable opportunity." . . .

Dr. Joseph Goebbels (1897–1945), center, the Nazi Propaganda Minister, was, like Hugh Nibley, a philologist. His erudition gave the Nazis intellectual credibility and his propaganda tactics were crucial to building the Third Reich into a massive totalitarian state to wage world war.

Having made his preparations for war, Hitler called together his military leaders on August 22, 1939 at Berchtesgaden and explained that the war had to come in his lifetime and he was now ready to strike, as another document showed, "I will give a propagandistic cause for starting the war, never mind whether it is plausible or not. The victor shall not be asked, later on, whether we told the truth or not. In starting and waging a war, not the right is what matters but victory."[5]

Hugh Nibley finished up at Berkeley and went to teach at Claremont College in California, and he and Springer continued to write each other. In the meantime, Hitler annexed Austria and—with the acquiescence of Chamberlain's British government— most of Czechoslovakia. Then, on September 1, 1939, the armed forces of Germany launched a crushing attack on Poland, and World War II officially began.

> **GUSTAVE GILBERT:** To create an 'incident' to provoke the planned attack on Poland, Himmler had obtained Polish uniforms, with which he dressed up concentration camp inmates and had them shot while "attacking" the Gleiwitz radio station [on the German-Polish border], to make it look like Polish "aggression."[6]

German forces quickly overran the Polish army. In less than three weeks they changed the map of Europe and killed 70,000 Polish soldiers, wounded another 133,000, and took 694,000 prisoner. Underneath the military statistics, the Polish people's lives were shattered with suffering that numbers can never quantify. The Nazis justified their actions in the worldwide court of public opinion as preemptive self-defense. Germany, in their view, was really a victim, and now Hitler had given the German people the nec-essary self-esteem and military muscle to stand up to their oppressors.

Hugh Nibley's letters at this time are mostly comic essays, and most of the subject matter is social criticism. His criticism is very critical indeed, and just about nobody is safe from his slashing wit. About his academic colleagues he writes:

> I'm dead sick of these textbook humanists. The émigrées with the big names are worse than the others: humbugs for the most part.

About the glamour of Hollywood:

> A community of professional entertainers dictating to the world; a cabal of exhibitionists and degenerates devising among themselves a universal design for living;[a] a ganglion of primordial plasm festering with exotic poisons, officiating as the brain of the age; don't let me go on! I may forget I am an optimist, expecting the best possible fate to

---

[a] A reference to *Design for Living*, a popular comic film made in 1933 by director Ernst Lubitsch from a script by Noel Coward and Ben Hecht and starring Gary Cooper. The movie has a frank and open attitude about sexual relations, including free love and homosexuality.

befall our generation, namely, its virtual destruction. Ja, komm Herr Je![a]

His comments about totalitarianism and its influence on American culture:

We seem already ripe for the doctrine of naked power, by which domination is a plain sadism and obedience a willful masochism. There is, I think you will agree, a significant relationship between the rise of Totalitarianism and the cult of nakedness. It is the reptilian nakedness of the Devonian age, that aeon when the world was filled with lush predatory and exuberant flesh, writhing with sleek, voluptuous, mindless creatures whose existence has become the type and pattern of our own. In nothing is the trend so plain as in the speeches of Mussolini, whose ideals of all people only the Japs seem to have realized.

Here he goes after immigrants and people who don't speak their native tongues in a way that meets his standards:

Hugh Nibley, Berkeley graduate student

I do detest that Syrian dialect; and after listening to [my Arab friend Sam] Tenis it makes me physically ill—just the sort of palaver you would expect from a lot of mooning oriental Christians that believe the soul of the virgin is carried about in the sleeve of St. Michael wrapped up in a damask napkin, and hold Moslem superstition in superb contempt.

[a] "Ja, komm Herr Je!" Yea, come Lord Jesus. Nibley is quoting a common German mealtime prayer and apparently calling for the apocalypse and second coming.

15

This was the age before political correctness, and in ways that would get him yanked off prime time today Hugh Nibley attacks the Germans, the English, the French, the Japanese, the Chinese, the Arabs, the media, the government, academia, and American culture. So does he approve of anybody? Yes, sometimes.

April 3, 1941

Dear Philemon & Bacchis,

I have withheld fire in the hopes of collecting enough ammunition for a real volley. At last it has happened; I am formally, legally, ritually engaged to be married! That, you may think, is not news, but wait until you hear who the engagee is—it is none other than Herta Pauly, the Prussian comet!!!!!!! Petite, exquisite, an incredible combination of unaffected elegance and volcanic energy, she has been everything from a dancer with Mary Wigman*a* to my own ace Greek scholar. Her father was *Oberintendant of the Berliner Stadische Oper* [Director of the Berlin State Opera] and other operas all over Germany until he got on the wrong side of Adolf, but her mother does not have to play up to the Nazis, because they play up to her, she being of the old Prussian military aristocracy (my Herta spent her childish days on a *Rittergut* [a manor or estate, such as those owned by feudal lords]): her sister is a Lutheran pastor (a rare office for a woman in the Reich) in Berlin. As for Herta, she is absolutely perfect in all respects (allowing for a pardonable sympathy with the German cause in the present debacle)—must be seen to be believed: Imagine a *hellblond* [platinum blonde] super-intellectual *Taubchen* [little dove] with form and motion like a Venus—the amazing strength and agility that only dancers, and good ones, can acquire, with enough humor for ten and enough generous affection to love even me. She is 27. Next to me, she declares, Bach is her grand passion (that gives you an idea). . . . You will be nuts about her. I don't think I can get north for Thanksgiving—couldn't think of deserting Precious. I have a very good car now, a Dodge.

Love and kisses from an expert,
HN, Junker-to-be by marriage.

P.S. The happy day's to be some time in December.

a Mary Wigman (1886–1973) was a choreographer and modern dance pioneer.

So now he's met someone who actually meets his standards and whom he actually considers his match. He praises her breeding, her ethnicity, her social status, her physical attributes, and of course her intellect. His sweetheart's one flaw is her Nazi sympathies, which he dismisses as "pardonable." If an affinity for Nazis is so easy to shrug off, it's perhaps understandable that Jews would get less flexibility.

Unlike poles attract each other, and like poles repel each other: that's why I love the Jews; the fascists hate them because they so closely resemble them. Profound, eh? That relieves me on all scores. I dotes on that afflicted race, but I promise immediate violence to the unfortunate who mistakes me for one of them. Did I tell you about Goebbels? It's good enough to repeat if I did. That celebrated "*Swartzabgestumpftegermane*" [short, dark German] sent to the archives at Copenhagen for the genealogy of some of his relatives. Of course you guess the rest, but a poizinal friend of mine was working in those very archives at the time, and was on hand when the chief archivist furthered to that torch of Arya the painful information that his family tree was to be examined not in the city archives but in those of the Synagogue. My theory, you see. What else *would* you expect from a brash and brazen publicist like that?

There's an extra layer of irony in Nibley's joke about Goebbels' Jewish genealogy. In his letter Hugh Nibley threatens "personal violence" to anybody who would accuse him of being Jewish. But, as he knew perfectly well, he had at least as much Jewish blood as Goebbels, since his own great-grandfather was a Jew. Alexander Neibaur, the first Jew to convert to Mormonism, was the first dentist to arrive in the Utah Territory and the maker of Brigham Young's dentures. His daughter Rebecca married Charles W. Nibley, whose son Alex was Hugh Nibley's father.

No matter what sector of society is getting lambasted by Hugh Nibley's wit, the one thing that remains constant is that the measuring stick he uses to judge them is an aesthetic and intellectual tradition that has its roots in German culture. He is unabashed in his chauvinism—but then he was, after all, an Edwardian, and in his age Manifest Destiny was still the order of the day and political correctness had not yet come into vogue.

For those who forged a nation out of the American wilderness, as Hugh Nibley's

Alexander Neibaur, seated left, with his sons

grandparents had, the concept of inherent racial and cultural superiority was very important. We needed it to justify the way we built the nation and still allow ourselves to look in the mirror and see God-fearing, freedom-loving patriots rather than ruthless land-grabbers. We may have mixed feelings about it, but America wouldn't be what it is today without the feeling that we had a right to take over the New World. So it was Manifest Destiny—nothing less than the will of almighty God—that sanctified taking land from the natives and killing them when they objected, then using African slave labor and exploiting minority immigrants to build an economy on that land.

This idea of racial superiority was still very strong before World War II and, although those of us who grew up afterwards may like to think we would have been different, there was widespread ambivalence about Nazi racism all over America. Even among many of those who opposed Hitler there was a feeling that the Jews were at least partly to blame for their bad treatment at the hands of the Germans, and that even though Hitler went too far, well, the Jews had sort of asked for it.

HENRY FORD SR.: The Jew in Germany is regarded as only a guest of the people; he has offended by trying to turn himself into the host. There are no stronger contrasts in the world than the pure Germanic and pure Semitic races; therefore, there has been no harmony between the two in Germany; the German has regarded the Jew strictly as a guest, while the Jew, indignant at not being given the privileges of the nation-family, has cherished animosity against his host. In other countries the Jew is permitted to mix more readily with the people, he can amass his control unchallenged; but in Germany the case was different. Therefore, the Jew hated the German people; therefore, the countries of the world which were most dominated by the Jews showed the greatest hatred of

HITLER'S INSPIRATION

The leading voice in speaking out against the Jews in the early twentieth century was not Hitler or even any other German. It was none other than Henry Ford Sr., founder of the Ford Motor Company and the industrialist who popularized the assembly line, the man who is credited with having a large influence in creating the American middle class. Starting in 1919, Ford published a periodical called the *Dearborn Independent,* which was distributed through Ford car dealerships throughout the country and gained a wide circulation. The *Independent* published a series of articles which were later bound and sold as a four-volume set under the title *The International Jew, the World's Foremost Problem.* When he was in prison Hitler read Ford's writings; they were one of his inspirations in writing his own book, *Mein Kampf.* Ford is believed by many to have donated large sums to the Nazi movement, though an investigation found no hard evidence to prove the claim. The Ford company built a factory in Germany to help supply vehicles to the German army. In 1938 Henry Ford Sr. was awarded the highest honor ever given to a non-German by the Third Reich, the Grand Cross of the German Eagle.

After Pearl Harbor the Ford Motor Company issued a letter from Henry Ford retracting his earlier views and denouncing anti-Semitism, but many doubted the sincerity of his apology. The anti-Semitic history of the founder of the Ford Motor Company has been an embarrassment to the company, which has distanced itself from the views its founder expressed in the early part of the century. Ford's writings are still available and are often used in neo-Nazi writings and other anti-Semitic forums.

Germany during the recent regrettable war [World War I]. Jewish hands were in almost exclusive control of the engines of publicity by which public opinion concerning the German people was molded. The sole winners of the war were Jews.

. . . Jews the world over supply the energy of disruptive movements. It is understood that the young Jews of the United States are propagandists of an ideal that would practically abolish the United States. The attack is aimed, of course, against "capitalism," which means the present government of the world by the Gentile. The true capitalists of the world are Jews, who are capitalists for capital's sake. It is hard to believe that they wish to destroy capital; they wish to obtain sole control of it, and their wish has long been in fair way to fulfillment.[7]

Given these statements by Ford, this letter of Hugh Nibley's is pretty representative of thinking common in prewar America.

The indecently brief interval between this and our last note is inspired by the need to correct an ERROR to which we have brutally exposed your ingenuous and trusting mind. We said, to wit, that we *loved* the Jews. What was meant by that naked declaration was that we would endure them willingly *if* they could manage somehow or other either (1) to remember their religion or (2) to forget their race. So far all their effort is in the opposite direction; there is nothing more depressing than a talk with a rabbi: race, race, race, "our people," all the time, with a practiced and patronizing sneer for anyone simple enough, or incautious enough to refer to God. Then (though this hurts you I must tell all) there is that eternal and insidious ultimatum which they . . . thrust upon an indifferent and apathetic world. We are required namely to acknowledge not their equality but their superiority, and any failure to do so is *in itself* an act of persecution. Cruel cherce! No question of toleration: the quiet indifference of toleration, the tacit preoccupation which lets everyone go his way is instantly interpreted as contempt: silence can have only one meaning—scorn; nothing is so much resented as the simple give and take of equals in which they . . . can only suspect a cynical condescension or treacherous intent. No, either you acknowledge your masters in all things or else you are guilty of

German people's elected representatives at the Reichstag salute their Führer.

persecuting defenseless women and children. That's enough to give anyone a neurosis, and it is not the strangest thing in the world that the
peculiar and seemingly unaccountable *real* persecutions seem to be acts
of unbalanced neurotics verging on insanity. . . . As to the international
situation, I remain neutral but more against the allies than the
Germans. I think we shall see the end of that business yet, but not until
we have seen the end of a lot of other things. The world gets worse as
the end approaches.

*So Hugh Nibley was not that far from the mainstream of America in 1941. And
people can change their attitudes. Hitler did. In* Mein Kampf *he explains how youthful naiveté can cloud one's judgment on matters of race and culture:*

ADOLF HITLER: At home I do not remember having heard the word
[Jew] during my father's lifetime. I believe that the old gentleman

would have regarded any special emphasis on this term as cultural backwardness. In the course of his life he had arrived at more or less cosmopolitan views which, despite his pronounced national sentiments, not only remained intact, but also affected me to some extent.

Likewise at school I found no occasion which could have led me to change this inherited picture. . . .

Not until my fourteenth or fifteenth year did I begin to come across the word "Jew," with any frequency, partly in connection with political discussions. This filled me with a mild distaste, and I could not rid myself of an unpleasant feeling that always came over me whenever religious quarrels occurred in my presence.

At that time I did not think anything else of the question.

There were few Jews in Linz. In the course of the centuries their outward appearance had become Europeanized and had taken on a human look; in fact, I even took them for Germans. The absurdity of this idea did not dawn on me because I saw no distinguishing feature but the strange religion. The fact that they had, as I believed, been persecuted on this account sometimes almost turned my distaste at unfavorable remarks about them into horror. . . .

I cannot maintain that the way in which I became acquainted with them struck me as particularly pleasant. For the Jew was still characterized for me by nothing but his religion, and therefore, on grounds of human tolerance, I maintained my rejection of religious attacks in this case as in others. Consequently, the tone, particularly that of the Viennese anti-Semitic press, seemed to me unworthy of the cultural tradition of a great nation. I was oppressed by the memory of certain occurrences in the Middle Ages, which I should not have liked to see repeated.[8]

The youthful Hitler, influenced by his liberal father, was horrified at disparaging remarks about Jews and didn't want to see their medieval persecutions repeated. Hugh Nibley's parental influence was different. In one letter to Springer he writes:

Mamma . . . hates Jews worse than ever, because she has been reading in a book how the Jew Rubenstein exploited the gentile Tschaikowsky, and how the German Madame von Meck saved poor Peter from his mercenary clutches.

Nibley said he would never want his letters to Springer to see the light of day (which of us would want to be judged by history based entirely on our conversations with one locker room pal?), and it would be unfair to believe that the caustic, satirical voice in his letters to Paul Springer is all there was to the young Professor Nibley. There were times when he dropped the sardonic tone and wrote in a voice that was so different from the one he used with Springer that it hardly seems possible it could have come from the same person.

July 14, 1941

Dear Grandmother

I still hold you up as my model for the philosophic and well-balanced life, and I still continue to flaunt all the dictates of measure and restraint in spite of my good intentions. If I did not have you as a living example of how a person should act, I would put no faith at all in human wisdom and run hog-wild. So you see, it is very important that you continue to flourish for a long time to come—more people than you think depend on you for inspiration. If nothing else, it is a matter of importance in these crazy times to know what a sane person is really like, just as a matter of curiosity. . . . I like to ride out to the hottest and most desolate parts of the country to enjoy nature at her worst: there is infinite comfort in the conviction that the worst in nature is indescribably beautiful. So I sit like an idiot on the hot rocks and think of you as one living, as the Greeks put it, "according to nature," and wonder

Grandmother Margaret Reid Sloan with Hugh Nibley

if I could ever learn to do the same. If I ever succeed in being anything but a half-made fool, I shall attribute it more to the steady, undismayed spirit of my Grandmother than to anything else. You see, I can put into writing what I would never have nerve enough to say out loud.

Without his grandmother's guiding influence, Hugh fears he would go "hog-wild" in self-destructive binging. Of course, what he calls going wild is not "sex, drugs, and rock and roll," but this didn't leave him free of spiritual danger, and he knew it. He once said he was never tempted by power. "Ambition was never my vice," he said, "it was vanity." He recognized this flaw and once wrote to Springer about their shared addiction to intellectual naughtiness.

You musn't be annoyed at thinking about the writer at times; base thoughts, I am told, occur to every man now and then. Occasionally one thinks of you too with a despairing shake of the head and a muffled curse in one's beard: *Bismallah ar rahman ar rahim!* Did ever a son of man have so much mischief written all over him and so little within him? Is there another man alive who stubbornly presents his worst side to the world and hides his virtues as carefully as other creatures do their defects? One of Nature's Pranks. Should be a National Monument.

" *Bismallah ar rahman ar rahim!*: Common Arabic exclamation, "In the name of God the compassionate, the merciful!"

In rare moments throughout his life Hugh Nibley let his vulnerable voice speak, in certain very personal letters and private conversations. It's different. It's clear. It doesn't have all the intellectual decoration. There are none of the footnotes that form so much of the books he went on to write. The bitter Oscar Wilde acid isn't there. He's not hiding behind literary smokescreens. It's a less intellectual but more intelligent voice. It's filled with love but terrified to express it. From the time he was a small child this voice, this secret part of his personality, had been alive and strong, even though he kept it well hidden most of the time. Such passion is too tender for everyday use. It was easy with the intellectual, witty voice of the professor to baffle and impress his audience and do it without exposing the sensitive material in his depths. The scornful voice is much more confident than the loving, awe-filled voice, but it's also less representative of the real man. This pure, simple voice appears in letters and poems he wrote as a small child; and from the time he was an infant to his death just before his ninety-fifth birthday, this loving, hoping, insecure, yearning-to-be-better voice has never changed its tone or its tune in the slightest.

So Hitler portrayed himself—at least at one time—as a tolerant, open-minded liberal, while Hugh Nibley ranted like a racist Junker. Hitler managed to overcome his bleeding heart squeamishness about Jews. Under his direction the "school for good citizenship" at Dachau was followed by many more concentration camps. In 1940, soon after invading Poland, the Nazis built a large complex and named it after the nearby town of Oświęcim. History knows it better by the German form of the name: Auschwitz. With the methodical precision of engineers, the Nazis built warehouses for what they considered human waste and built gas chambers and crematoriums to dispose of those who were not the most useful as slaves. This was the National Socialist solution to what they called "the Jewish problem." One Jew who found himself in Auschwitz was a young psychiatrist named Viktor Frankl. He survived, and later wrote about his experiences from a psychological point of view in his book Man's Search for Meaning:

> **VICTOR FRANKL:** The daily ration consisted of very watery soup given out once daily, and the usual small bread ration. In addition to that, there was the so-called "extra-allowance," consisting of three-fourths of an ounce of margarine, or of a slice of poor quality sausage, or of a little piece of cheese, or a bit of synthetic honey, or a spoonful of watery jam, varying daily. In calories, this diet was absolutely inadequate, especially taking into consideration our heavy manual work and our constant exposure to the cold in inadequate clothing. The sick who were "under special care"—that is, those who were allowed to lie in the huts instead of leaving the camp for work—were even worse off.
>
> When the last layers of subcutaneous fat had vanished, and we looked like skeletons disguised with skin and rags, we could watch our bodies beginning to devour themselves. The organism digested its own protein, and the muscles disappeared. Then the body had no powers of resistance left. One after another the members of the little community in our hut died. Each of us could calculate with fair accuracy whose turn would be next, and when his own would come. After many observations we knew the symptoms well, which made the correctness of our prognoses quite certain. "He won't last long," or, "This is the next one," we whispered to each other, and

when, during our daily search for lice, we saw our own naked bodies in the evening, we thought alike: This body here, my body, is really a corpse already. What has become of me? I am but a small portion of a great mass of human flesh . . . of a mass behind barbed wire, crowded into a few earthen huts; a mass of which daily a certain portion begins to rot because it has become lifeless.[9]

Did Hugh Nibley make any connection between his own cavalier attitudes and these horrors on another continent? In his academic world he was more concerned with ideas than fighting over scraps of bread to stay alive. But still, underneath his diatribes against all the unworthy elements of society, he was always most critical of himself. Behind the glib attitude there is fear of the impending war, fear of what he would have to endure, surely, but even more fear of what he might become if he failed to stand up to what he knew would be a test of his own moral mettle.

HUGH NIBLEY: I had some marvelous dreams that were fulfilled. I call them my "five o'clocks." I'd wake up at five o'clock and find myself dreaming I was in a situation that actually occurred later on. I dreamed the sinking of the Hood[a] when I was teaching at Claremont. I found myself on the deck of the Hood leaning on the railing with a British officer as the ship was sinking. There I was talking to this officer and he said, "The Russians are to blame for this." I don't know why he said that; they were expecting some support or something. I went up the steps to the library the next morning and I met a student. I said, "The British are about to lose their biggest battleship, the Hood." He said, "How do you know?" I said, "I just saw it sunk today."

And there was one very strong dream where I woke up one fine morning swimming around in beautiful balmy tropical waters, very blue and so forth. I was swimming around by the side of a large ship, and there were explosions and a lot of smoke pouring up, and I swam around to the side of the ship to see what it was and I looked up at the ship and painted across the side of the ship it said "Arizona." I had this dream before the attack on Pearl Harbor.

---

[a] *HMS Hood:* Sunk by the German battleship *Bismarck* on May 24, 1941, the *Hood* was actually a battle cruiser rather than a battleship and not the biggest ship in the British fleet as Nibley describes it later. She was sunk less than ten minutes into the battle of the Denmark Straits when her ammunition exploded. Of more than 1,400 men on board, only three survived.

USS Arizona *sinking after being attacked at Pearl Harbor, December 7, 1941*

FRANKLIN DELANO ROOSEVELT: Yesterday, December 7, 1941—a date which will live in infamy—the United States of America was suddenly and deliberately attacked by naval and air forces of the Empire of Japan. . . .

No matter how long it may take us to overcome this premeditated invasion, the American people in their righteous might will win through to absolute victory. . . .

Hostilities exist. There is no blinking at the fact that our people, our territory, and our interests are in grave danger.

With confidence in our armed forces—with the unbounding determination of our people—we will gain the inevitable triumph—so help us God.

I ask that the Congress declare that since the unprovoked and dastardly attack by Japan on Sunday, December 7, 1941, a state of war has existed between the United States and the Japanese Empire.[10]

The Pearl Harbor attack destroyed or disabled 18 American warships, including eight huge battleships. Of the 394 military planes on the island of Oahu, 188 were destroyed and another 159 were damaged. In less than three hours America's ability to wage war in the Pacific was reduced to almost nothing. Up until that day the country had continued to debate war. President Roosevelt wanted to get involved and did everything he could to help the Allies, but he couldn't get the Congress to unite behind him and actually go to war. Many Americans were opposed to getting tangled up in what they considered other peoples' business. Others had sympathies for the Axis powers. As for Hitler, he was never afraid of the allied democracies. Albert Speer, the Third Reich's Minister of Armaments and War Production and a man very close to Hitler, would later write:

ALBERT SPEER: The Americans had not played a very prominent part in the war of 1914–18, [Hitler] thought, and moreover had not made any great sacrifices of blood. They would certainly not withstand a great trial by fire, for their fighting qualities were low. In general, no such thing as an American people existed as a unit; they were nothing but a mass of immigrants from many nations and races.[11]

Hitler was more worried about his totalitarian neighbor, the Soviet Union, despite what he considered its people's Slavic racial inferiority. His great disdain for democracy

FDR signs declaration of war

was based on what he believed was a democracy's inherent inability to act. Unlike those trained to follow the iron will of a dictator, democracies were weak and ineffective because they didn't know how to give and take orders without question as he had trained the National Socialists to do. Waging the aggressive preemptive warfare Hitler wanted was impossible when common people question the intentions and methods of their leaders. What Hitler never realized was that although it is very hard to get a large, diverse democracy to approve going to war, once the whole mass of the people do make the decision for war, the collective will of the millions becomes stronger than even the most hardened will of a despot. On December 7, the Japanese attack did what FDR,

Churchill, and all the many advocates of America's entering the war hadn't been able to do. The bombs and torpedoes crippled the American military, but at the same time they served to unite the United States.

ADMIRAL ISOROKU YAMAMOTO: I fear we have awakened a sleeping tiger and filled it with a terrible resolve.[a]

A huge nation made up of hundreds of ethnic groups and millions of points of view suddenly congealed together as a single force. A country that had been debating the war, as Hugh Nibley and Paul Springer had been doing, suddenly galvanized its collective energy into winning the war. One evidence of the feeling Pearl Harbor galvanized was an intense and widespread hatred of the Japanese, including those whose families had been American citizens for generations. Behavior that would be considered unthinkable racism years later became commonplace. Yes, there were those still opposed to the war, but their voices became very few and very quiet after December 7, 1941.

PAUL SPRINGER: The propaganda was very strong in 1940 and '41, especially after Pearl Harbor. After Pearl Harbor you were a heel if you didn't want to—the expression was—"break through the Nazi Line and set the Rising Sun." There were lots of songs the soldiers sang on that, including me.

HUGH NIBLEY: I was involved in a sort of think-tank in Claremont—"War Aims and Peace Objectives," it was called. Claremont College President Russell M. Story, who was one of the two great men I have ever known, brought me into the think-tank because I could take shorthand, and he was always very nice to me. It was funded by the Rockefellers, and I remember Thomas Mann[b] was there and Albert Einstein visited. These high-powered intellectuals would talk about the war and what it all meant, and I would take notes.

Letter to Springer, early 1942

Dear People, and Sir,

Do you realize that it was more than a month after apprising you of my espousement before I got a rise out of you? I will admit you were

[a] Isoroku Yamamoto (1884–1943): Japanese admiral who planned the attack on Pearl Harbor. He had lived in America and been educated at Harvard. He promised the Japanese government that he could slow down the Americans by destroying their Pacific fleet, but he worried that America's productive potential meant his country could not prevail in a protracted war. This quote is popularly attributed to Yamamoto, but a search for the original source indicates it may have come from the screenwriter of *Tora! Tora! Tora!*, a Hollywood movie about the Pearl Harbor attack.

[b] Thomas Mann (1875–1955): German writer who won a Nobel Prize for his novel *The Magic Mountain* in 1929.

WAR SONGS

Within hours of the raid on Pearl Harbor the American recording industry began its counter-offensive on the Axis. Here are some of the many songs Paul Springer and others were singing to stir the country's patriotic feelings:

"Get Your Gun and Come Along, We're Fixin' to Kill a Skunk"
"A Cranky Old Yank in a Clanky Old Tank"
"Let's Put the Axe to the Axis"
"Good-bye, Mama, I'm off to Yokohama"
"Remember Pearl Harbor"
"You're a Sap, Mister Jap"
"Last Page of *Mein Kampf*"
"Leave the Dishes in the Sink, Ma"

Here is an excerpt from "We're Gonna Have to Slap That Dirty Little Jap" by Bob Miller, recorded by Carson Robison and His Orchestra, possibly the source of Springer's quote on the facing page:

We're gonna have to slap
That dirty little Jap
And Uncle Sam's the guy who can do it
The Japs and all their hooey
Will be changed into chop suey
And the rising sun will set when we
  get through it. . . .

American propaganda poster

right when you did answer: Sturm & Drang—24 hrs. of it a day with my Teutonic passion-flower; it got very tedious. We called it off; she *is* utterly wonderful, but as you know I'm a person of definite limitations. . . . We have just had a sort of purge here. It seems that two of my particular friends on the Scripps [College] staff turned out to be big-time Nazi agents. Which there are perhaps three people in Claremont who had not suspected steadily for the past two years. As spies these two are *the* prize ninnies: I could carry it off more subtly in darkest Japan. I feel that I'm about to embrace a not too unwelcome pretext for breaking with a moribund academic profession; just now I am writing to Washington about it.

Hugh's mother, Agnes Sloan Nibley, or "Sloanie," as she was known, was a very energetic woman who planned her children's lives in great detail. He was very careful what he wrote to her, since she had a penchant for getting involved to an uncomfortable degree.

Dear Mother:

I think I shall find a chance to break with the despicable and corrupt teaching profession. . . . I'm broke now and expect to stay that way—the austere life is the only one I can enjoy; you may think it strange, but I find the good, homey atmosphere simply suffocating. May I be boiled in oil if I force a congenial and comfortable home on anyone;[a] if the war keeps up even this plush-bottom generation may learn that joy lies in another direction and a world far removed from cozy beds and double-rich Sundaes. . . . You must permit me to send you money—avalanches of it; because after all I did tell the draft board I was.

But he was aware that many other men who were also providers for their families were being drafted as the country moved into the reality of wartime. Later he wrote to Springer:

Did you know that all the national forests, etc. are to be closed to the public in June? I wonder if that goes for inland and desert regions such as the Z--n. Still have sweet thoughts about that place. . . . There is a good deal of philosophical reflection going on in many quarters these days, following the recognition that we are living in a declining world; that war is nature's way of correcting those sins against abstract justice

[a] A vow he kept.

which is not abstract at all, but which, as Solon of old observed, merely seems to be so because it bides its time. It is really quite overwhelming to think that we are all going to get what we deserve. . . .

Early on the morning of his thirty-second birthday he had another of his vivid dreams.

HUGH NIBLEY: It was another one of my five o'clocks. I looked up and there, by the foot of my bed was President Story. When I went to school later that morning they told me President Story had died during the night.

March 27, 1942

Dear Mother,

It's nice to have reached the point where a year here and there doesn't much matter. A man is only worth what he produces; nothing else matters, and that depends not on credits, reputation, experience, office or anything in fact that most people find impressive. The only strictly honest man I've ever known, President Story, died last night of a stroke. I find the circumstances significant; suppose I shall soon be moving on.

Your polemic on the Jews is very depressing. They have just as large a proportion of their numbers in the war as the rest of the people, and are quite as exposed to danger, I can assure you from inside information. It is true that the Oriental in them refuses to be washed out, but when the hypocrisy in the rest of us has become as white as snow, then and not until then have we a case against them. For Reid's sake I beg of you to let up on that hysterical theme—it can cause him a great deal of trouble, as it has cost even me not a little loss. Those things get around, you know. . . . I hear a report that I have been reclassified in the local draft board to

Sloanie Nibley

1-A. What's to be done with all these books is my only care in the world on that score. Can't you, sweet parent, be a little teeny weeny bit philosophical and not so wildly emotional about everything? . . . We are living under an economy of scarcity, you know (did you hear about dear old red-white-and-blue Standard Oil's role in creating the present rubber shortage?)

The news from the war was bad all over. The Germans had reached Sebastopol in Russia and had just taken Tobruk and El Alamein in Northern Africa. U-boats were sinking Allied ships daily. The Japanese dominated the Pacific and were advancing across it toward the American coast. In addition to taking numerous South Pacific island chains, they had moved on Alaska and occupied American territory in the Aleutian Islands. America had been caught unprepared and was trying desperately to get ready for a war that it was already in up to its neck. To Paul Springer, Hugh Nibley wrote:

If I didn't hate boats and get strange diseases on the water I would join the Navy. It might be wise to dicker with various govt. agencies, but I strongly feel that salvation does not lie in that direction. Come what may, our concern is to do the right thing and let the opportunists do the smart thing—in the end we shall see which course is the wiser.

Give your spouse a fervid but ethereal kiss for me,

X-79

With the world even more crazy than usual, Zion Canyon seemed like the only place on earth a young scholar could find any peace.

In 1942 Brigham Young University was holding its regular summer school, and members of the Nibley family were gathering there at the

Paul Springer and Hugh Nibley

34

STANDARD OIL, PART I

This parenthetical mention of Standard Oil would not be the last time the name of that company would come up in Hugh Nibley's experiences with World War II. The story of Standard Oil of New Jersey and rubber involves the cooperative relationship between the American company and the giant German conglomerate I.G. Farben, and it involves much more than rubber. It is chronicled and documented in The Crime and Punishment of I.G. Farben *by Joseph Borkin.*

JOSEPH BORKIN: On December 7, 1941, Japan attacked Pearl Harbor, and the United States was suddenly faced with a monumental rubber crisis. It was blocked from its main source of natural rubber in Southeast Asia—just as Germany had been blocked from its source of saltpeter in Chile during World War I. Desperate measures were called for, and rubber was soon tightly rationed. A campaign was started by patriotic citizens to collect rubber goods of all kinds for possible recycling into tires. It was a futile if laudable enterprise. These enthusiasts learned, to their dismay, that rubber bathmats could generally be turned into new rubber bathmats but not into tires. The United States would have to rely on synthetic rubber for tires. However, the American rubber and chemical companies were completely unprepared to mass-produce a synthetic.

The U.S. Senate held hearings on the matter, as Borkin reports.

JOSEPH BORKIN: Scripps-Howard's Thomas L. Stokes, a Pulitzer Prize-winning reporter, described the atmosphere in the committee room.

"Members of the Senate Defense Committee sat grim and visibly shocked as Thurman Arnold . . . testified. . . . [Truman] was particularly indignant about a memorandum by Frank Howard . . . made at The Hague, Netherlands, October 12, 1939, after the outbreak of war, in which Mr. Howard said 'representatives of I.G. Farbenindustrie delivered to me assignments of some 2,000 foreign patents and we did our best to work out complete plans for a modus vivendi which would operate through the term of the war whether or not the U.S. came in.' . . . That last phrase sent a shudder through the committee room."

. . . Hardly had the committee convened when Senator Robert M. La Follette of Wisconsin embarked on an attack on international cartels generally and the I.G.-Standard arrangement specifically.

"Recently, Standard Oil of New Jersey was found by the Antitrust Division of the Department of Justice to be conspiring with I.G. Farben . . . of Germany. I.G. Farben, through its maze of international patent agreements, is the spear-head of Nazi economic warfare. By its cartel agreements with Standard Oil of New Jersey, the United States was effectively prevented from developing or producing any substantial amount of synthetic rubber.

"The penalty administered on Standard Oil for its part in this obstructionist arrangement was a court 'consent decree' which provided a $50,000 fine and a temporary—strictly temporary—and only partial suspension of the monopoly patent privileges which estopped full United States use of granted patents. . . .

"It seems to me that the Standard Oil of New Jersey consent decree is a real victory for Standard Oil Co. . . . All the consent decree does . . . is guarantee that Standard Oil will hold those patents for I.G. Farben . . . until the day when Standard Oil can render an accounting to I.G. Farben, and return the patents."[12]

CLAREMONT COLLEGES
CLAREMONT, CALIFORNIA

aug 16 '42

THE GRADUATE SCHOOL

To Abu Zaid, Prince of the Beni Hilal and
     Leader of the Great Hajj

Verily He who placed before our feet the expansive (lit. "stretched-out")
Deserts and they are full of sand and plant and animals creatures without
number they are creeping and running and flying in the air above the heads
of those they are beneath them in their flying etc... *** ... and as to
what follows verily I am attempting the extreme of effort that given me by
God may He be exalted that I should come to thy meeting with the quickest
of that which is possible and it is the rulership and the government and
what is of the military and the power which is up/them (lit. "her") and perhaps it may be if God will they are permitting me I should depart to thy
meeting but I am not ceasing I am ignorant that which is being about-to-do
the government so I pray God he causes me to arrive upon the city in which
are dwelling in it you along with your family the noble the generous and
thy wife and she is like the moon shining round bright there being no
clouds before its face and verily I if I have arrived in the city of the
Holy Faranjy (supply "it is well," "so be it," etc.) and if not and already
it is the noon of the day of the Assembly so I am not coming because I
cannot but God is powerful over all things and it may be I shall and it
is on the morning of that day and if not I have not but God is the knower
so may he whiten thy day and make cool thine eyes and is writing to thee
this writing thy friend and he hoping our meeting be if God will may he
be exalted

                              Ras Malfoof

(Free render: I think I can make it; but if I am not in S.F. by Fri. noon
don't wait. The govt. is touchy and I must make sure there will be no
sudden orders to report)

Letter to Paul Springer, July 16, 1942

dormitories between 700 and 800 North in Provo, Utah. A young girl of sixteen, the daughter of a Swedish immigrant widow, had come there to study music for the summer. Her mother, who had at one time worked as a maidservant in the household of one of Hugh Nibley's aunts, had none of Sloanie Nibley's sense of style and driving ambition for her children. The Swedish mother had, however, purchased a cello as part of a package deal that included six silver spoons, which were much more interesting to the mother than the instrument. But the daughter loved that cello and found music to be a refuge from a world full of the drudgery of getting through the Great Depression. Now the daughter had taken the cello and traveled down from the Salt Lake Valley, where she and her mother lived, to study music in Provo for the summer. Later she recalled seeing part of the

Phyllis Draper

Nibley family there that summer: Sloanie the matriarch; Reid, the youngest son at nineteen; and Barbara, the baby of the family, who was then sixteen. Sloanie had decided that Reid was to be a concert pianist and Barbara was to have a career singing opera. They too had come to study music for the summer at BYU.

The imposing Sloanie made an impression that stuck with the young cellist. The older woman bustled about, complaining loudly that the service and accommodations were not up to her standards. The Nibley children, who had received the best in music lessons and instruments from infancy, were more accomplished than the Swedish widow's daughter with her secondhand cello. In fact, this young girl had almost nothing in common with Sloanie Nibley's children. She was a simple girl from a background where talk focused more on how to get by than on solving the cultural ills of the world— exactly the kind of talk Hugh Nibley often viciously attacked in his letters. Her name was Phyllis Draper, and if she had little in common with the Nibley family, she had far less in common with Hugh's ex-fiancée, Herta Pauly, the "super-intellectual Prussian comet." As Sloanie Nibley waited impatiently for Hugh, her favorite child, to arrive in

Provo, there was no way she or any of them could know that Hugh Nibley would some-day be Phyllis Draper's husband. A lot had to change before that could happen.

Three times from the "burning rocks of Zion" Hugh wrote to his mother that he would be late—then later—in meeting her in at BYU. But finally he left Zion and went to Provo.

Letter to Springer, Aug. 5, 1942

Reverendissimus viator,

No sooner had you faded from the view in fair Provo than my esteemed ancestress appeared with the instantaneous decision we should return by the shortest (because of tires) route to the haunts and heats of So. Calif. In which hot and humid corner of the Fatherland we have just arrived after a single day of driving. It was painful to pass again within the full view of the walls of Zion without turning aside to pause again in its awful precinct. My grand magnum opus[a] has been accepted for publication—in 1944. Just think what things will be then, with the world rushing from worse to worse in the meantime. . . . The draft board is still marking time and the whole situation is as ever teeming with quiet fun. . . . For the rest you know as much news as I do, since we have explored pretty well in the last decade of days that bright and happy, albeit narrow, vale in which our opinions do not clash. I have received communication from various students posted in the great military camps expressing impatience at my delay in joining them and rather spitefully insisting that all has been prepared for my arrival—less solicitude would be appreciated, it looks bad on a number of counts. Give my greetings to your excellent parents (whose forebearance [sic] borders on the miraculous) and your neglected spouse, and bear with me till we meet again *Gott weiss wo.*[b]

HN

[a] *My grand magnum opus:* His doctoral dissertation

[b] *Gott weiss wo:* God knows where

He was right. There was no telling in the summer of 1942 what kind of a world would see his published thesis when it came out in 1944. As for Hugh Nibley and Paul Springer, the two friends would not see each other or the burning rocks of Zion again until the Axis fell. When they finally did meet again, it was in a different world.

2

YOU'RE IN THE ARMY NOW

HUGH NIBLEY: President Story died and I had a talk with the new man who took over. He didn't like Mormons. He said, "You know, you are not one of us." I could feel the tension growing, so I left. I said, well this certainly justifies me in pursuing a patriotic duty.

PAUL SPRINGER: I don't think Hugh was a jingo.[a] I mean he was not a wild-haired patriot; he wasn't going to save the world or anything in particular. I don't think he was unduly patriotic but I think the idea of being drafted was very unpleasant to him and he felt he would rather volunteer and get into it on his own motion rather than being dragged in by his feet like I was.

HUGH NIBLEY: I had taken a lot of ROTC in high school and college. Mother insisted that if there were a World War II that we be officers. She said, "You go into ROTC and you'll never have to slug it out in the mud; you'll have a comfortable war." So the first year in the ROTC in Los Angeles High School I was such a soldier I got the proficiency medal. It was a big ROTC unit, and I got the number one soldier proficiency medal, the highest honor they gave. Colonel Mudgett bestowed it. Then of course I rebelled against it and got into trouble with Colonel Mudgett.

---

[a] *Jingo:* "One who brags of his country's preparedness for fight, and generally advocates or favors a bellicose policy in dealing with foreign powers; a blustering or blatant 'patriot'; a Chauvinist" (*Oxford English Dictionary*).

RESERVE OFFICERS TRAINING CORPS
LOS ANGELES HIGH SCHOOLS
LOS ANGELES, CALIFORNIA

This is to certify that HUGH W. NIBLEY

HAS COMPLETED THE first YEAR OF THE PRESCRIBED COURSE IN THE R. O. T. C. OF THIS

INSTITUTION AND HAS OBTAINED THE REQUIRED PROFICIENCY IN THE SUBJECTS THEREIN AS

INDICATED ON THE REVERSE SIDE HEREOF AND IS ENTITLED TO ENTER 2nd year COURSE.

CONDUCT Excellent   CHARACTER Excellent   PHYSIQUE Good

GIVEN UNDER OUR HANDS AT THE Los Angeles HIGH SCHOOL

LOS ANGELES, CALIFORNIA, THIS 26th DAY OF January 1925.

R. H. Housh
PRINCIPAL

John J. Mudgett
Lieut. Colonel, U. S. Army
ASST. P. M. S. AND T.   L. A.   HIGH SCHOOL

APPROVED:

Susan M. Dorsey
SUPERINTENDENT OF SCHOOLS

E. H. Clark
Colonel, U. S. Army
PROFESSOR MILITARY SCIENCE AND TACTICS

Hugh Nibley's proficiency citation

SLOAN NIBLEY:[a] Hugh didn't care for gym as we were going to high school, and if you took ROTC you didn't have to take gym, so he took ROTC. He couldn't stand the officers, but when there was something interesting that would break the routine he was glad to join in or contribute. For example, they were having the big yearly review, and a group of them showed up with an "Awkward Squad." There were eight of them, and they were well organized and well drilled, and they drilled up and down the field with Hugh with them, making all the wrong moves, doing everything contrary to regulations. It was like an Abbot and Costello routine and it was at the head of the whole review, showing what they thought of the army.

HUGH NIBLEY: I'd had too much army; I didn't like it. Colonel Mudgett would take me in for serious talks, not about being *against* the army but treating it too lightly. I was no longer the perfect soldier I had been before. Colonel Mudgett and Mother were good friends and that helped some, but I was fed up. It was a lot of nonsense is why. He was still fighting the Spanish-American War. He'd been a sort of hero in the Spanish-American War and that's the way we learned to do things. To quell any sign of rebellion or independence, that's why we were there.

PAUL SPRINGER: I bent myself double to find the best way possible to dodge the draft because I was just beginning to make money, and the idea of going in for $20 a month, $21 a month, was not pleasant. I wasn't really afraid of being shot at, but it was the financial embarrassment of it. Hugh put it to me this way: "The trouble with you is," he says, "confronted with a situation, there are several things you can do: you can do the smart thing or you can do the right thing. But *you* inevitably do the *easy* thing." He rather keynoted that, too. He was rather right, too.

To Paul Springer, summer, 1941

. . . For some reason the local draft board seems to have taken a shine or a violent aversion to me, I cannot tell which; at any rate they are stubbornly averse to deferring me, even though I'm safely beyond the 28 year mark—seem determined to see what I look like in a uniform. . . .

[a] *Sloan:* Alexander Sloan Nibley (1908–1990), Hugh's older brother, was a screenwriter and husband of Linda Stirling, a star of the movie serials of the forties.

INDUCTION

Four days before Hugh Nibley was inducted at Fort MacArthur, a man who had a great deal in common with him went through the same process. Max Oppenheimer Jr., who would later cross paths with Nibley, wrote about induction in Los Angeles in his memoir, An Innocent Yank at Home Abroad.

MAX OPPENHEIMER: Induction into the Army was a dehumanizing process. Experience has taught the Services that the transition for new recruits from civilian life to the military must be absolute. As in all military operations, the element of surprise is paramount. We handed in our personal effects, our last physical link to civilian life, to be shipped back to relatives or friends. Our fears of failing the physical proved quite unfounded. With the Army in dire need of bodies, a vertical corpse pushed along the recruit line would have had a fair chance of passing. There was a psychological exam, but I should guess only a flagrant deviant would have flunked that. By early evening we had taken the oath and been supplied with a Service record and Form 20, detailing our biographical data and civilian qualifications. As enlisted wards of the Army we had been issued our new olive-drab uniforms and personal effects free of charge. We now were OD from the skin outward. This standardization, together with the new title of Private indiscriminately granted to all, should at least have inspired in us a feeling of *esprit de corps.* What keeps up morale under such circumstances is that everyone is in the same, shall we say, to reflect the general mental state of most, leaky ship.

We were sent to Fort MacArthur, outside of Los Angeles, in itself an electrifying morale-raising name, and arrived rather late at night. We handed the envelope containing our records irretrievably to a Sergeant (henceforth our personal data would remain confidential even to us), who scanned them casually, as though he were thinking, "What are they unloading on us today?" Glancing at my record, he raised his head with these ominous words, "You got more degrees than a barometer, ain't you?"

The Army travels on its stomach, preferably a full one. We were invited to a late supper, our first encounter with an Army mess hall. Then came the important lesson of how to make up a bunk bed with blankets so tight that a dime, dropped on it, will rebound at attention and the ensemble pass a First Sergeant's inspection, removing the scowl from his face. The next event was to be a surprise. Deemed refreshed after 17 hours of energizing initiation into a new lifestyle, we were informed that we would now take the two-hour Army General Classification test, an IQ test determining our future in the Army and our chances of becoming an officer. Despite the late hour, I achieved a safe score somewhere in the high 120s or low 130s, sufficient for OCS. It had been a very long day.

In the morning, rather early, we were informed that the high scorers would go to the Army Air Corps. As we discovered subsequently, this preliminary triage was not perfect. A few illiterates managed to slip through the cracks. In any event, I was now the proud wearer of insignia with wings and could thrust out my chest to the "Off We Go Into the Wild Blue Yonder" song. All of a sudden, I had this passing, but sinking, feeling that this was the point of no return. I could see Uncle Sam pointing his finger at me: "You're in the Army now!"[1]

HUGH NIBLEY: Finally I just went and enlisted. Enlisting was the simplest thing to do, no complications or anything. We took the big red car down Hollywood Boulevard and enlisted in the old Pacific Electric building downtown on September 28 of 1942. I had to go in a room where you take off all your clothes and get a medical examination; then I got on a bus and went down to Fort MacArthur at San Pedro. I was kept up till three in the morning with delays; then I had to go and take the intelligence test and practically flunked it because I was so tired out. No, actually I didn't flunk it. The man who gave me the test was a friend of mine, a medical student and a member of the Church too, and he came in and congratulated me and told me I got the highest score they'd ever had. But I would've done better if I'd had enough sleep. This friend of mine told me I was going to St. Petersburg, Florida, where the air force had this business.

Meanwhile they were short on the garbage detail, so I was taken over to work right after taking the intelligence test. My job was to follow the garbage truck around this big camp and empty the cans into the truck, and I did that. And I did that the next day, and the next day, and the next day. And then finally the sergeant in charge says, "I can get you a permanent job here as a garbage man and keep you out of the war; you're the best I've ever seen." I thought it over. It was a good offer, running after this garbage truck for the rest of the war. But I didn't want that for a permanent job. There were guys that went in as lieutenants, and when I got there I was carrying their bags because they had come, these snobs, from Eastern families and immediately got commissions with no trouble at all. I guess I could have pulled strings, things like that, but I didn't. No, I just got into the army as a buck private. As a garbage man. In the air force they were short of weathermen, so I went to be trained as a weather observer.

The first thing, of course, I went to Florida for basic training. I was with a lot of great kids, mostly Southerners, and delightful people they were. They were as naïve as all get-out. And there were Greeks and people from New York. They had me leading the calisthenics in the morning: hup, two, three, four, hup, two, three, four! I was good at that. I don't know why they picked me out. I was muscular in those days.

October 9, 1942

Dear Mother

I have a very elaborate address, now

Pvt. H. Nibley
586th Technical School Squadron
Flight no. 126-C
Edgewater Hotel
St. Petersburg, Florida

All this is descriptive of a rather sumptuous setting. Any setting would be enchanted by the wonderfully bemusing quality of the air, which is strangely dreamy & exhilarating. Everything is fun—such a hilarious sensation for a change, simply to play the game & enjoy the show. The last few days have been nothing but a round of tests, from which no results are as yet available. Easy & pleasant. I find myself rather surprisingly in a non-combatant branch of the air-force, but one which promises to be anything but unexciting. . . . Everywhere I am running into the Utah element [i.e., Mormons]—you can usually spot them because they are the pleasantly cracked ones in any group. The train trip was by all odds the pleasantest journey I ever made. The Southern mind and the Southern Soul are yours for the asking—anyone who can count up to 4 or spell two out of ten common words is a damn Yankee. Please *don't* send anything.

Love
Hugh

HUGH NIBLEY: They had these refectories[a] there that had everything the soul of man could demand. They had frozen strawberries and all this stuff, and yet it was like hell. There was something so regimented about it, it was mechanical. It was like Disneyland. Everybody marched in line, it was brilliantly lit, and everything was so clean and smart and the way it should be, and you could have anything you wanted to eat, and so forth and so on. And it was sickening. It was horrifying. And the first time I went to Disneyland I said, this is like hell would be, a plastic Early America. Everything was phony. It's all built on a formula that doesn't have any charm for me, and I don't know why people should want to go to Disneyland—it's

[a] *Refectory:* "A room for refreshment; *esp.* in religious houses and colleges, the hall or chamber in which the meals take place" (*Oxford English Dictionary*).

so depressing! None of it is real, and there are all these young Mormons conducting you around and telling you what to do and where to go.

The war was changing people's lives all over the world, taking them from what was familiar and what they had chosen and forcing them to go down paths they would never have taken if the war had not intervened in their lives. On another continent, other men were being introduced into other camps. Viktor Frankl describes what it was like:

VIKTOR FRANKL: When one examines the vast amount of material which has been amassed as the result of many prisoners' observations and experiences, three phases of the inmate's mental reactions to camp life become apparent: the period following his admission; the period when he is well entrenched in camp routine; and the period following his release and liberation.

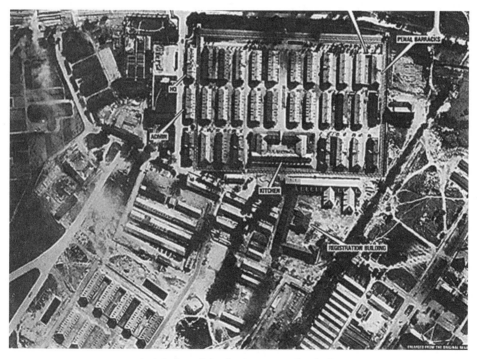

Aerial view of the death camp at Auschwitz

The symptom that characterizes the first phase is shock. . . .

. . . Auschwitz—the very name stood for all that was horrible: gas chambers, crematoriums, massacres. Slowly, almost hesitatingly, the train moved on as if it wanted to spare its passengers the dreadful realization as long as possible: Auschwitz!

With the progressive dawn, the outlines of an immense camp became visible: long stretches of several rows of barbed-wire fences; watch towers; search lights; and long columns of ragged human figures, grey in the greyness of dawn, trekking along the straight desolate roads, to what destination we did not know. There were isolated shouts and whistles of command. We did not know their meaning. My imagination led me to see gallows with people dangling on them. I was horrified, but this was just as well, because step by step we had to become accustomed to a terrible and immense horror. . . .

In psychiatry there is a certain condition known as "delusion of reprieve." The condemned man, immediately before his execution, gets the illusion that he might be reprieved at the very last minute. We, too, clung to shreds of hope and believed to the last moment that it would not be so bad.[2]

Hugh Nibley's experience was different.

Dear Mother

This is one of those super-snooty places, very much like the Coronado Hotel.[a] I am in a deluxe cottage on the lagoon sharing a room with but one other occupant & with the original hotel beds. The food is as elegant as the surroundings. After all the tests & exams at St. Petersburg they told me I could go to any technical school in the air force. . . . My application with the Intelligence is still cooking—they are all satisfactorily impressed and I may get a whack at the Near East before you think. Meantime what lies ahead is a period of basic training—very jolly and picturesque, amid these tropic lagoons with their odd fishes and fowl and stunning exuberance of vegetation. Pleasantest of all are the frequent and prolonged rest periods (that is, to *me* they seem that way) when one can really get a lot done. Since I must be a scientist for a

a The Hotel del Coronado in San Diego, built in 1888, is a famous fixture on the Southern California coast.

while, I am gobbling up mathematics in an ecstasy of zeal—it is a long pent-up appetite which I had almost despaired of ever satisfying. It is heavenly stuff. . . . Contrary (of course) to everything you hear, there is no great thirst for correspondence in the camps—letters in fact are a distinct nuisance. . . . The food is good and sleep is abundant, I have put on 7 pounds and never get tired. . . .

Hugh Nibley, Clearwater, Florida, 1942

Nov. 13, 1942

Dear Mother,

It is duty and duty alone that dictates this communiqué, for there is certainly very little worth writing about. Everyone else around here spends all his spare time reading and writing letters—if you should hear one of these masterpieces you would wonder about many things. . . . I'm quite happy with army fare, but I have eaten so much of other warriors' boxes from home—you simply can't get out of it—that I am embarrassed at being unable to reciprocate. So we hereby lift the ban on such vain objects without in the least suggesting any degree of compliance with such a brash hint. Sloan suspects the war may end in a hurry—ha! It won't end that way if we are the winners.

The weather is hot and sultry—very tropical with new birds and animals appearing with every change of the wind. . . . You wouldn't believe how strongly the presence of growing and living nature captivates the whole spirit with a kind of overpower[ing] conviction, a feeling of acceptance and love of whatever is, which is quite Yogi.

Love and kisses
Hugh

HUGH NIBLEY: After we finished basic training there was a long period of kitchen police[a] while we were waiting in this big hotel in Clearwater for our session of

---

[a] *Kitchen police:* Also known as "KP," this was scullery work such as scrubbing pots and peeling potatoes. Though assigned by the army, it had nothing to do with police work.

weather school to begin. My first assignment during this time was typically army. It was the eve of Thanksgiving and I was scrubbing toilets out with a big scrubbing brush, and an officer came to me and said, "Come with me and bring the brush." He took me to where there was a huge pile of celery; they were preparing it for the officers' mess the next day. He said, "Clean this celery off."

I said, "With this brush? I just used it for cleaning toilets."

"That doesn't make any difference. If it's shiny and clean, that's all we want to know," he said. "That's an order!"

So here I was helping the officers get diarrhea or whatever it was by cleaning celery with a toilet brush for their Thanksgiving feast, which I couldn't even attend, of course. So I was having my subtle revenge. That's so typically army, but it's the sort of thing you find all the time going on.

October 17, 1942

Springerlein

. . . So far I have had nothing but fun in the army. You would love it, & become an officer in no time & have everybody hating your guts. This service is taking languages (& little me) quite seriously. . . . I repeat, I can't imagine anyone who would fit more naturally into this outfit than yourself. These guys (the right ones, that is) are anything but dumb. Brahms is at a premium, and none fears to speak the truth. Pleasanter company in a pleasanter setting cannot be imagined. I am sure Nelly would be right welcome too, even at the risk of slighting some minor statutes of the military—she might come as an entertainer or something—you could surely get that much out of the draft-board.

Siegheil,
Hugh

HUGH NIBLEY: My next assignment was almost as good as the celery. They found out I knew shorthand and immediately some weasel-faced officer gets a hold of me. His business was to go underneath the telephones in the officers' club, and I went with him to take shorthand notes. We had wires and made connections and listened to all the officers' calls to see if any officer should say anything critical of the colonel. He was the commander of the base and was bucking for a star, you see, and he wanted

CATCH-22

JOSEPH HELLER: Bologna turned out to be the most rewarding event in Captain Black's life since the day Major Duluth was killed over Perugia and he was almost selected to replace him. When word of Major Duluth's death was radioed back to the field, Captain Black responded with a surge of joy. Although he had never really contemplated the possibility before, Captain Black understood at once that he was the logical man to succeed Major Duluth as squadron commander. To begin with, he was the squadron intelligence officer, which meant he was more intelligent than everyone else in the squadron. True, he was not on combat status, as Major Duluth had been and as all squadron commanders customarily were; but this was really another powerful argument in his favor, since his life was in no danger and he would be able to fill the post for as long as his country needed him. The more Captain Black thought about it, the more inevitable it seemed. It was merely a matter of dropping the right word in the right place quickly. He hurried back to his office to determine a course of action. Settling back in his swivel chair, his feet up on the desk and his eyes closed, he began imagining how beautiful everything would be once he was squadron commander.

While Captain Black was imagining, Colonel Cathcart was acting, and Captain Black was flabbergasted by the speed with which, he concluded, Major Major had outsmarted him. His great dismay at the announcement of Major Major's appointment as squadron commander was tinged with an embittered resentment he made no effort to conceal. When fellow administrative officers expressed astonishment at Colonel Cathcart's choice of Major Major, Captain Black muttered that there was something funny going on; when they speculated on the political value of Major Major's resemblance to Henry Fonda, Captain Black asserted that Major Major really was Henry Fonda; and when they remarked that Major Major was somewhat odd, Captain Black announced that he was a Communist.

"They're taking over everything," he declared rebelliously. "Well, you fellows can stand around and let them if you want to, but I'm not going to. I'm going to do something about it."[3]

to know about any criticism of him from the officers. And so we took down everything that was spoken by the officers over the phones in the officers' telephone booth. This is the army. This is how they trust each other. It's right out of *Catch-22*.

December 5, 1942

Dear grandmother

Army life is far from being an unmixed evil. First of all, while one commonly hears the complaint of long and tedious hours, I must confess I have never had so much free time, nor used it so profitably. Nine weeks in Florida have been a carnival—all the strains and shocks of trainings have been nothing but fun, thanks to a lesson learned long ago—the secret is to remain as detached from everything as a disembodied spirit, viewing even one's own activities as something rather distant and amusing. Seen in this light, the pattern of our feverish and ill-considered career present some striking features. What strikes one most forcibly from the first is the fact that the people of our world are guilty of the tragic mistake of acting and thinking like animals, like mindless insects or some species of shell-fish, to live and breed for a date and then disintegrate and leave nothing behind but a pestilential odor. . . . It is marvelous how little the people of our time are inclined to challenge and examine anything. It is only because the race has become a pack of sheep that absolute dictators can spring up anywhere without opposition. But enough of this Jeremiad. If there is no greater distress than to watch the world rushing into ills they know not of, and to feel ourselves strongly seconded by powers greater than our own. Even if we stood quite alone, it would be enough to know that we are in the right. But we do not stand alone. Certain as I am of the presence of a mighty host, I would beg the other world to withhold its fire, so to speak, till we show them what we can do unaided. I cannot be too grateful to the Lord for allowing us the flattering liberties we enjoy, but I am afraid things have almost reached the point where we have demonstrated our incompetence to the full—it will soon be time for heaven to intervene, and then we can expect no end of surprises. My own position is certainly an amusing one. Could I ever have dreamed that someday I would be preparing myself to be an aerial warrior—and thoroughly enjoying it? My role as a soldier I have long anticipated. After all I ran like a fanatic through the cities of the Rhine preaching nothing but death and destruction, until I had no authority for such extravagant behavior, (which frequently earned the censure of my fellows) except the Doctrine and Covenants.[a] I expected with perfect confidence the present and violent destruction of Karlsruhe, Mannheim, Ludwigshafen[b] and other such towns, all of which were really rather well warned. But though I looked for a time "when peace would be taken away from the world and the Devil would have control of his dominion,"[c] I never dared to think the Saints could be *happy* in the midst of such a world. But now I say, "why not?" The gospel is cut and fashioned to weather the strain of perfectly horrible environments, and wherever you have the gospel that is heaven—in the awareness of its truth we may have a fullness of joy at any time.

I think of you very often and wonder at the great and far-reaching influence of your wonderful life; I am sure you cannot imagine the good you have done or the distant repercussions of your ceaseless effort and sacrifice in this weary world. I expect to go abroad quite soon and will write you again before I do.

Love to all in Portland, but mostly to you,
Hugh

HUGH NIBLEY: After basic training I went to weather school in Urbana, Illinois. I started doing hard math and things like that, and I'd stay up all night long working on it because I was conscientious.

December 18th, 1942

Dear Mother

This place is *vast;* such an endless expanse of very "technical" looking buildings and such seething masses of uniforms of every type and

---

[a] *The Doctrine and Covenants (D&C):* A volume of Latter-day Saint scripture consisting mostly of revelations received by Joseph Smith in the early nineteenth century.

[b] The Allies believed they could break down the German war machine by attacking production sources in German cities and breaking the will of the German people at the same time. At the time Hugh Nibley wrote this letter the Allies had not yet begun to bomb Germany with the intensity they would eventually reach, but they had succeeded in creating the first firestorm in Hamburg, destroying 70 percent of the city and killing 30,000 people. While German skies rained bombs, by night from the British and by day from the Americans, it was not as effective as the Allies hoped in destroying production. And, like the English in the battle of Britain, the German people seemed to grow more determined the more they were bombed, a phenomenon that seems to have foreshadowed the American reaction to the bombing on a much smaller scale of New York City and the Pentagon in 2001.

[c] "For I am no respecter of persons, and will that all men shall know that the day speedily cometh; the hour is not yet, but is nigh at hand, when peace shall be taken from the earth, and the devil shall have power over his own dominion" (D&C 1:35).

denomination—all very "World of Tomorrowish" and you are welcome to the next thousand years if it's going to be like that; and give me a few quiet decades on a distant island. But the weather is gorgeous. Not at all like Florida, you might guess, but very icy and windy and grey, with bare trees and bleak expanses of perfectly flat white plains. . . . We have become quite a little mathematician and work great big problems, sometimes passing within view, almost, of the right answer. . . . Now that it can be told, I *nearly* ended up as a commando, for I weigh 158 pounds and am so strong I scare myself and in training I was *superb*. But suddenly they needed weathermen and being in charge of the group I got a peek at the records and lo I was so exceedingly high as to score that how could I be anything else? The answer may be forthcoming.

Love and kisses,
Hugh

Jan. 25, 1943

Dear Mother

Try as I do, I can't believe that somewhere the sun is warm and the sky clear, even though as a weather-man I should know that such a state is entirely possible. . . . For your enlightenment, sweet ancestress, the officer business in the Army is very different from that in the Navy. No one can think of being a high and mighty until he has been through Officers Candidate School, which lasts three months at least, and *no* one can even apply for admission to that jute mill until he has been in the Army at least three months. But why should I be an officer? By most counts I would make a rather bad one. If I am even a worse weather observer, that, I can assure you is much nearer the type of thing you recommended in your last. I still think I can get out of this pseudo-scientific time-wasting. If we must be nasty let's do it in a big way. . . .

Love,
Hugh

[continued on the same page]

Such a lot of letter writing at these posts! We can be sure, when the day of wrath shall come it will find this generation absorbed in giving and taking correspondence. Such zeal! Such unrelenting application! And to what? You should have some of these letters read to you (that happens here whether you like it or not) you would understand my admirable and self-sacrificing resolve *never* to write a note unless there is at least a reasonable certainty that the lives, fortunes and sacred honor of no less than seventy times seven church-going tax-payers depend on it. *Why* should *anyone*, I would like to know, want to hear from *me?* I refuse to be party to this morbid and degrading practice of penning notes that have no more to convey than the above. Please understand this and be advised.

Love and kisses
Hugh

Feb. 18, 1943

Dear Mother,

When I say I haven't time to write I am telling the truth. The Air Corps is split wide open between two factions, one that thinks effective fighting is what counts and the other that looks before everything for shiny buttons and snappy salutes. The old guard is in the saddle here and so everyone must be a full-time technician and at the same time a full-time grenadier. So for once in the army I have no spare time at all. I'm sending back the bathrobe, first because I have no use for it (when *will* you give me credit for knowing what I need and what I don't) and second because bathrobes are not allowed here. But I have almost worn the garments* out and could use a *couple* of pair (not ten please!). Only two more weeks of this (a dozen or so examinations) school. I am in no hurry about the officers school, what with 20 years of war ahead. 3 cheers for the Russians, upon whom, incidentally, Communism seems to have had anything but an enervating effect. I wish we had some of their morale. Nothing tickles me like the New Pretensions of our own land-of-the-Comic-Book-and-Soap-Opera to do the World's Realistic Thinking for it. With finals coming up, please don't expect anything for at least two weeks.

Love Hugh

---

* *Temple garments:* Ceremonial underclothing worn by devout Mormons to remind them of their faith. Temple garments are believed by many to have both spiritual and physical protective power for the wearer. The military makes allowances for Mormons to wear these items of non-typical GI clothing, as they do for some other religious items for other sects.

THE BATTLE OF STALINGRAD

Hitler needed the Russian oilfields and access to the Middle Eastern oil to keep his war going. When his troops got to a city in southern Russia named after his Soviet rival dictator, the battle got personal. He ordered his armies to take Stalingrad and not to retreat under any circumstances. Stalin, equally determined not to let Hitler take his namesake city, ordered the Soviets not to give up a square meter. From August 1942 to February 2 the next year (from about the time Hugh Nibley went to Zions Canyon until he was in the middle of his weather training) the Germans and the Russians slugged it out, taking, losing, and retaking the same shattered buildings over and over. The Russian winter came and the Russians cut the Germans off from their supply lines, but Hitler still would allow no retreat. Starved, frozen, exhausted, and out of ammunition, the Germans finally disobeyed their orders to die where they were and surrendered. Casualty figures vary, but the Soviets lost around half a million soldiers and the city of Stalingrad was reduced to rubble. The Germans lost between one hundred and two hundred thousand dead, with ninety-one thousand taken prisoners, almost all of whom died in the Soviet gulag either during the war or in the years following it. But a loss even greater to Germany was its myth of invincibility. It was the turning point of World War II. The Russians had turned the tide, and from Stalingrad on, the Germans began to play defense.

American propaganda poster

HUGH NIBLEY: I finished the weather school in Illinois and became a weather observer at Godman Field. That was in Kentucky by Ft. Knox. It was a very important place, and it was rather exciting because there were only six weather observers there. We worked in two-man teams—on twelve hours, off twelve hours—around the clock, me and a jolly Irishman from New York called McCann; he was very smart. They would bring food in on a cart so you could eat as you were going along, and I'd eat while I was making diagrams, and profiles for flights to Cuba, and things like that. And every fifteen minutes we had to send out these weather observances—humidity, temperature, and all these readings—we'd get them together and send them out on the wire regularly. I'd just dash it off on the teletype and get all the necessary weather data to go all over the country because they didn't have weather satellites or anything like that.

March 8, 1943

Dear Mother

Thanks for the caramels and undies. The food is pretty awful here, but it was no tragedy to leave Chanute [Illinois] where they went on camp rations on March 1; the one decent thing about that mechanical nightmare was the food.

March 20, 1943

Dear Mother

The Colonel yesterday told me they have done what they could here about my commission—the rest is up to Washington which, of course, will do nothing at all about it. . . . I may go abroad and I may not. Hey, the phone for me—very confidential—it seems (tho you mustn't breathe a word) that I am quitting weather some time next week and going into intelligence. That means I will be an officer but *that* is nothing to swoon about. These poor flying officers barely know enough to be efficient [unclear]—there! We get a flash notice at this very moment, one of them has just cracked up a P-38. So we go on paying the price of trying to make everything cheap and easy. I have to rush.

Love,
Hugh

HUGH NIBLEY: One night some officer was drunk and he was flying to Cuba and took off and flew into Bear Mountain, a knoll at the end of the runway at Godman Field. He smashed up his plane and got himself smashed up or killed, I don't remember which, I think it was killed. And of course I had made the report on the maps and I had sent him off with a blessing. So 3:00 in the morning I get this call and I thought, oh boy, this is it. Court martial at least. I'm going to be cashiered[a] or something. But it wasn't that at all. A letter, a 5-star notice, had come from Camp Ritchie. They wanted me transferred to Ritchie in a hurry because they were planning the invasion of North Africa, and they'd heard that I had had some Arabic, so they wanted to get me up there. The commandant, the guy in charge of the weather system at Godman Field, said, "Well, you'll be a major tomorrow, my boy!" Because this was a 5-star, and they didn't come for everybody, you know. So they immediately whisked me up to Camp Ritchie—very secret—for Intelligence.

[a] *Cashier:* To dismiss from service or fellowship

April 1, 1943

Dear Mother and Dad

. . . I am no longer in the Air Force, but find myself suddenly in the unassailable and inapproachable Adjutant General branch, to wit, Intelligence. On my way to Maryland . . . on business of a rather exalted nature, so I am writing in great haste from Cincinnati, never knowing but what every syllable from now on will be censored without mercy. Thanks for the c-n-d-y. Will write later about things. Almost sorry to leave my New Kentucky Home, but spring is now on the circuit and the East should be beautiful.

Love,
Hugh

Private Hugh Nibley wearing the wings of the Army Air Force

3

THE HALL OF CROOKED MIRRORS

Prior to World War II, the United States military had no centralized Intelligence service. The beginning of what would eventually become the Intelligence Corps (and later the Central Intelligence Agency and the many other agencies dedicated to gathering and analyzing information about America's enemies and friends) was a relatively small group of soldiers gathered together in a Maryland National Guard facility called Camp Ritchie.

HUGH NIBLEY: This is a dream I've had: somebody says, "Ah! here comes the great scientist, the great mathematician! He's going to solve this problem." And then, of course, I don't know a thing about it, and I'm absolutely utterly miserable. It's criminal! That's been with me all my life, so I've always overcompensated, always over-killing in preparation for examinations and so forth. I had to be at the head of the class. That's how I got into this Intelligence mess.

> Dear Mother,
>
> After the red gullies of Kentucky, the Blue Ridge Mountains would be a pleasant change but for a touch of bronchitis—a mere trifle for which I am being allowed to rest my head off; once the Army gets you in a hospital you have to be violently healthy before they even smile at the thought of letting you out. . . . If it keeps me from starting school here on the 15th I shall be fit to be tied. Not that I love army schools—weather wasn't bad but I certainly learned more in one 12-hour 2-man shift at Godman Field than in all the fuss and fury of Chanute.

If, as Hitler believed, ethnic diversity is a source of national weakness, Camp Ritchie had to be the weakest place on earth. Nowhere in America was ethnic diversity more prevalent. The camp was built near what is now known as Camp David, the presidential retreat. Its official title was Military Intelligence Training Center or MITC.

Dear Mother:

I can't tell you anything about this place—it's just mud and the army. . . . Here we have the latest shipment from continental Europe—a bad and shop-worn lot, for the most part;—brash, ill-mannered men, quick to exploit every situation for personal gain. Yet among them are a few a little lower than the angels.

There aren't a lot places or groups of people in the world where Hugh Nibley would fit right in, especially in the United States Army, but if there was such a place and such a group, it was the MITC at Camp Ritchie and the strange crew that gathered there. In addition to language skills, the one thing all the Ritchie men seemed to have had most in common was an extremely unusual personal history. Here, among the men Hugh Nibley called "a little lower than the angels," were men who became his lifetime friends. One was George Bailey, who later gained renown as a scholar and wrote the best-selling Germans, *which is his memoir of the war. Another Ritchie pal of Hugh Nibley was Max Oppenheimer Jr., a scholar of Spanish literature and one of the pioneers of the current U.S. Intelligence establishment. Then there were two men who shared an occupation that would make them irresistibly attractive to Hugh Nibley—George Allen of Philadelphia and Lucien Goldschmidt of New York were dealers in rare books.*

The following description of life in Camp Ritchie is assembled from the memoirs of Bailey, Oppenheimer, and Allen and an interview with Goldschmidt.

GEORGE BAILEY: If . . . Camp Ritchie has not entered world literature, it is only because the phenomenon of it has proved too difficult to grasp and transmit in any coherent way. Camp Ritchie was basically a pool—not to say "cesspool"—of language talent; it harbored every conceivable—and in some cases inconceivable—kind of immigrant: there were barracks housing Russians, Greeks, French, Italians, Spanish, Indians (American and Hindu), Icelanders, Laplanders, Mexicans, Albanians, Ruthenians,

Macedonians, Slovenians, Wends, Hungarians, Welsh, Algerians, Syrians, Montenegrins, Ceylonese, Eskimos, Tunisians, Turks, Georgians, Azerbaijani, Uzbeks, Chuvash, Cossacks, Kozakhs, Mongolians, Basques—to name but a few. Basically, nevertheless, the camp was German.[1]

LUCIEN GOLDSCHMIDT: Ritchie was a very small army camp; there were never more than eleven hundred or twelve hundred people at the top and often fewer, which by army standards is very little. Many of them had been selected because they had particular skills or knowledge in language, which didn't prevent them from having a Ukrainian bartender from the lower East side [of Manhattan] but also the son of Thomas Mann,[a] the poet Peter Veerick, Prince Shashavadseh, Bahoutmanstoff,[b] and any number of odd and unexpected phenomena.

GEORGE ALLEN: It was probably the nuttiest camp in the country, though I realize there is considerable competition for that title. The camp commandant, a General Charles G. Banfill of the air force, used to buzz the camp in a Piper Cub to qualify for flight pay.[2]

MAX OPPENHEIMER: Before long, I gathered the distinct impression that MITC should have stood for Military Institution for Total Confusion.[3]

GEORGE BAILEY: The soldiery and, to a considerably lesser extent, the officers' corps at Ritchie were a hodgepodge of European intellectuals. There was a high percentage of academicians, writers, poets, novelists (Klaus Mann and Stefan Heym[c]), stage producers and directors, musicians, choreographers, dancers, singers (Sergeant

[a] Klaus Mann (1906–1949) was the son of Thomas Mann and also an author. He left Germany during Hitler's rise to power and came to America. Best known for his novel *Mephisto*, he died in France from an overdose of sleeping pills.

[b] I have been unable to find any information on these men, probably because the text used here is a transcription of an interview with Goldschmidt done in 1983, and the transcription contains spelling errors of foreign words and names.

[c] Stefan Heym (1913–2001), a Jewish writer born in Germany, immigrated to America in 1935 where he edited a German-language, anti-Fascist newspaper in New York and wrote his first bestseller, *Hostages*. During the McCarthy purges, Heym returned to Europe and lived in East Berlin from 1953 until his death.

William Warfield[a] as an example of the non-European performing artist: he was in charge of the recreation hall), psychiatrists, psychologists, engineers, playboys, and sportsmen (during my time we had three erstwhile mountain climbers credited with first ascents of various Alpine peaks).[4]

LUCIEN GOLDSCHMIDT: David Rockefeller,[b] then only a first lieutenant, was teaching French Army identification, and it was not below his dignity. The lieutenant for whom I worked when I went to Italy was Professor King—I mean *Lieutenant King*—who then became one of the outstanding hispanists of our time.

GEORGE BAILEY: The Post Exchange at Camp Ritchie resembled the Tower of Babel after construction had been discontinued: an Icelander reciting a saga in Old Norse over a strawberry milkshake was a commonplace. Passages from the Upanishad in the original Sanskrit could also be heard during an informal discussion among GIs refreshing themselves after a field exercise.[5]

LUCIEN GOLDSCHMIDT: In Camp Ritchie, like in most army posts, a great deal of illogical activity goes on. No one could really explain why Camp Ritchie had gotten a contingent of native-American Indians from the west, Indian boys, some of whom had never seen a shower before they came, and the army used them mainly to portray Nazis. The rationale was that they were different, I guess, and that they could, without language abilities, do things like, for example, be shown across a ravine on the other side moving in a formation, and then we, the neophytes, would be asked to identify what weapons they had, what units they might represent, and whether they had given any secrets away by passing through that forest. What the Indians thought about it, I couldn't tell you.

GEORGE BAILEY: Those who prided themselves on the breadth of

---

[a] William Warfield (1920–2002), an African-American baritone famous for his opera, musical, and concert singing, was probably best known for his stage and movie roles in *Showboat* and *Porgy and Bess*.

[b] David Rockefeller (1915-) is a businessman, philanthropist, and member of the wealthy Rockefeller clan that gave Rockefeller Center its name. He received a Ph.D. from Chicago University and served as secretary to New York Mayor Fiorello H. LaGuardia and assistant regional director of the United States Office of Defense, Health, and Welfare Service before he, like Hugh Nibley, enlisted in the army as a private.

their linguistic achievements would frequent the PX merely to test their ability to identify all the languages spoken there. The Upanishad provided the inspiration for the name of a language invented solely for the purpose of confounding such people: the artificial language was called "Upmanshipad"; it boasted a vocabulary of more than two hundred words, enough for a limited conversation and just enough to pique the curiosity of overhearers to the point where they would humbly ask which language was being spoken. The avoidance of any similarities with major European and Asiatic languages set exacting requirements for the concoction and hence took time. I knew a sergeant at Ritchie, Hugh Nibley, formerly professor of ancient history at Pomona College, who spoke sixteen languages tolerably well and whose nodding linguistic acquaintanceship included twice that number.[6]

LUCIEN GOLDSCHMIDT: No one could say at that point with whom we might have to fight, so they trained people in Scandinavian and other things that they never used. We never sent American troops to Scandinavia, but who could tell? I mean, who could tell what who would do? There were French classes, there were German classes, there were photo interpretation classes. We were in the German class—section A, I believe, of the seventh class. The seventh class came at a reasonably propitious moment because, while we didn't know it, they were then beginning to think of the invasion of Western Europe and to prepare people. There are groups of 25, or whatever, that form a section, and you quickly notice that there are several that are really very interesting people like Hugh Nibley or Ulrich Frandsen,[a] or like one or two others, with whom one could exchange opinions, thoughts, hopes.

I think both Hugh Nibley and myself were very glad to be at Camp Ritchie because it seemed to us that we could certainly do something more useful, something more constructive, in such an environment; and being prepared for Intelligence work of this type [was preferable to] being equipped to handle a mortar or something in an environment where we would be somewhat lost. But it seemed to us that out of this group of people we would be able to come out better, more useful. If already we had to spend three years away from our normal occupations, this at least seemed to make sense to us.

[a] Ulrich Franzen (1921-) went on to become a prominent architect whose work was especially influential in New York City.

GEORGE BAILEY: One of the main courses of instruction at Ritchie was Interrogation of Prisoners of War (IPW). To this purpose a cadre of fluent German speakers was cultivated to act as freshly captured prisoners of war in simulated interrogations. For the sake of verisimilitude they usually wore German uniforms (this also provided a test of the examinee's knowledge of German army rank and branch insignia) and goose-stepped around the camp in formation. They were trained to act the part of the different types of German the interrogator was likely to meet on the field of battle. Some were briefed to respond only to the subtle approach, some to the legalistic dismantling of the significance of their military oath, others would "spill their guts" only when browbeaten and hectored at the top of the interrogator's lungs. There was one, and he was famous throughout the camp, who was allowed to play it by ear—he could react to any interrogator whichever way he chose. Some of these men were professional actors. (The late Peter van Eyck[a] was one of them. He always played a high-ranking Prussian staff officer,

American soldiers in German uniforms for intelligence training

---

[a] Peter van Eyck (1911–1969) continued to play German officers long after the war in movies such as *The Longest Day* and *The Bridge at Remagen.*

arrogant but correct; he would respond with extremely valuable information if the interrogator could find a way to appeal to his code of honor.)[7]

HUGH NIBLEY: Lucien ended up as an officer because he was such a marvelous interrogator. The reason was that Germans—all the German males—were mortally afraid of their schoolmasters. Lucien had gone to a famous Protestant school in Berlin and his parents were from a distinguished family in Brussels. He was medium height, but thin and severe and gray—you know, the *eminence gris.*[a] He had this marvelous vocabulary, and he was a typical German schoolmaster, very strict, and he knew German kids were just terrified of their teachers, so he'd stand and he'd talk to German prisoners like a schoolmaster. "Are you sure you're telling me right? You'd better tell me where it is, and don't you lie to me!" And they'd spill their guts. Lucien was marvelous at interrogation. I was awful.

[a] *Eminence gris:* A gray eminence, a person respected and feared for his age and power.

> Dear Mother
>
> I finished my course here yesterday, but for the next week or so I must be engrossed in a series of problems to decide whether I am a total loss or whether perchance some of my more appealing qualities may be salvaged for military purposes. Hope for the best, but never try to decide what the "best" may be. You see the darkness and craziness of things has me quite bemused since I entered the hall of crooked mirrors we call Intelligence. Expect no lucid communications for a time yet.
>
> Love to all
> Hugh

HUGH NIBLEY: I was not kept as an interrogator at all. I couldn't frighten anybody; they'd all start laughing at me. They knew I wasn't serious. Well, I was serious, all right, but when I tried to be tough it would just send them. They would risk shedding their discipline just to laugh at me. No, I was not a good interrogator, so they put me into Order of Battle.

LUCIEN GOLDSCHMIDT: Hugh Nibley decided that he would not like to be an interrogator. The idea of pressing others—soldiers who were under orders not to reveal information—to press them to reveal it seemed morally unpleasant to him. He therefore, wisely, went into that section called Order of Battle.

HUGH NIBLEY: In OB we had to learn all the organization of the German army—extremely complicated—and I was the best at it. We had to be tested all the time on German uniforms. We'd dress somebody up and they'd ask, "Is he a field marshal or what is he?" You had to know the insignia, and you had to memorize the units of the German army. So I thought I'd show them up, and so every week they'd list the order of the grading, and I was number one on the list for the first three weeks in a row. And then I said, "What the hell," and let it all go. I didn't care about it anymore. I said, "That's it. There's no point to being here. The officers will get the top spots anyway." But I memorized every unit of the German Army so I could tell you things like the Seventeenth SS Panzergrenadier Division had been moved from this village to that village or something.

LUCIEN GOLDSCHMIDT: In many ways [Hugh] was different from the average G.I.—wasn't always badgering sergeants to give him a pass to go to New York or to go somewhere, often under invented pretexts. Some [of those at Ritchie] obviously didn't catch on at all [to what kind of a person Hugh Nibley was]. A person who

Interrogation Prisoner of War (IPW) class at Camp Ritchie. Hugh Nibley is top row, second from left. Lucien Goldschmidt is in front row, third from right.

wasn't telling any dirty jokes, who wasn't bragging, didn't come into their ken. On the other hand, those who were perhaps more thoughtful, more attentive to the people around them—a number of them were very interested and perhaps even fascinated. I think that I remember telling some of the other students, having discovered it early, "This is not a person like the others." Not only did he carry things like the Koran in Arabic and Thucydides in Greek in his fatigues with him, but he also would exchange coffee for powdered lemon juice or other things that seemed far more desirable.[a]

One of the first times I saw the depth, so to speak, of his knowledge was in a map-reading exercise where we had maps with Arabic or Turkish writing. Lieutenant Church called on him just to say what a *wadi* was. All Lieutenant Church undoubtedly wanted was for him to say that it's a stream that is dry much of the year and then other times there is a rivulet or a river. But once launched, he began to say that yes, that is what it meant, but one had to understand it properly, that the root indicated that it really meant to stand with one foot on the dry land and one foot in the water, and that this had, historically, the following explanation. And Lieutenant Church got increasingly concerned about the scholar delivering a lecture when all he had wanted, obviously, was a simple answer, half a sentence. And there you could see that, if challenged, Hugh Nibley would rise to the occasion.

There were quite a few views we shared, and there were quite a few we didn't share. We shared, I think, a basic consensus about war being a regrettable thing, but the Nazis were not something that should take over, and that, well, if you were going to fight, this at least was a worthwhile thing to fight for. And where we didn't perhaps agree was on certain methods or certain aspects of that war. I would think that I, on a whole, was more optimistic about the President and some of the intentions [of the administration] than Hugh Nibley might have been, although that too was open to change from time to time. He was often pessimistic; he altogether regarded that we were at the end of the times, that this was like the end of the Roman Empire, the fourth century, and that more disasters were ahead of us. We

---

[a] The Mormon health teaching called "The Word of Wisdom" disallows coffee drinking by Latter-day Saints. The powdered lemon juice Goldschmidt refers to is the dehydrated lemonade that came in GI rations.

would speak perhaps about early Christianity, which interested him very much. And then, I imagine, we must have spoken about religion. . . . What he appreciated was if you searched for more knowledge, more approach to the basic truths. He was also rather interested, I think, in the obviously Jewish heritage of Christianity, and therefore, even though he surely couldn't find in me a very good interpreter of Jewish antiquities but simply a person entirely Jewish by background, I represented something that he was not that commonly familiar with.

Hugh Nibley was getting an entirely different view of Jews from what he had heard from his mother. Now he was not only studying what was happening in Europe, but he was also hearing from his fellow soldiers, many of whom had been there recently and were refugees from the Reich. Some soldiers in Ritchie were actual escapees from concentration camps. Suddenly, swimming in an ethnic and linguistic soup, he was no longer in an environment where white Anglo-Saxon Protestants were in the majority. Mormons often use the word "gentile" to refer to non-Mormons, but in Camp Ritchie Hugh Nibley found himself in the minority, a true "goy."

GEORGE BAILEY: Most, but by no means all, of the Germans [at Ritchie] were Jews. Of these it was said that some had been born Jewish, some had achieved Jewishness, and some had had Jewishness thrust upon them.[8]

HUGH NIBLEY: There were the Vienna Jews and the Berlin Jews, and they hated each other's guts. The Berlin Jews believed *they* were cultivated and the Vienna Jews believed *they* were cultivated, and oh boy, the way they'd go at each other! But anyway, it was nice knowing both groups, because there were some famous people, some famous pianists and artists and scientists and things like that.

Though Ritchie's training kept him busy, Hugh Nibley also found time for some extracurricular activities. On leave in New York, he found Lucien Goldschmidt's rare bookshop very attractive—and only partly because of the books. Goldschmidt had a charming assistant. Hugh wrote to his mother about her.

I hesitate to describe the many perfections of the lady-love until I can be sure of success. She is quite a miracle—almost too much to hope for. I am in my usual condition of doing too many things at once. The situation is saved by the great opportunities one has to learn new and rather revealing things about the world. I think I have said before that a more strange and wonderful assortment of people never gathered . . . together than at this almost too-too dramatic place. A combination of a Tibetan Monastery and Noah's ark it is, with Grand Hotel and the Magic Mountain quite out of the running.

Love,

Hugh

New York, Sept. 23, 1943

Dear Mother,

I have been living behind a seven-walled barricade of censorship. The work has been interesting and may become exciting and that is all I can tell you about it.

Yesterday we went through another graduation ritual—my third Army diploma—it represents some extremely intensified and specialized work—not too hard but very exhausting; also very revealing. It has been a year since we got into this mess and as yet we have acquired neither rank nor honors. But the year has been anything but wasted as it is no small thing to get access to the main-spring of the whole machine; and how else could one have met this work of perfection who herewith gives me permission to submit a report on her qualities. The name is Anahid Iskian, which is Armenian because she is descended from that particular branch of the House of Israel. She is extremely sought after because she is beautiful, vivacious, brainy and generous, with a boundless fund of know-how and a joyous sense of humor. . . . As a side-line she conducts the Armenian Congregational Choir, which does not prevent an active and growing interest in the gospel.[a] . . . It would be nice if I could get a furlough long enough to see you-all before going across, but that is doubtful. I am more convinced than ever that this war will bring about no good. I must end now in a great hurry

Love

Hugh

[a] *The gospel:* A term often used by Latter-day Saints to mean Mormon theology.

JOHNNY'S GONE FOR A SOLDIER

Hasty marriages were very common among American soldiers, sailors, and marines rushing off to war. Many of these ended sadly for GIs who received "Dear John" letters telling them their wives weren't going to wait after all for husbands they barely knew. Hugh Nibley's friend Max Oppenheimer writes of his marriage in An Innocent Yank at Home Abroad:

MAX OPPENHEIMER: We were secretly married on October 14, 1942. We spent the night in a motel where the clerk asked me if this was a "quickie." (The breakdown of American Puritan morality was already looming.) It was not a "quickie"; over 50 years later we are still married! . . . We had little time together. I spent the night of the 23rd alone in a cheap hotel near the Los Angeles railroad station. At 6:00 A.M., on October 24, 1942, I reported to the Army Recruiting Station in downtown Los Angeles.[9]

While the training, interesting new friends, trips to various libraries on the Eastern seaboard, and his new "lady-love" must have been a great diversion, there was an ugly shadow looming on the horizon: the war was getting closer. The allies were making gains, but the end was still far from certain.

HUGH NIBLEY: The first Ritchie men going over to invade Africa were all Italians. Of course it was top secret. They were taking off at three in the morning from a special airfield at Ritchie, so all the Italians went down to sneak off over to Africa, and when we got down to the airfield all of the Bronx was there. All the Italian families, Italian flags—they had their lunches; they had their sausage and their picnics; and they celebrated; they sang songs. It was a typical Italian reunion like the Knights of Columbus Day or something like that. That was our security—everybody comes to see them off. The Germans knew everything we were doing.

The British and Americans finally beat the Germans in Africa, after initial defeats and some stumbling by an inexperienced general named Eisenhower who was commanding his first battle. The Russians stopped the German offensive at Kursk in the largest tank battle in history and were urging the Americans and British to quickly open a second front in Western Europe to take some of the heat off them. The Allies had signed an armistice with Italy, but the Germans had occupied Rome. There was a lot of fighting yet to be done, and Hugh Nibley's time was coming.

Oct. 29, 1943

Dear Mother

This day ends a strange and eventful furlough. After a couple of days among the Amish in the Pennsylvania Dutch country (the autumn colors were incredibly brilliant) I ended up in New York where a whirlwind courtship culminated in a flat refusal. Hence in a cumulo-nimbus mood to Washington. I have been made a Master Sergeant and in the great press of affairs take the liberty to saddle you with all my financial affairs on this continent. That means you will receive an allotment of $100 a month plus a war-bond. Such a sum would only embarrass me in the field—as it is I will get $40 a month—and you might find use for it. The enclosed bond was picked up during a drive. I will let you know what and when I can.

Love

Hugh

Hugh Nibley's passion as a scholar was always to get to the root of things, the original sources, and that's just what he was supposed to do as a member of an Order of Battle team. His training was to learn everything possible about what was going on, to put together all the little pieces to make up the big picture. Now he was supposed to do in a military scenario exactly what he had been trying to do as a scholar with the history of human knowledge. His training complete, and newly promoted to the rank of master sergeant, Nibley the scholar was on his way back to Europe to pit his mental and physical strength against the massive empire and the apocalyptic war machine Hitler had built up since the younger Elder Nibley had last crossed paths with him in the restroom of a Bavarian beer hall.

4

GIRDING THE LOINS

By the time Hugh Nibley completed his training at Camp Ritchie, the tide of the war had started to turn. The catastrophic defeats Hitler's armies experienced in Eastern Europe at the hands of the Soviets had shattered the image of Nazi invincibility. The British had forced the Axis to give up trying to hold Africa; in this they had help from the Americans, whose inexperienced troops went through some initial missteps in the African campaign but in the process learned valuable lessons. The Japanese were on the defensive in the Pacific; much of the Imperial Navy had been destroyed; and the Japanese occupation of the Pacific, which had happened with such lightning speed the year before, was being slowly rolled back island by bloody island.

Lucien Goldschmidt had been sent as an interrogator to Africa, then to the 82nd Airborne Division in Italy where the Allies were making some progress moving up the peninsula. Mussolini was out of power, and the Italian army was no longer a major factor in the war, but progress was difficult against the Germans who were still in Italy. Meanwhile, Stalin was demanding that Roosevelt and Churchill fulfill their promise to open a major front in Western Europe to force Hitler to fight on two fronts and take pressure off the Soviets. Allied troops and equipment were massing in England, but there was still no clear plan for how they would be used to invade the continent and squeeze the Reich from both sides to conclusively end the war and obliterate Hitler's power to terrorize the world.

HUGH NIBLEY: I was at Ritchie quite a while, about eight months, then in late October I got on the *Queen Mary*[a] and we set a speed record for crossing the Atlantic, docking in England after only five days at sea. We had a whole division on the ship, and if the U-Boats had gotten that they would have had a real prize. You can bet they were hunting for it.

The Queen Mary *sails for Europe*

After we got off the *Queen Mary* we boarded a train and went to the worst camp in England. The conductor came around and started talking to all the soldiers about where we were going because he had heard we were on our way to a very famous place in Staffordshire near Lichfield. The conductor told us it was a legend, known as the worst military base in England with the most terribly strict

[a] The *Queen Mary*, launched in 1934, was the fastest ocean liner of its day and one of the most luxurious until it was fitted as a troop carrier in 1940. Hitler promised the Iron Cross and $250,000 to anyone who could sink her. She still holds the record for the most people ever to fit on board one ship—16,683.

Victorian methods. That's where we were being sent to get us toughened up. When we got there, it was just as horrible as the conductor said.

> Dear Mother,
>
> . . . The place [is] called Whittington Barracks—very cold, dark and stony, with 150-years deposit of coal smoke and Empire tradition. Incidentally, the more you see of this sort of thing the clearer it becomes that the Empah[a] is nothing but a cheeky bit of window-dressing; top to bottom, it is pure eyewash.

HUGH NIBLEY: There were these old Victorian barracks full of smoke from coal stoves, and the army was so notoriously strict there everybody muttered about it. Whittington Barracks was really a sort of prison camp. But with the big buildup of allied troops in England they were overcrowded everywhere, so that's where they put us. We hadn't been assigned to our units yet, so we were temporarily attached to the British army, and it was a mess. After eight months of Intelligence training I ended up drilling with the British army all day because we weren't assigned to units. It was a horrible place, getting up and marching and everybody cheating like crazy. The British were wonderful at that. They had these dense fogs in Lichfield, and there were times when the British would all form up in their lines and then suddenly the fog would come in and they'd just melt away and nobody knew where everybody had gone. They were all over at a place called Naffy's drinking coffee and having donuts. And then before the fog let up they'd find their way back around and form up again.

If you were British you had no chance at promotion or recognition unless you were a member of the right family. You could've won the Congressional Medal of Honor three times in our army, and you still wouldn't be mentioned in the British dispatches unless you were a member of a certain family and unless you were an officer. Enlisted men would never get mentioned for valor or things like that; that was reserved for officers. It was the darndest method you ever saw.

---

[a] "The British Empire was the largest empire the world has ever known. It was known as "the Empire on which the sun never sets."

"TOMMY"

Rudyard Kipling

I went into a public-'ouse to get a pint o' beer,
The publican 'e up an' sez, "We serve no red-coats here."
The girls be'ind the bar they laughed an' giggled fit to die,
I outs into the street again an' to myself sez I:
   O it's Tommy this, an' Tommy that, an' "Tommy, go away";
   But it's "Thank you, Mister Atkins," when the band begins to play—
   The band begins to play, my boys, the band begins to play,
   O it's "Thank you, Mister Atkins," when the band begins to play.

I went into a theatre as sober as could be,
They gave a drunk civilian room, but 'adn't none for me;
They sent me to the gallery or round the music-'alls,
But when it comes to fightin', Lord! they'll shove me in the stalls!
   For it's Tommy this, an' Tommy that, an' "Tommy, wait outside";
   But it's "Special train for Atkins" when the trooper's on the tide—
   The troopship's on the tide, my boys, the troopship's on the tide,
   O it's "Special train for Atkins" when the trooper's on the tide.

Yes, makin' mock o' uniforms that guard you while you sleep
Is cheaper than them uniforms, an' they're starvation cheap;
An' hustlin' drunken soldiers when they're goin' large a bit
Is five times better business than paradin' in full kit.

Then it's Tommy this, an' Tommy that, an' "Tommy, 'ow's yer soul?"
But it's "Thin red line of 'eroes" when the drums begin to roll—
The drums begin to roll, my boys, the drums begin to roll,
O it's "Thin red line of 'eroes" when the drums begin to roll.

We aren't no thin red 'eroes, nor we aren't no blackguards too,
But single men in barricks, most remarkable like you;
An' if sometimes our conduck isn't all your fancy paints,
Why, single men in barricks don't grow into plaster saints;
   While it's Tommy this, an' Tommy that, an' "Tommy, fall be'ind,"
   But it's "Please to walk in front, sir," when there's trouble in the wind—
   There's trouble in the wind, my boys, there's trouble in the wind,
   O it's "Please to walk in front, sir," when there's trouble in the wind.

You talk o' better food for us, an' schools, an' fires, an' all:
We'll wait for extry rations if you treat us rational.
Don't mess about the cook-room slops, but prove it to our face
The Widow's Uniform is not the soldier-man's disgrace.
   For it's Tommy this, an' Tommy that, an' "Chuck him out, the brute!"
   But it's "Saviour of 'is country" when the guns begin to shoot;
   An' it's Tommy this, an' Tommy that, an' anything you please;
   An' Tommy ain't a bloomin' fool—you bet that Tommy sees![1]

Whittington Barracks, Lichfield, England

The camp was commanded by a little Irishman from New Jersey called Colonel Kilian.[a] He was a politician—that's how he got the job—and he was enormously vain. He must have been insane; we all had to bow down and worship him. To show how he'd run the camp, we'd have movies at night, and he'd deliberately keep everybody standing at attention while he'd go get his political friends. And everybody had to stand at attention until he came in, and he would march into the movie half an hour or an hour late with his political cronies, and we'd have to salute this little roly-poly Jersey politician, as corrupt as they come, and *then* we could sit down and watch the movie.

> **MAX OPPENHEIMER:** Our entire group proceeded to Lichfield Barracks near Manchester, an ancient Roman military encampment. The Commanding Officer, Colonel Kilian, we soon discovered, was marching to a different drummer and ran things very much his own way. He had, it appeared, set a goal to court-martial everyone in sight.[2]

HUGH NIBLEY: One night Colonel Kilian came in drunk and he was challenged—as he should have been—by a black soldier on sentry duty. This soldier wouldn't let him in until he gave the password, and for that Colonel Kilian wanted to sentence him to ten years hard labor. All sorts of things like that happened. But this Colonel Kilian, he was insane. Absolute power will drive most men insane—it would certainly drive me insane—but how can you tell if a man in absolute power is insane? It has happened so many times.

After a few weeks at Whittington Barracks we were sent to London, and I started working at the Intelligence Office at Hyde Park Corner. There were some Americans there along with the British, but the atmosphere was typically British—the one-upmanship and the bitter conflict and very smart talking and everybody putting everybody else down and everybody climbing over everybody else trying to get the best jobs. The tension was terrible, but fortunately I ended up with Miss Crawford. When I was

---

[a] Some of Hugh Nibley's information is wrong in this case. Colonel James A. Kilian, the American commander at Lichfield, was a career army officer from Nebraska, not a politician from New Jersey. Other parts of his memories of Kilian are borne out by other sources.

LICHFIELD

Hugh Nibley isn't the only one who thought Colonel Kilian was out of control. Colonel Kilian and Whittington Barracks at Lichfield later became the subject of a book, *Lichfield, The U.S. Army on Trial,* by Jack Gieck. To summarize what Gieck reveals:

Whittington Barracks gained the nickname among soldiers of "Colonel Kilian's Concentration Camp." After the Normandy Invasion, the camp was used as a "repple-depple" replacement camp supplying fresh troops to units in the field. Many of the soldiers at Lichfield were wounded combat veterans waiting to heal enough to return to the front, but an unusually large number of men at the camp had been court-martialed for petty infractions and given harsh prison sentences. The stockade was overflowing with men who might have been fighting the Nazis, but who instead were doing hard labor for such crimes as coming back from leave a few hours late or speaking back to an officer. And prisoners reported that brutal torture and humiliation were the daily routine in the stockade. The result was the death of American soldiers.

After the war, charges were brought against some of the guards at Lichfield. The trials started with the court-martial of a single, low-ranking, noncommissioned officer. A young assistant prosecutor the army assigned to the case, Captain Earl Carroll, believed the abuse at Lichfield came from more than a few noncom bad apples. When the sergeant on trial called Colonel Kilian as a character witness, Captain Carroll kept him on the stand for a full week with questions that drove the colonel to fits of rage and transformed the trial into an examination of deeply rooted corruption and megalomania. It eventually led to wide-ranging prosecutions that went all the way to the top. The defense? Nearly identical to that being used across the Channel at the same time in the trials of the Nazi leaders in Nuremberg: We were just soldiers following orders. But in this case the torturers were not Nazi fanatics; they were American soldiers torturing American soldiers. Colonel Kilian was convicted of allowing the atrocities to occur. He was fined five hundred dollars and eventually retired on a military pension.[3]

Colonel Kilian receives the Legion of Merit medal a few weeks before his court martial.

at Ritchie there was a big fellow called Tucker—"Mr. Tucker from Washington"—a great big black-haired fellow whose hair was all varnished with artificial dye.

MAX OPPENHEIMER: Tucker (whom I was to meet again in 1956 in the Office of the Assistant Chief of Staff for Intelligence at the Pentagon) came from Washington to lecture to us, and we visited his office in the Pentagon one day during the course. The OB section consisted of Tucker and two enlisted men. Later, several graduates from the first OB class joined his staff. At that time I was envious of them, but I soon changed my mind. That was not where the action was to be!

Tucker was a hairsplitting, i-dotting, scholarly, if pedantic, sort of man, but his creation of the red *Order of Battle* book and its contribution to the war effort were absolutely invaluable. We have him to thank for our start in this area of Military Intelligence. Years later, when I worked with him during the Korean War, I felt truly sorry for him. Outside the soulless, sanitized, bureaucratic world of the Pentagon, he might have enriched our planet in more humane ways. He served us well in World War II by providing us with the springboard to start shaping our own roles in the campaigns to come.[4]

HUGH NIBLEY: Mr. Tucker came down from Washington to tell us the real inside story on international intelligence. He kept telling us the time would come when we might get to see the great Miss Crawford. "There is a woman in the British War Office who knows more about the war than anybody else: Miss Crawford!" Well lo and behold, first thing after I get into London I'm assigned to work for Miss Crawford. She was in the top of British Intelligence, and she worked on the top floor of the Admiralty Building.

So I went to see Miss Crawford. I went over and showed my credentials at the Admiralty and went to her office. She didn't show up at 8:00. She didn't show up 9:00. She didn't show up at 10:00. Finally she came in a little before 11:00. I said, "I've been here since 8:00," and she bawled me out. "We don't come in that early!" So pretty soon it was 11:00 and we all had to go up to the roof—for tea, of course. There was a big lineup of people that went clear around the roof of the building waiting for tea. So we waited for tea, and that took about an hour and then lunchtime came after that. That's the way they were living life at the Admiralty.

Miss Crawford was a little tiny woman with a tremendous mass of red hair all fluffed up, and she was always fussy and excited. "Now where did I put that, where did I put that?" My job was to help her compose the guide to the invasion of Normandy, which was a big book with a bright red cover called *Invademecum*, which is Latin for "invade with me."[a] It contained all the instructions you had to know about the German army if you were invading Europe, all our information on all the German units we were facing. It was absolutely top secret. That's why it was bright red, so it could be spotted at a distance.

So after tea and lunch we finally got back to the office, and Miss Crawford got her stuff out and we got busy on the *Invademecum*. My business was compiling information on all the top officers and their connections in the different units of the German army. Miss Crawford said, "Let me get my files." She goes to her desk and gets her files, which consisted of a couple of shoeboxes full of notes she'd cut out of newspapers. She just cut them out of magazines and newspapers, German and otherwise, and that was her source of information, because they would tell where the important people were socializing. She'd see in some society column a mention of a German general who'd been a guest at a particular spa or something with his wife, and that indicated the Germans were moving some unit somewhere and we'd guess about it. And the great Miss Crawford, the mastermind of British Intelligence, would construct a picture of the German order of battle out of this shoebox full of clippings from popular magazines. What a way to run military intelligence compared to what you've seen in the movies!

I had this notebook, a small diary I kept in the lining of my coat. We weren't

---

[a] *Invademecum:* A play on *vademecum,* "a book or manual suitable for carrying about with one for ready reference" (*Oxford English Dictionary*). *Vademecum* is Latin for "come with me," so the *Invademecum*—"invade with me"—was a manual on the German military for soldiers to carry into battle.

"The planning and execution of Operation Overlord was brilliant. Naval, ground, and air forces cooperated with precision. Logistics and supplies were well coordinated. It appeared that great lengths were taken to attend to the most minute details. A small booklet entitled 'Invade Mecum' (invade with me) was given to platoon leaders before the D-day invasion. It contained detailed drawings of every hamlet and village in the Normandy area, with the location of major buildings in the village, such as the mayor's home, city hall, the public utility building, and the telephone exchange; in some cases it even gave the names of the mayor and the director of utilities. The booklets proved an invaluable source of information to the combat troops." (Belton Y. Cooper, *Death Traps: The Survival of an American Armored Division in World War II*, 10.)

Aircraft spotter on the roof of a building in London, with St. Paul's Cathedral in the background

supposed to keep diaries in military Intelligence, but I made notes in this special handwriting, shorthand and other things, and I knew the Germans could never read that. Nor could anybody else, but if they'd known I was keeping a diary I would have been in trouble.

DIARY ENTRY, JANUARY 2, 1944: Slept until eleven, went to church on Nightingale Lane. Rather bleak. Returned in the evening with Trujillo and read *1001 Nights.* Watched flak and rockets during the raid.

JANUARY 3, 1944: Worked all day in the War Office. . . . Heard about the socialist governments of Switzerland and Italy. Very hush, hush. In the War Office there is talk about drumming up interest for the Italian King. They are dreaming up very dangerous things to establish a king in Italy. Very nasty. Anything to stop the reds.

HUGH NIBLEY: Our whole concern was the communists—we weren't worried about Hitler very much. We wanted to see a king in Italy; that would help stop the communists. And of course King Victor Emanuel supported Mussolini, but we liked Victor Emanuel. What a mess!

In London I was buying books like mad, particularly from one used book dealer named George Salby. He was a gigantic man, and he'd just bought two Arabic libraries from two famous Arabists that had just died. He didn't put the books up on shelves but piled them up, and he knew where every book in the shop was. So here was this huge library collection, and they were just piled up in his shop, so I just picked and chose like mad. I took the last money I had in the Claremont bank and paid for them, paid him $800 for this huge pile of books—they were worth far more than that. Salby said he'd send them to me after the war. I trusted him. I had nothing written or anything like that, and sure enough after the war along came the books.

Hugh Nibley had not achieved the officer status he had predicted and his mother had wanted for him. Still, he was not where his mother had dreaded he might go, in infantry as a foot soldier who would have to "slug it out in the mud." In his line of Intelligence it looked as though he would be able to use his languages and research skills and stay pretty far away from the really nasty part of the war.

HUGH NIBLEY: Since I wasn't any good at interrogation at Ritchie I had been transferred to Order of Battle, which was actually quite an honor, only top people got into OB. The Order of Battle teams had three members, an officer and two sergeants. There were fifteen OB teams chosen at first, and I was to be on team number five. Now one reason the OB teams were so prestigious and such a desirable assignment in army Intelligence was that we understood they were to be attached only to army groups or corps, and that was about as high and as safe a job as you could get. When I was assigned to OB everybody told me, "You will never go lower in your assignment than army group or army." So the OB teams were very high up, very exalted, except for one team that was to be kept for actual battlefront interrogation.

    MAX OPPENHEIMER: I graduated from the second OB course. . . .
    As . . . members of the first-ever OB teams in the U.S. Army, we

were charged with a heavy responsibility and could now hope to play a crucial role in the war. We would always possess, at the disposal of Intelligence and Operations staffs, even Commanding Generals, the most up-to-date knowledge of the enemy forces opposing us. My self-esteem rose considerably.[5]

HUGH NIBLEY: So when I had finished my work with Miss Crawford I went to the British War Office, where they were going to give out the unit assignments to the OB teams. We were up on the top floor of the British War Office late at night. They had a special wooden structure built up there because they didn't have enough space, and we were standing in this little dark hall waiting for the judgment. Braun, our lieutenant who spoke with a thick German accent, went in to get our assignment with Weigner, the other member of our team. They were in there a long while; then Weigner came out white as a ghost, his eyes popping out, sweat streaming down his face. He leaned up against the wall and rolled his eyes, gasping, "Mama mia, mama mia! We're it!" Then Braun came out and said, "We're it. We got the dirty assignment. OB Team Number Five is to be attached to the 101st Airborne Division."

All the rest of the OB teams were to be a good twenty miles from the front, but we were it: we had to go to the front line and report front-line intelligence. Not from corps or from army group or the fancy places where you have dinner on a tablecloth. We were the ones for the suicide mission. We would be attached to the 101st Airborne and would be the first to land in Normandy.

DIARY ENTRY, JANUARY 12, 1944: I am to go to an airborne division. Given like a death sentence.

HUGH NIBLEY: Braun, the lieutenant in charge of our team, had an accent so thick you could cut it with a knife. He was very superior. Weigner, the other non-com on our team, was a scion, the only son of a rich Jewish family in New York; and both of them were worried to death about what would happen to them. They were just sick about it. Weigner dragged me all over to visit every fortuneteller in London, which swarmed with fortune tellers because soldiers were coming to get

Fires from German bombs illuminate St. Paul's Cathedral, London.

their fortunes told. He wanted to get good news, but all he got were character readings.

In November 1943, the Allied leaders—Stalin, Churchill, and FDR—had met in Teheran, where Stalin argued strongly for the western Allies to put all their efforts into the plan called Operation Overlord, the invasion of Western Europe. The Russians were tired of waiting, and Stalin urged Churchill and FDR to open the western front by the first week of May. Four days after Hugh Nibley was assigned to 101st Airborne (which would come to be known as the Screaming Eagles), General Dwight Eisenhower was named Supreme Commander Allied Expeditionary Forces to oversee Overlord. An American was chosen for this job because so many of the men and much of the materiel going into the battle were American. But the actual command of the battle would be in the hands of the British hero of North Africa, General Bernard Law Montgomery, who was preparing the master plan for the invasion. The plan was to strike in the spring or summer of 1944, and in January planning was already underway.

DIARY ENTRY, JANUARY 24, 1944: Our departure is 100 percent fouled up. At 3:00 we call the office. I swim.

HUGH NIBLEY: While I was swimming down at the YMCA Club in the lower end of London there was an air raid. We were right in the way, and bombs landed all around the swimming pool. At the YMCA you always just swam in the nude in those days. Bombs were going boom, boom, boom, boom all around, and you never knew when one would hit the pool. Then the lights went out, and I was swimming around in total darkness. I felt rather exposed too, because we didn't have bathing suits.

I reached Newbury, the headquarters of the 101st, on an unbelievably dark and stormy night in a terrible January when the rain and the wind were awful. We lived in tents without light or heat on top of a very windy hill with gliders tied down all around us. The mud was pelagic, the food unspeakably vile and very scarce. (At the foot of the hill a black supply company lived on chicken and ice cream, but we never saw any of that unless we had some excuse to visit them.)

Up there in Grenham Lodge on the top of the hill on the upper floor of the church in the castle, we had a map room with all Normandy laid out. We were preparing to invade Normandy, and I was quickly informed what the role of the division was to be in the invasion: namely, to spearhead the whole operation, landing four hours ahead of anyone else. My job was to keep the map that showed everything we knew about where the German units were and what we were expecting to encounter when we went over. I had to sit there at night to guard the map. The Germans would easily have given a billion dollars to see it. It showed everything we were going to do. I would have to keep awake all night to guard it with guns and hand grenades. I would also receive reports on what was going on across the Channel: who was holding a position, what they expected to happen, and what they observed from where they were. But I felt like I was only there to observe. I didn't feel like a participant at all.

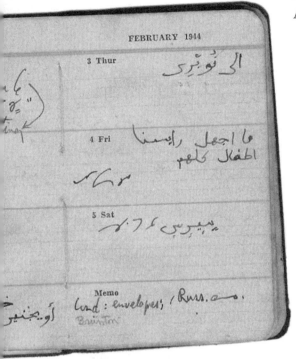

A page from Hugh Nibley's diary

DIARY ENTRY, FEBRUARY 4, 1944 (written in Arabic): What an ignorant boob our leader is!

It is not clear who the leader is that Hugh Nibley was referring to in this entry. On the day Nibley wrote the entry, the 101st was commanded by the very popular General William Lee. On the following day Lee had a heart attack and was temporarily replaced as commander of the division by the Assistant Division Commander, General Donald F. Pratt. A few weeks later, on March 14, Lee's permanent replacement, General Maxwell Taylor, took over the division.

HUGH NIBLEY: The commander of the 101st Airborne was General Maxwell Taylor, and he was a real fire-eater. He was a wonderful guy, always full of spirit. He was all very military and this and that, but when it's the real thing it's exciting to be with. I liked Taylor. He got me all excited; he was very gung-ho. He was what a general should be, very picturesque. I got to be very close to General Taylor. He knew a lot about military history, and that's why he liked me. We had CPXs—command post exercises—where we would go down to southern England together to see where we could rehearse exactly what was going to happen at Normandy so everybody would know exactly how the operation was going to work. This was Operation Overlord we were practicing for, and we'd duplicate everything that was going to happen on the other side of the Channel to practice for the invasion. On these exercises we'd sleep among the leeks and practice the invasion during the day. General Taylor would come to talk with me, and we'd take walks together. He'd talk, not about the war, but about history and the like, and the officers would be quite jealous because here I'd be, an enlisted man, talking with the general all the time. It annoyed them.

General Maxwell Taylor, commander of the 101st Airborne Division, addresses his men.

Since our undertaking was to be something unique in its kind, a great many practice runs had to be gone through, and after each one things looked blacker. It is fantastic how many things there are to go wrong in an airborne operation. Everybody who saw what was going on was worried to pieces, and I was wistfully envious of the simple rifleman who had no idea what he was in for. After I had been sworn to undying secrecy, General Taylor gave me an assignment; and I set about wising everyone up on the strength, disposition, and honest intentions of

General Gerald Higgins, Chief of Staff, 101st Airborne Division

the Germans. Every Thursday night I had to give a two-hour lecture to all the officers of the 101st on the German army and German warfare. You can imagine how popular that made me with the officers. They would have to sit there like ramrods—Taylor was very strict—and I would have to give them lectures about ancient wars and strategy and tactics. I had a devil of a time getting material. I'd go to the library in Reading, anything like that. But I kept going; he didn't fire me. I gave lots of lectures to all the units, and the questions the boys asked on those occasions called for all the comfort I could give them. I lied until I even cheered myself up.

As a member of the OB team attached to the 101st I was in division Headquarters Company, which included the unit's administrative personnel. The officers I worked with were all good men, these military men. They were sort of idealists, you know, and they had to put up with an awful lot. There was General Donald Pratt, the Assistant Division Commander. Anthony McAuliffe was Division Artillery Commander; I think of him riding around in a jeep, crunched down as far as he could crunch, but he was the same as many of the other officers, a diligent, removed sort of guy. I got to know Colonel Jerry Higgins (later General Higgins), a tall redheaded fellow from Idaho. I think he was a Mormon. I remember at the end Major Paul Danahy, the G-2—by then he had become Colonel Danahy—he said, "I'm getting out of this as soon as I can." I said, "Why's that?" He said, "Because I've had to say yes too many times when I wanted to say no." But that's how you get ahead, by saying yes.

DIARY ENTRY, FEBRUARY 10, 1944: *Orde Dies: post hoc nullas seritet nules epistulas nisi jocundas atque vitam milit. laudantes.* [Order of Day: From now on no letters will be written other than those which are cheerful and in praise of military life.]

HUGH NIBLEY: There is such a thing as a private war. I was interested in observing what would happen, but I wasn't really in it, so I felt more like an observer than a participant preparing for the invasion. It was curious—when we had our operations and went through our drills out on the British coast, here we were on these gun emplacements from World War I, which were made earlier to resist the invasion of Napoleon, but they had also been Roman fortifications before that, and here we were, manning the same positions for the same war. We hadn't moved since the time of the Romans. It was the same thing.

One day Winston Churchill came to visit us. Our headquarters at Grenham Lodge was just south of Newbury and just outside of Newbury was a little village. Churchill came down to this little town, and the people lined the road to cheer him. He was coming to give us a pep talk. (Everybody gave a speech to the 101st; the final talk before the invasion was given to our boys by Eisenhower—that's the 101st.) Well anyway, along comes Churchill, and all the women and children cheer him wildly as his car drives along the road. Then he tells his driver to stop. The driver stops, Churchill gets out, stands to the side of the car and begins relieving himself. He had an honor guard and everything else, and he ordered the whole thing to stop. At the same time, he flashes the "V for Victory" sign. And all the women and children? It doesn't faze them in the least. Well, that was the great Winston Churchill. If you can do a thing like that in full sight, you're an unusual man.

I was to be number-two man in the number-one glider, and we rehearsed the glider landing many times. We were using these huge, terrible gliders made entirely of plywood, invented by a Hungarian called Horsa. They were very impractical, but we used to ride around in them. It was amazing how they could jerk those massive things into the air, two at a time, pulled by a C-47 Dakota[a] buzzing along down the runway at about 55[b] miles per hour. They'd barely fly and a lot of them smashed up—a lot of men were killed in training; it was a tragedy.

Horsas were experimental gliders, and they tried to figure out ways to get them up into the air because they were bigger than the C-47s, and a lot heavier, and you had to get going down the runway full speed before they could ever hope to take off. So they'd wind a rope of pure silk around and around and around and we'd sit in those darn things and wait. You could see the rope unraveling as the plane sped

[a] The C-47 "Dakota" was the workhorse cargo plane of the American military in World War II.

[b] Takeoff speed for the Horsa was actually closer to 85 miles per hour.

NOTHING TO HIDE

Hugh Nibley was not the only one to witness Churchill's lack of squeamishness.

JONATHAN SIKORSKY: Walter Thompson, Churchill's personal body guard, recalled that shortly after Churchill arrived at the White House, he went upstairs to his suite to unpack and bathe. While Churchill was splashing about in the tub and inspector Thompson was checking over the room, there was a knock at the door. Thompson opened the door and was surprised to find President Roosevelt in his wheelchair all alone. Thompson remembered the President looking "curiously beyond me, not with fright but with something very unlike approval." Thompson turned around to see Churchill standing in man's most natural state, smiling cordially, a drink in one hand, a cigar in the other. When Roosevelt tried to excuse himself, Churchill insisted that he come in. In Thompson's words, "the Prime Minister posed briefly and ludicrously before the President," then said, "you see, Mr. President, I have nothing to hide."[6]

Churchill, Taylor, Eisenhower, General Donald Pratt, and a naval officer, on the occasion of Churchill's visit to the 101st

up, then finally the rope went tight, and because it was pure silk it would stretch without breaking, and you'd feel this jolt and you'd slowly go down the runway and wonder whether it would take off or not. Horsa himself said he wouldn't go into one of those for a thousand pounds.

MAX OPPENHEIMER: What we did not realize was that the entire concept of Intelligence teams, which were to remain assigned to MIS (Military Intelligence Service) while attached to armies, corps, divisions, and regiments, was still in its infancy and never had been implemented. No one in the U.S. Army knew about us, and the idea of MIS had to be sold to the various combat units. They had to be indoctrinated, briefed, and convinced about the services they might expect from us and how our teams could support their Intelligence collection efforts. Imagine the scenario: a senior officer, G-2 (Intelligence officer) of a corps or division, pretty set in his

Horsa glider

ways and not ready to take into his confidence a bunch of new recruits, some without Basic Training, others foreign—some from Germany—many with a thick foreign accent, merely because they spoke a foreign language most likely better than English. Their training at Ritchie, a place he never heard of, would hardly impress him. Can't you see such an officer welcoming with open arms a uniformed individual approaching his desk, leaning over and with both hands on it, smiling self-satisfied and with supreme confidence, saying with a thick accent, "I *sh*peak *z*even lang*uitges,* und *Tje*rman da best." We joked about it later, but such incidents occurred.[7]

HUGH NIBLEY: Because there had never been an Order of Battle team attached to a division like ours, there were no procedures established for us to get the information we were supposed to have. To get it we had to break all the rules of priority and procedure, and we became adept at falsification and intrigue, plain and fancy gate-crashing, and advanced prevarication. The Swan Inn was right at the foot of the hill where the Castle was and there was no army around, and that was where you could pick up underground information from the natives. There were all these local people in the inn who would sell information—someone who knows this, someone who knows that—because they were spying on everything around there. It wasn't much good, mostly information about what we were going to do, what units were going where, and so forth.

For one of our practice operations we went off down to Land's End, down at the southwest end of England. The conditions on the English side of the Channel were very much the same as conditions on the other, and down there we had the imitation of Normandy set up on the beach full-scale so we could practice the landing. It was called Exercise Tiger, and was a disaster. We were putting on a show, and the Germans found out what was going on there and came and spoiled the show with submarines and torpedo boats. We were just faking it, practicing the landing, and they came right in and started shooting. We lost five hundred men just rehearsing the Normandy landing on the English coast. It was a hell of a mess, a horrible thing. The army kept it top secret, of course.

EXERCISE TIGER

On April 22–30, 1944, the Allies conducted a large-scale rehearsal of the landing at Utah Beach, which was to include getting the U.S. 4th Infantry Division, with some 25,000 men and 2,750 vehicles, onto ships and landing craft, then onto the beach in Normandy to link up with the airborne forces that had come in by parachute and glider. Several days into the exercise a group of German torpedo boats found a convoy of ships carrying troops and supplies. The Germans sank two ships and damaged a third. It might have been worse except several German torpedoes failed to explode. Many casualties were the result of soldiers who hadn't been trained to use their life preservers properly and inflated them in such a way that they floated head down. Seven hundred forty-nine men were killed, far more casualties than the 4th Division suffered in the actual landing at Utah Beach. The casualties were buried in a mass grave and their families were told they died in the invasion. Although many Allied soldiers and sailors witnessed the catastrophe, details were kept secret and the full extent of the Allied losses were never known by the public until documents relating to it were declassified in 1974.

Loading a jeep into a landing craft during practice exercises for Operation Overlord

MAX OPPENHEIMER: I and many others never knew until 45 years later, from reading about it, that 749 of our men died in the E-boat attack, [and] were buried in a mass grave, and the whole affair kept secret for security reasons.[8]

HUGH NIBLEY: We were actually supposed to go into action before D-Day in an operation in which the 101st was to land in Le Havre, which would have been pure suicide because the Germans had tremendous reinforcements there. It's a big port and they had it very heavily fortified, and the 101st was to land there from the air. At that time nothing was prepared; we weren't ready for anything. It would have been absolute suicide. They called it off when they saw what insanity it would have been. But of course Max Taylor was very gung-ho; he always wanted to be right in the front. When they called off the operation everybody breathed a sigh of relief, but not Max. He had to put on his show. He threw down his hat; he kicked the

Sand tables were detailed models, including miniature buildings, of the area where an operation was to take place.

sand table; he turned it over and stomped on it. He was furious. He cursed everyone because they'd robbed him of his chance for glory. And he was as glad as the rest of us were that we didn't have to go. He was glad; I'm sure of it—he wasn't a fool. But he had to put on a show. That's Max. That's the military.

From then on we faked it to make it look as if we meant to land at Le Havre. We did everything. We had false airfields in the east of England; we had false planes to make it look as if we aimed for Le Havre, whereas the whole thing was actually aimed at the Cotentin Peninsula.

May 4, 1944

Dear Mother,

The words of parental advice which closed your last were a happy reminder of that unfailing power of imagination which so often in our childhood introduced an element of glad surprise into otherwise prosaic situations. Please go on thinking that way about our present activities, and I promise never, never to break this spell. For one thing it's not permitted. To remind me to see, for example, Hugh Brown,[a] is much the same thing as suggesting I drop in at the Mexico City Zoo next Thursday, or borrow the Grand Lama's toothbrush. . . .

Love to all
Hugh

The British Isles were crammed with American soldiers whose problems, according to the music hall comedian's joke, were that they were "over-paid, over-sexed, and over

[a] Hugh B. Brown (1883–1975) was the President of the British Mission for The Church of Jesus Christ of Latter-day Saints. He had served as an officer in the Canadian Army in the First World War, and was also assigned as Military Coordinator for all Mormon servicemen. In addition to being a Church official, he was a family friend from the same region of Alberta as Hugh Nibley's mother. At this time his mission had virtually no missionaries, since they had all been sent home at the outset of the war.

From Hugh B. Brown's letter to his son, Hugh C. Brown, a pilot in the Royal Air Force:

"I am with the soldiers daily, as you know, and have my heart-to-heart talks with them, and though they here know nothing of the 'real thing,' still the fact that they are to go and that no longer can they direct their own lives or follow their chosen courses has a sobering effect, and they mature so fast that the change is plainly seen from one visit to the next. What a shame that so many of them will have to finish in another sphere what they now hope to accomplish here. I think I'm not pessimistic, but I know too well that war plays no favorites.

"As for you, Hugh, I feel and have always felt that you are to be spared, not because He loves you more than others, but that you have a great work to do after the war—you must carry on where I leave off" (Firmage, *Abundant Life*, 99).

This was the last letter Hugh B. Brown wrote to his son, who was killed in action soon after it was written. Hugh B. Brown went on to become one of the foremost leaders of the Church as First Counselor to Church President David O. McKay.

here." Most of them were training hard for missions that could very well put an abrupt end to their young lives, and they let off steam, as would be expected, with liquor, local girls, and swing music. But not Hugh Nibley. His solace had always been in nature and in solitude. In the States that meant Zion Park. In Britain he found a near equivalent.

General McAuliffe briefs glidermen of the 101st.

April 8, 1944

Dear Mother,

. . . Farburgh in the Scottish Highlands was heaven—not a soul in uniform, the people unbelievably kind and generous, as if the lost remnant of a better world had taken refuge in these lost volcanic wastelands. . . . Very many of the Highlanders have lived all over the world (including your lovely "land of orange-groves and jails,") and returned hither to tend sheep and hoe the soil about their "weems"ᵃ in the manner of 15,000 B.C. I think they are wise.

DIARY ENTRY, MAY 7, 1944: On this day the war should end.

HUGH NIBLEY: In May of 1944 I predicted the war would end in Europe on the 7th of May, 1945. I made that prediction when we were out on one of these exercises in rural England. I was walking along and I said to myself, "When is this thing going to end?" I remember I took a whole day and walked over a field for a long time, and I figured out according to such-and-such this should happen, and this has been going on so long, and so-and-so should reach this objective by such-and-such a date. And it occurred to me that it was May 7, Dad's birthday. I thought,

---

ᵃ *Weem:* "The name applied in Scotland to a cave or underground dwelling-place used by early inhabitants of the country" (*Oxford English Dictionary*).

this would be a good day for the war to end, on Dad's birthday, and wrote it in my diary.

In his letters Hugh Nibley often took on a prophetic attitude in talking about what the world and the people of America were about to experience. Now he was moving toward the reality of his own predictions. What he called the "plush-bottom generation"—himself included—was training hard for a ride into Normandy that would clearly be anything but comfy. Now as an Intelligence sergeant he was forecasting the future again, this time as part of his official military duties. But it was no longer glib prose in letters to Springer. Now he had to look men in the eyes and tell them to their faces, and in detail, what they were about to experience.

HUGH NIBLEY: In the four weeks preceding the invasion it was my painful duty to brief all the unit officers down to company level on what roles they were supposed to play and tell them what they could expect from the Germans. I knew where the invasion was going to be and everything that was going to happen, but I didn't know when, of course. (I knew that too, actually.) General Taylor said, "Now you tell them exactly how it'll be, the type of work they're supposed to do, the terrain and the like. You cannot tell them where it will be, and you cannot tell them when it will be, of course. That is absolutely top secret. Don't say when or where, just 'soon and near.'"

And all the soldiers, all these boys I briefed, had the same question. It was very sad. They said, "Have we got any chance of survival?" It was sad because they were so eager to know what chances they had, which is fair enough to ask, but some of them, like the pathfinders, didn't have a prayer. They were practically suicide missions, and we knew it was going to be bad business. It was pretty bad describing what it would be like, and naturally we couldn't reassure them or anything like that. The reassurance that the general gave them was to say, "Sergeant Nibley will be going in among the very first, so he's not going to just give you cold comfort, or anything like that, you know." So I couldn't feel very smug about lecturing all these officers.

Weigner, who was so worried and dragged me around to all the fortune tellers in London, artfully managed to get himself transferred, after months of string-pulling, just before the invasion. But my luck was almost as good. They had me

PATHFINDERS

CORNELIUS RYAN: The task of this advance guard of the invasion, a small, courageous group of volunteers, was to mark "drop zones" in a fifty-mile-square area of the Cherbourg peninsula back of Utah Beach for the 82nd and 101st paratroopers and gliders. They had been trained in a special school set up by Brigadier General James M. "Jumpin' Jim" Gavin. "When you land in Normandy," he had told them, "you will have only one friend: God."[9]

A pathfinder sets up equipment to help paratroopers find the landing zone.

down as the number-two man in the number-one glider, and I had practiced the glider landing and was all ready to go. Then just before the invasion they said, "Nibley, you have to take the jeep over by sea because General Pratt wants your place on the glider." I didn't argue about it because you don't argue with a general, and I was not exactly sick at heart at being told that I would have to come by sea and land on the beach. So I was taken off the glider and instead I had to take our jeep over.

> **LEONARD RAPPORT AND ARTHUR NORTHWOOD JR.:** A young officer who, in England, had worked very closely with General Pratt remembered him thus: "From a first impression of General Pratt—that he was a well meaning but dated officer—my respect for him grew continually. He was a sound tactician, sincere and loyal, definitely close to the junior officers and troops with whom he worked. . . . Originally designated to command the water lift into Normandy, he was as tickled as a schoolboy when it was decided to permit him to enter the combat area by glider."[10]

HUGH NIBLEY: General Taylor told some amusing stories sometimes. During our final preparation for the invasion he told us one about Marshal Saxe,[a] the famous French field marshal from the Wars of Devolution.[b] Marshal Saxe was briefing his officers before one battle and one of the officers was rather amused and said, "Marshal Saxe, I see your knees are knocking together." He said, "Yes, and they'd knock a lot harder if they knew where I was taking them." And General Taylor gave us that as our story to send us off.

DIARY ENTRY, MAY 16, 1944: At 2:30 in a pouring rain we drive into Pontllanfraith via Monmouth.

HUGH NIBLEY: I had to go up in the mountains of Wales and take the jeep to where we were preparing secretly for the crossing. We went by way of Monmouth,

---

[a] Maurice Comte de Saxe (1696–1750) held the position of Marshal of France and was one of the greatest generals of his age.

[b] Wars of Devolution were fought in 1667–68, when Louis XIV of France claimed ownership of the Spanish Netherlands and invaded, drawing Sweden and England into the wars as well.

driving in the middle of the night. Of course we had to drive blacked out with our lights off, and I got so impatient because we were getting all mixed up driving around in the dark. At one point we came to a place where we could see there was a signpost in front of us and I said, "What the hell. I'm going to stop, regardless, and turn on these damn lights." And so I turned on the lights, and there was this road sign right smack in front of me, not ten feet away, and it said: "Nibley 2 miles." That was a real shocker. We thought the Nibleys were up in Scotland all the time, but I later discovered in a history of England that this was where the battle of Nibley Green was fought that changed the fortunes of the Plantagenets.[a]

Pontllanfraith was the Welsh place where we were marshalling for the crossing for the invasion of Normandy, the last place we were to be in Britain. It's back in the hills and hidden, and that's where I was to waterproof my jeep and get it ready to drive through the water on the beach in Normandy. You had to fix a pipe up from the carburetor and seal the engine with this creosote grease so the jeep

[a] The battle of Nibley Green was between the armies of two barons who had a dispute over land. It was the last private pitched battle in England and the last battle of the War of the Roses.

Testing a jeep's waterproofing

wouldn't stall in the water. I worked hard at it; the beach at Normandy goes out for miles; and if the jeep stalled before I got to shore I'd be a sitting duck.

We had a tent in Pontllanfraith, and I was bivouacked with a group of Irish policemen who were going over with the rest of the invasion force to be military police. Every morning they would take out this bottle of whiskey and pass it around. "Breakfast of champions!" they'd all say, and each one would take a drink and pass the bottle. "Breakfast of champions!" I didn't partake of the "breakfast of champions." It might have helped me if I had.

Back in America, Sloanie Nibley, who was cut off from receiving any direct communication about what her son was up to, recorded her feelings.

SLOANIE NIBLEY:

> Dear Lord he has thought for the finer things your gifts to all
> The sunrise from a mountain top a dashing waterfall
> The soft sweet color of the desert in the early morn
> The splash of flaming red that defies the coming dark
> The hiding little violet, a waxy hyacinth, the charming sweet pea,
> Each one a heavenly fragrance all its own
> These three his favorites
> And books—his honored friends from every land
> Hundreds of them piled high in boxes waiting.
> The destroyer's hand feels all too near this night
> Dear Lord be with him, let thy power touch him
> That his courage will not fail
> Bring him home
> Thank you Lord

5

NORMANDY

DIARY ENTRY, JUNE 2, 1944: On the ship in Bristol Harbor.

GENERAL DWIGHT D. EISENHOWER, SUPREME COMMANDER, ALLIED EXPEDITIONARY FORCE: Soldiers, Sailors and Airmen of the Allied Expeditionary Force: You are about to embark upon the Great Crusade, toward which we have striven these many months. The eyes of the world are upon you. The hopes and prayers of liberty-loving people everywhere march with you. In company with our brave Allies and brothers-in-arms on other Fronts you will bring about the destruction of the German war machine, the elimination of Nazi tyranny over oppressed peoples of Europe, and security for ourselves in a free world. . . .

I have full confidence in your courage, devotion to duty and skill in battle. We will accept nothing less than full victory!

Good Luck! And let us all beseech the blessing of Almighty God upon this great and noble undertaking.[1]

HUGH NIBLEY: The 101st Airborne Division were to be the first to land in Normandy. Their assignment was to land on either side of the Cotentin Peninsula to prepare an area cleared out so others could come and land on Utah Beach. Because General Pratt had taken my seat as number-two man in number-one glider, I was to take his jeep over and meet up with the division at a farm behind Utah Beach near the village of Ste.-Mère-Église. On June second the jeep was on

Ships, with balloons attached for snaring attacking planes, move toward Normandy.

the boat and we were ready to go. Then on June third there was a tremendous storm. We hadn't put out of Bristol Harbor yet, so we waited it out in Wales. The storm delayed our landing by one day, so we had to cross the next morning. One of the natives there in Bristol said, "The last time we had a storm like that was the day World War I began."

The landing was meant to be on June 5, so the ships loaded with men, machines, ammunition, food, and the myriad other tools of war set to sea on June 2 in order to be in place at the right time. The largest armada ever assembled waited, each ship and man and machine assigned a time and place on the enormous stage. But the weather was too rough. The men sat on the boats and waited as the landing was postponed. Having set the giant machine in motion, it looked as though Eisenhower might have to do the unthinkable—call it all back.

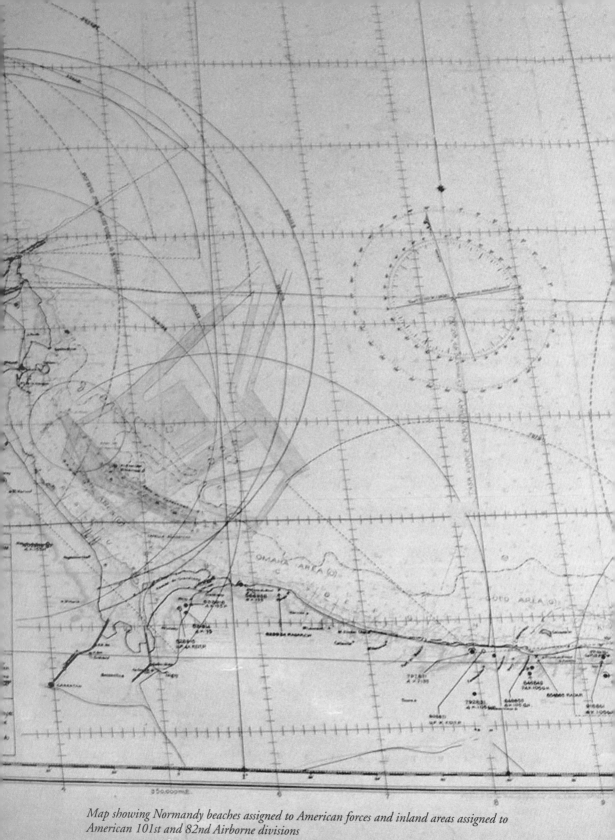

Map showing Normandy beaches assigned to American forces and inland areas assigned to American 101st and 82nd Airborne divisions

Soldiers wait their turn to go ashore.

WINSTON CHURCHILL: Conditions were bad, typical of December rather than June, but the weather experts gave some promise of a temporary improvement on the morning of the 6th. After this they predicted a return of rough weather for an indefinite period. Faced with the desperate alternatives of accepting the immediate risks or of postponing the attack for at least a fortnight, General Eisenhower, with the advice of his commanders, boldly, and as it proved wisely, chose to go ahead with the operation, subject to final confirmation early on the following morning. At 4 A.M. on June 5 the die was cast: the invasion would be launched on June 6.[2]

DIARY ENTRY, JUNE 4, 1944: Sail past Lundy Island. We are the leading ship.

Stephen Ambrose described the strange position of a human being wielding great power over the lives of men and nations in his biography of Eisenhower.

STEPHEN AMBROSE: A minute earlier he had been the most powerful man in the world. Upon his word the fate of thousands of men depended, and the future of great nations. The moment he uttered the word, however, he was powerless. For the next two or three days there was almost nothing he could do that would in any way change anything. The invasion could not be stopped, not by him, not by anyone. . . . Eisenhower sat at his portable table and scrawled a press release on a pad of paper, to be used if necessary. "Our landings . . . have failed . . . and I have withdrawn the troops," he began. "My decision to attack at this time and place was based upon the best information available. The troops, the air and the Navy did all that bravery and devotion to duty could do. If any blame or fault attaches to the attempt it is mine alone."[3]

WINSTON CHURCHILL: In retrospect this decision rightly evokes admiration. It was amply justified by events, and was largely responsible for gaining us the precious advantage of surprise. We now know that the German meteorological officers informed their High Command that invasion on the 5th or 6th of June would not be possible owing to stormy weather, which might last for several days.[4]

As Hugh Nibley's ship moved toward the shores of France, his fellow members of the 101st made their final preparations for the assault from the air.

CORNELIUS RYAN: Nobody, from enlisted men to generals, seemed eager to challenge the fates. Over near Newbury at the headquarters of the 101st Airborne Division, the commander, Major General Maxwell D. Taylor, was holding a long, informal session with his senior officers. There were perhaps half a dozen men in the room and one of them, Brigadier General Don Pratt, the assistant division commander, sat on a bed. While they were talking another officer arrived. Taking off his cap, he tossed it onto the bed. General Pratt leaped up, swept the cap onto the floor and said, ". . . [T]hat's damn bad luck!" Everybody laughed, but Pratt didn't sit on the bed again. He had chosen to lead the 101st's glider forces into Normandy.[5]

HUGH NIBLEY: There was quite a flotilla crossing with us. The thing that most impressed me about the war was how much more dramatic, more spectacular, more theatrical it was than you could ever imagine it to be, especially a big invasion.[a] The gigantic scale on which things were happening was amazing. On the night before we went ashore in Normandy I spent the whole night up on the deck watching the fireworks, and the destructive power I saw was just unbelievable. They say the Normandy invasion was

General Don Pratt

the biggest military operation ever undertaken, and you could see it. I felt the same thing on the mission that I had felt in the training exercises—once again I was observing without participating.

The whole thing was extremely visible from where I was. The ships were all lined up at anchor waiting for the time to go, and I sat up on deck all night and watched as the Germans tried hard to get our ship. Planes bombed us all night. They kept flying over again and again and again, but they didn't hit the ship. They must have been very new at it. The planes would come in very slow, very

---

[a] "Altogether there were 2,727 ships, ranging from battleships to transports and landing craft that would cross on their own bottoms. They came from twelve nations—the United States, Great Britain, Canada, Australia, New Zealand, South Africa, France, Belgium, Norway, Poland, Greece, and Holland. . . . On the decks of the LSTs were the Higgins boats and other craft too small to cross the Channel on their own. There were 2,606 of them. Thus the total armada amounted to 5,333 ships and craft of all types, more vessels—as Admiral Morison pointed out—'than there were in all the world when Elizabeth I was Queen of England'" (Ambrose, *D-Day*, 170).

Antiaircraft tracers light up the sky off the coast of Normandy.

deliberately—they sounded like coffee grinders—and they'd drop their bombs and go on their way. It seemed like the bombs would come within inches of the boat, and they completely bracketed the ship with great plumes of water that would shoot up over us and thoroughly wash the decks and shower us and fill the air with an overpowering, sickening smell of cordite. It was brilliant, but they never hit us. I was the only one on the deck at night because I wanted to see the sights. All the other guys were down below, which I thought wasn't a safe place to be—so I spent the whole night up there.

Then we came up the Normandy coast in the morning, and we got the jeep ready.

My fate seems always to have been first in line. Our ship headed the convoy and, as if that were not enough, our party was to be the first ashore when contact was made with the division.

Priest saying mass for troops as they approach the Normandy coast

DIARY ENTRY, JUNE 6, 1944: Pass Bill of Portland and land across vast masses of flak in the morning. A ship next to us goes down in about 8 minutes.

HUGH NIBLEY: When I was very sick in Claremont I had impressions of the war, those "five-o'clock" dreams. In one I had dreamed vividly of a ship going down with black smoke pouring from it. I saw it as plain as anything. And then I saw it again right next to us off the beach there in Normandy. I was on the troop ship waiting to land and a ship right next to us was hit by a shell from the shore. There was a great cloud of black smoke and it sank, just as I had dreamed at Claremont.

The Germans tried hard to get our ship because it was the one right at the head. They knew it was valuable, so they were showering 88s onto the ship. I don't know which wave I was in—a lot of infantry had already landed—but the beach wasn't very well held. I stood at the head of the rope ladder for half an hour talking to a chaplain. After the ship next to us sank, a speedboat went by and a British officer with a bullhorn yelled, "You must land at once; your cargo is vital! Your cargo is vital; you must land at once!" They needed our jeep, so I had to be the first one there to land. So we immediately loaded the jeep into a landing craft.

I had rehearsed the glider landing many times, but this was the first time I had

SINKING OF THE *U.S.S. CORRY*

CORNELIUS RYAN: Off Utah the *U.S.S. Corry's* guns were red-hot. They were firing so fast that sailors stood on the turrets playing hoses on the barrels. . . . The Germans had been firing back—and hard. The *Corry* was the one destroyer the enemy spotters could see. . . . [Lieutenant Commander] Hoffman decided to move back before it was too late. "We swung around," recalls Radioman Third Class Bennie Glisson, "and showed them our fan-tail like an old maid to a Marine."

But the *Corry* was in shallow water, close to a number of knife-edged reefs. Her skipper could not make the dash for safety until he was clear. For a few minutes he was forced to play a tense cat-and-mouse game with the German gunners. . . . Finally, satisfied that he was away from the reefs, he ordered, "Hard right rudder! Full speed ahead!" and the *Corry* leaped forward. . . . Tearing through the water at more than twenty-eight knots the *Corry* ran headlong onto a submerged mine.

There was a great rending explosion that seemed to throw the destroyer sideways out of the water. The shock was so great that Hoffman was stunned. . . . The mine had cut the *Corry* almost in half. . . . The twisted pile of steel that had once been the *Corry* thrashed through the sea for more than a thousand yards before finally coming to a halt. Then the German batteries zeroed in. "Abandon ship!" Hoffman ordered. Within the next few minutes at least nine shells plowed into the wreck. One blew up the 40-millimeter ammunition. Another set off the smoke generator on the fantail, almost asphyxiating the crew as they struggled into boats and rafts.

The sea was two feet above the main deck when Hoffman, taking one last look around, dived overboard and swam toward a raft. Behind him the *Corry* settled on the bottom, her masts and part of her superstructure remaining above the waves—the U.S. Navy's only major D-Day loss. Of Hoffman's 294-man crew thirteen were dead or missing and thirty-three injured, more casualties than had been suffered in the Utah Beach landings up to this time.

Hoffman thought he was the last to leave the *Corry*. But he wasn't. Nobody knows now who the last man was, but as the boats and rafts pulled away, men on the other ships saw a sailor climb the *Corry's* stern. He removed the ensign, which had been shot down, and then, swimming and climbing over the wreckage, he reached the main mast. From the *U.S.S. Butler,* Coxswain Dick Scrimshaw watched in amazement and admiration as the sailor, shells still falling about him, calmly tied on the flag and ran it up the mast. Then he swam away. Above the wreck of the *Corry*, Scrimshaw saw the flag hang limp for a moment. Then it stretched out and fluttered in the breeze.[6]

The USS Tide burns off the coast of Normandy. Portions of the ship's masts, possibly with details that would reveal American technology, have been painted over by censors.

done a landing from sea, and that Normandy beach, the way it stretches out, it looked like miles and miles to shore.

I went down to the LCT[a] without orders. They had just lowered my jeep into the landing craft, and I was going down the rope ladder into the jeep when I had a thought that troubled me. I thought, "Joseph Smith slipped up when he had elephants in the Book of Mormon. The Americas didn't have any elephants." Then it suddenly occurred to me: "The elephants are only mentioned in the book of Ether. That's the archaic period. They could have been around then very well. They're not mentioned in the Nephite story at all."[b] I had this thought as I was coming down the ladder into the landing craft and that suddenly corrected my perspective on the problem, and I said, "That's just the thing! That's just right! How very happy I feel!"

There was a big French battleship blazing away right next to us, and the Germans zeroed in on us with their 88s as we put the rope over the side and started to swarm down into the landing craft. As soon as I got down the rope ladder, the very spot where I should have been waiting on the ship was hit by an 88, and half a dozen tankmen were blown up. The chaplain I had been talking to was wounded. The landing craft went in as far as it could, and then there were still a couple of hundred yards—quite a way to go yet. I climbed in the jeep and revved her up. I had packed it with sand bags so we could get some hold on the sandy beach, and five or six guys loaded on so we'd get some traction on the bottom. We couldn't afford to float around; we had to have traction. In we went with water up to our necks, and the pipe going up in the air, and all the guys who jumped on to help weight it down yelling, "Go Nibs! Keep going! Keep going!" All I had to do was press on the gas and it would go straight ahead, and it didn't stall at all in six, seven feet of water. The jeep did handsomely. It plowed right in and we were making towards the shore—buh, buh, buh, buh, with water up to our necks and the men cheering, "Go Nibs, go!" It must have been quite spectacular.

We were the first jeep to come in, so naturally the German 88s on the shore

[a] LCT: Landing Craft, Tank

[b] The Book of Mormon contains the stories of ancient migrations from the Middle East to the Americas, which Mormons believe to be accurate historical records. The bulk of the book is occupied with immigrants who left Jerusalem around 600 B.C. There is also, however, the history of an earlier migration at an unspecified date, and it is this one that Nibley remembered contained the references to elephants.

GIs climb down from their ship into their landing craft, as another landing craft moves toward the shore.

tried hard to stop us, first landing shells in front and then behind, and followed us all the way in, but they didn't hit us. There was one command car ahead of us driven by a big red-headed Kentuckian, and that disappeared and was never seen again. The 88s were splashing on all sides and jets of water were going up—it was an exciting ride. I wasn't afraid, I was too busy thinking about whether those wheels on the jeep would make contact and we'd keep going. If you lost your momentum, *that* would be frightening. But your heart is pounding, your adrenaline's up, it's that excitement that nature provides as your protection that keeps you from being paralyzed by fear. As I'd heard it said so many times, in battle you're too busy or too excited to be frightened. So I was thinking about the jeep and

Landing craft moves toward a Normandy beach, D-Day.

where to find our position and the like. Fear is the unknown, the uncertainty—there's always that nagging fear when you don't know what the score is. If you know what the danger is, that's not so bad.

I did a good job of waterproofing the jeep because it got to shore very well through that long, stretched-out beach that goes out forever at low tide. A lot of them stalled in the water, but mine didn't. We moved ahead and they cheered us on and we landed all right with German gunners popping 88s at us all the way; then we got up to the road and everybody scattered in all four directions. We were given instructions on how to find the headquarters. Everything was to be gauged by a certain windmill, which was to show us where we were. Of course they bombed the daylights out of it before we came, and there was no windmill in sight.

A waterproofed jeep moves through the water toward Utah Beach.

Everybody wandered around all over the place; I blundered into places. Things were going bad. Very bad.

The first thing after landing, I did something I thought I could never do. We were trying to get to a farm there, and I was about to eat this bar of hard, bitter chocolate.[a] We were pinned down and they started shooting in our direction, so we got into foxholes. There had just been a battle there recently, and I jumped into a foxhole that was full of spattered brains. There was a helmet full of brains, and it was just a bloody mess in there, and I still had this chocolate bar in my hand. Well, I immediately lost my appetite. And then, after a few minutes, I was so hungry I calmly ate the chocolate in this grave just as unconcerned as anything. I never

---

[a] Among the GI's equipment was the D-ration, a high-energy chocolate bar to be used as a quick snack to keep a soldier going when a full meal was not possible.

thought I could do a thing like that, but apparently you can shut off certain parts of the brain. I thought I could never face that sort of thing—it would be terrible; I'd lose my appetite. But you have to eat. I thought, "Well, this is the way war's going to be, might as well get used to it." I wouldn't do that again, though.

And then when I popped my head out of the foxhole, what were growing there? Great big red poppies! Just like the World War I poem: "In Flanders Fields the poppies grow between the crosses row on row . . ." I thought, "Here we are, no progress at all, back where we started. What's the use? We stand dead still. What a world we live in!"

It's funny, you live in your own world at times like that. There are these things that go through your head in battle, like at the end of *The Magic Mountain* of Thomas Mann, the main character keeps singing to himself the song about the tree, *Der Lindenbaum;* it kept running through his head. You think of things like that on these mournful occasions.

The airborne landing the night before had not gone according to plan.

STEPHEN AMBROSE: When [the planes carrying the paratroopers] crossed the coastline they hit the cloud bank and lost their visibility altogether. The

"IN FLANDERS FIELDS"

John McCrae

In Flanders fields the poppies blow
Between the crosses, row on row,
   That mark our place; and in the sky
   The larks, still bravely singing, fly
Scarce heard amid the guns below.

We are the Dead. Short days ago
We lived, felt dawn, saw sunset glow,
   Loved and were loved, and now we lie
   In Flanders fields.

Take up our quarrel with the foe:
To you from failing hands we throw
   The torch; be yours to hold it high.
   If ye break faith with us who die
We shall not sleep, though poppies grow
   In Flanders fields.[7]

HUGH NIBLEY: Utah Beach was rather pleasant compared to other landings like Omaha Beach, but we did have German artillery on the beach just north of where we landed; and the first road we came to the Germans had already closed the bridge and retaken the road. From then on it was rough.

pilots instinctively separated, some descending, some rising, all peeling off to the right or left to avoid a midair collision. When they emerged from the clouds, within seconds or at the most minutes, they were hopelessly separated. Lt. Harold Young of the 326th Parachute Engineers recalled that as his plane came out of the clouds, "We were all alone. I remember my amazement. Where had all those C-47s gone?" . . .

General Taylor . . . the commander of the 101st landed alone, outside Ste.-Marie-du-Mont. For twenty minutes he wandered around, trying to find his assembly point. He finally encountered his first trooper, a private from the 501st, established identity with his clicker, and hugged the man. A few minutes later Taylor's aide, Lieutenant Brierre, came up. The three-man group wandered around until Taylor, in the dark, physically collided with his artillery commander, Brig. Gen. Anthony McAuliffe. He didn't know where they were either.

Brierre pulled out a flashlight, the generals pulled out a map, the three men ducked into a hedgerow, studied the map, and came to three different conclusions as to where they were.[8]

Horsa glider meets hedgerow

HUGH NIBLEY: They were shelling the hell out of the beach at that particular time. There was a little road that I followed and found the headquarters. At the farm where the headquarters should be there, nobody was there but a couple of officers; the rest had all gotten lost or been taken and everybody was dirty and frightened. And they told me immediately, "Well, Braun's been killed; he's been shot." Lieutenant Braun, like Weigner, had been worried about getting killed. He felt he would be; he was worried sick about it. The Germans picked him up right after he landed and found some intelligence documents on him, and he spoke English with a very thick German accent, so they shot him on the spot. The other member of our team had also been killed.[a]

A crashed Horsa and its casualties

The murderous Horsa gliders were used with disastrous impact. It didn't break my heart when General Pratt had taken my place in the glider and, as it turned out, he was killed in the landing sitting in my seat. The rest of the crowd in my glider were all banged up and captured. The rest of the division had been scattered all over the place. One battalion of the 502nd, one of our crack regiments, were dropped 55 miles away from their target.[b] The flak was too heavy and the army air force pilots didn't want to go in, and they started dumping the paratroopers early. Apparently many of them landed in a marsh, and a lot of them were drowned. But it turned out getting scattered was the best thing that could possibly have happened, because it threw the Germans off completely. They didn't have any idea what was happening. They didn't know where we were going to land or where to counterattack or anything. So Hitler held back his crack armored divisions in Paris, and he insisted they would have to go to Le Havre, because that's where the main attack was going

[a] Weigner had transferred out of the 101st just in time to avoid D-Day and Hugh Nibley did not remember the name of his replacement; it is uncertain exactly what became of him. Max Oppenheimer offers one possible explanation: "I heard that the Sergeant [in the 101st OB team] . . . came in on a glider around D-Day, became entangled in a tree top, and was picked off by a German bullet" (Oppenheimer, *An Innocent Yank at Home Abroad*, 172).

[b] This appears to be an exaggeration. While many paratroopers were dropped far from their targets, *The U.S. Army Atlas of the European Theater in World War II* shows the farthest any troopers from the 101st landed from their intended drop zones was 21 miles, while some troopers from the 82nd Airborne Division were dropped as far as 25 miles from their targets.

to be. We put on a bluff that fooled them that time, and it saved the day. If they'd let those armored divisions go, they would have pushed us right back into the sea. Also, the 101st were awfully good, and even though it took a while to get the division back together, it really ruined things for the Germans.

Zilske, an old hardened master sergeant of the 101st, said the worst night he ever went through in his life was the first night we occupied that farm where we set up division headquarters. As I said, there was nobody there when I arrived but a couple of officers, and the place had all been blasted. The first sergeant of the company was killed also. I was just going to sleep when Major Danahy said, "Nibley, you're the ranking non-com in the company; you'll have to put up a defense around the farm tonight." We were expecting a German paratroop attack, and I was appointed to set up the perimeter in the field line to hold it against the attack because so many of the other noncommissioned officers had been taken or disappeared.

Most of the troops the 101st were facing on D-Day were low-quality coastal defense units. But not all, as Ambrose points out:

STEPHEN AMBROSE: Just before dawn, Colonel Heydte[a] got . . . his orders. He should attack with his regiment northward out of Carentan and clean out the area between that city and Ste.-Mère-Église.

Heydte set out confident he could do just that. He had under his command an overstrength regiment that was, in his opinion, worth two American or British divisions. His paratroopers were tough kids, seventeen and a half years old average age. They had been six years old when Hitler took power. They had been raised in a Nazi ideology that had been designed to get them ready for precisely this moment. They had an experienced and renowned commanding officer, a professional soldier with a record of audacity.

The 6th Parachute Regiment was a quintessential creation of Nazi Germany. The Nazis had brought together the professionalism of the German army with the new Nazi youth. They gave it new

---

[a] *Oberstleutnant Friedrich August Freiherr von der Heydte:* Commander of the 6th Fallschirmjaeger (parachute infantry) Regiment

equipment. They would hurl their best against the best the Americans could put into the field. "Let them come," Goebbels had sneered.

Now they had come, and they were in scattered pockets, highly vulnerable. As the first of the sun's rays appeared, Heydte and the elite of the Nazi system marched off to take them on. The first significant counterattack of D-Day was under way. Fittingly, it would pit an American elite force against a German elite force, a trial of systems.[9]

German paratroopers

HUGH NIBLEY: I started to dig a foxhole along the line, and I was surprised at how easy it was to dig. But it turned out the place where I was digging had been an old privy at the farm, and I was digging into some not-very-nice dirt. So I got out and had to dig again. What a mess! Everything was frantic. We were expecting an attack, digging foxholes, setting up this defensive line, and then suddenly came a gas alarm. We'd always been taught that phosgene gas smells like new-mown hay, so when a young lieutenant smelled new-mown hay he sounded the gas alarm right away. But he didn't realize that this was June and everything in Normandy smelled like new-mown hay because they'd been mowing hay all around. But this lieutenant smelled it and immediately sounded the alarm, so I put my gas mask on. But I had waterproofed it for crossing the Channel and it was all stopped up with clay, so I couldn't breathe through it. I sucked—no breath at all. And that was panicky because here was a gas alarm going off and at the same time I was trying to set up a perimeter because we were expecting a German paratroop attack any minute. Luckily it was a false alarm and it wasn't gas at all.

On that first night I did something I never did before or since. I put an old piece of corrugated iron over my foxhole and covered it with dirt. Then all night German planes flew back and forth dropping these butterfly bombs.*a* They were supposed to have a psychological effect; they made a terrible noise and lots of flashing. And in the morning the top of my foxhole was just sticking like a porcupine with splinters of steel, and there I was safe and sound under my roof.

Because the airborne landing had been so scattered, it threw everything into hopeless confusion. We were confused; the Germans were confused. My first real taste of combat was there at the farmhouse near Ste.-Mère-Église. There was a counterattack; and General Taylor was in his glory. He was so happy! He said, "I always wanted my men to smell the smoke of battle!" You couldn't see anybody, the smoke was so thick. As far as noise is concerned, the artillery doesn't bother you so much; it's all the small arms going off that make such a terrific noise you can't hear anything. Very, very dense smoke everywhere, nobody knows what's going on, the leaves and branches keep showering down. You keep looking to see if you can see anything through the smoke and bang at nothing with your trusty carbine and hope you won't hit anybody—I mean it would be sad if you did. When I had Colonel Mudgett in high school ROTC he taught us Spanish-American War tactics, and the first thing you did was to set the windage on your gun sight, if you can imagine. After World War I they developed a new theory of battle: it was just pure firepower; and that's what they taught us in college ROTC. That was the change between wars, in World War II you just saturated the place with fire *en*

General Maxwell Taylor waves from the door of a C-47. The D-Day jump was Taylor's fifth and earned him his paratrooper wings.

KILLING

Hugh Nibley's statement that "it would be sad" if he hit an enemy does not show him to be much of a soldier in the sense we are used to seeing in Hollywood movies. But Dave Grossman, a former army Ranger and a psychologist, shows that just by pulling the trigger Nibley was one of a small minority of combat soldiers.

DAVE GROSSMAN: Prior to World War II it had always been assumed that the average soldier would kill in combat simply because his country and his leaders have told him to do so and because it is essential to defend his own life and the lives of his friends. When the point came that he didn't kill, it was assumed that he would panic and run.

During World War II U.S. Army Brigadier General S. L. A. Marshall asked these average soldiers what it was that they did in battle. His singularly unexpected discovery was that, of every hundred men along the line of fire during the period of an encounter, an average of only 15 to 20 "would take any part with their weapons." This was consistently true "whether the action was spread over a day, or two days or three."

Marshall was a U.S. Army historian in the Pacific theater during World War II and later became the official U.S. historian of the European theater of operations. He had a team of historians working for him, and they based their findings on individual and mass interviews with thousands of soldiers in more than four hundred infantry companies, in Europe and in the Pacific, immediately after they had been in close combat with German or Japanese troops. The results were consistently the same: only 15 to 20 percent of the American riflemen in combat during World War II would fire at the enemy. Those who would not fire did not run or hide (in many cases they were willing to risk great danger to rescue comrades, get ammunition, or run messages), but they simply would not fire their weapons at the enemy, even when faced with repeated waves of banzai charges.[10]

A replica of the clickers used by the airborne troops at Normandy

masse. So I banged away. I made them keep their heads down, but I don't know if I ever hit anything. It could have been, just shooting blindly that way.

We had a way of identifying other Americans in the confusion. They gave us little toy frogs like they used to give away in shoe stores. They made a click-click noise, so all our boys had those frogs, and if you ran into someone you didn't know or you saw somebody behind a tree you just went click-click, and if they went click-click, click-click in answer you'd know it was one of ours. The frogs were a good way of identification in the dark without speaking, and the sound carried very well. It was ingenious but it didn't last long, because the Germans soon found out and they started picking up frogs too and it started making trouble.

DIARY ENTRY, JUNE 8, 1944: Still

The invasion had been successful, but it was behind schedule. General Montgomery had boasted that he would take the city of Caen at the east end of the Allied beachhead within thirty-six hours, and he was nowhere near to achieving that objective. In the American sector there was a gaping hole between Omaha Beach in the east and Utah Beach at the west end of the Allied lines. In that gap stood the town of Carentan, which was heavily guarded. The landings could not be called truly secure until the beaches were all linked up. The 101st had to take Carentan.

DIARY ENTRY, JUNE 9, 1944: Plane drops 2 great mines and ruins my jeep.

HUGH NIBLEY: The mines were supposed to destroy the whole country. You don't hear much about them. They weren't bombs; they were land mines.[a] That was after

---

[a] It is unclear exactly what kind of mine this was. Land mines, including large anti-tank mines were sometimes dropped from airplanes. Although they lay on top of the ground and were therefore visible, they served as a delaying tactic since they forced advancing troops to take time to clear the mines.

D-Day; maybe it was two days. Everybody was running around, and we didn't know if it was day or night. General Taylor put our headquarters over toward Carentan on a spit of land going out with the sea on one side and a big canal on the other. Years afterwards at Paul Springer's place, I talked with some of the officers who had been there at the same time, and they were saying that it was the insanest thing that ever happened when General

A jeep destroyed by a mine

Taylor set up his headquarters out there. We were stuck on this peninsula out there, and all the Germans had to do was cut us off and our headquarters company was in the soup. So the first thing the Germans did, they charged down the road right to the place where we were. But we stopped them. There was an awful a lot of shooting but they didn't get through, and we were saved that time.

In Intelligence our business was to overrun and loot enemy headquarters as soon as we could. This is the thing they always taught us in Ritchie: how to take over the headquarters the minute it fell into our hands. Often you would find the last company clerk there, having to type out his morning report. He wouldn't surrender until he was finished. The conscientious German has to finish his morning report, and *then* he will surrender. Of course he knows it doesn't mean anything at all, but it's that attachment to duty—you just have to keep going to the bitter end.

Of course I had to look over their papers. We had to figure out what units were being moved where and immediately report back to Intelligence. We had to know what we were up against, where they were coming from, where they'd been shipped from, where they had been at their last station, where they were going now. We had to know all these things so we'd know what to be ready for. Every German soldier had to have his paybook with him, and that listed the places he'd been, the units he'd been attached to, and so forth. It had valuable information in it; so we'd take their paybooks and get information that way. They weren't supposed to, but they all kept diaries too. Typical German thoroughness. They would diagram everything—always these geometrical diagrams—and they would list the officers in the unit and so forth, and they would joke about Hitler and write, "On this day Private 'So-and-so' decided to go over and get out of the war."

About the third day in Normandy we were having a very bad time in this little farmhouse we were trying to hold on to by the skin of our teeth. Finally somebody from the navy got through. It was Tom Hungerford, who had been a student of mine at Claremont; in fact, he had been a student in a one-man class. He had got to be quite a high officer in the navy, and when we saw each other we immediately embraced. The officers didn't like that at all. We weren't supposed to talk to officers that way. But he called in some artillery fire from the sea because we couldn't get any. Their guns were very accurate and very valuable to us.

I was right next to General Taylor all the time. His tent was just a few yards from my foxhole, and I acted as interpreter for him on numerous occasions in Normandy, including for Russian prisoners. But Taylor was an idealist. We hadn't been there more than three days, fighting over Carentan, when he called me and said, "Sergeant Nibley, I want you to take a message to the colonel of the German regiment over there. I admire him. He's put up a good fight. I'll send you over with a white flag, and you can invite him to tea."

The Germans admired Taylor, too. They called him *"der letzte Gentleman"*— the last gentleman. So I changed my tunic and got ready to go invite Colonel Heydte of the German 6th Parachute Regiment to tea. They called it off at the last minute, but that General Taylor, he was storybook. He got his ideas out of storybooks, and you could tell that he wanted to act like a storybook character himself.

I had another friend, Dave Bernay (he got the Silver Star)—we were very good friends in the 101st. Bernay was a Jew, very short, just five feet tall, big schnozz— he was a character. And very tough. Boy, was he a tough little Jew! He'd been born in Germany and his family escaped, and he didn't like the Nazis at all.

Little Dave Bernay went down with Colonel Danahy—well, Major Danahy

GERMAN SOLDIERS SURRENDER

DAVE GROSSMAN: One interviewer of World War II POWs told me that German soldiers repeatedly told him that relatives with World War I combat experience had advised, "Be brave, join the infantry, and surrender to the first American you see." The American reputation for fair play and respect for human life had survived over generations, and the decent actions of American soldiers in World War I had saved the lives of many soldiers in World War II.[11]

ASIAN POWS

LUCIEN GOLDSCHMIDT: One forgets it now, there were so many unexpected groups of people [in the German army]. For example, among the prisoners were Tatars and Kalmyks. I have in my recollection a scene that is unforgettable: we were still in England—we had not gone to the continent—and there was some sort of factory that had been filled with these auxiliary troops of the German army, who had been captured in the very first onslaught [at Normandy]. Obviously at that time we had no space in France to keep these prisoners, so they had been brought to somewhere near an industrial city of northern England. And there was this scene with these naked Asiatics, being driven, on the double, around that arena while being sprayed with anti-lice and anti-bug and various sprays. It was one of these things that you believe, perhaps, a very advanced filmmaker might think up, but could not realize. You visualize this arena, which was basically an assembly floor, I think, in a factory, and these guys being made to run, and these American noncommissioned officers were spraying them with these powders. These people didn't know enough German to read their paybook, you know, vulgar Tatars. So the army did not only face German soldiers, and Hugh Nibley had to be ready for many emergencies, or many unexpected developments.

Asian POWs, in German uniforms, probably conscripted from parts of the Soviet Union the Germans had invaded

at that time—they went down together to St. Lo. At the time the Germans were there and the allies were nowhere near it. It was a very important center to take. Bernay went on this expedition, a scouting reconnaissance, and he ran right into the Germans and went right through the middle of them. It was nighttime and he was right in the midst of them and came away undetected because he knew how to lie still, though at one point he had to lie still in a ditch while some German urinated all over him and he didn't dare make a motion.

Dave Bernay was an awfully good interrogator. Because the officers knew he was a Jew and that he had no love for Nazis, they'd assign Dave to interrogate the SS men who would never give up, and they would just melt in his presence. The Germans were scared to death of him and the ones he interrogated told him everything he wanted to know, because he wouldn't fool around with these tough SS men. This little Jew would break them real quick. He had a trench knife that he kept very sharp, and when he started interviewing a German, he would take it out and begin by flicking the buttons off their jackets as he went. "Is that so? Was it anywhere near the bridge that it happened?" Snick! another button, one by one, moving up, and up, and up, and by the time he got to the top button they'd tell him anything he wanted to know. Lucien Goldschmidt would get the same effect by being the schoolmaster. Little Dave Bernay[a] got his answers flicking buttons off.

Dave and I had our foxholes right together, and we fixed them up into a big fancy super-foxhole. We put parachute silk all over it, nice and clean. The silk parachutes were very convenient; you'd find them all over and you could just use them. So we lined our foxholes with silk. We had some long talks there.

One day I was asleep, all covered up in my foxhole, and Dave came running up and said, "Get up! Grab a carbine and come quick! The Germans are in Carentan, and they're going to attack!"

And I heaved an enormous sigh of relief and I said, "Thank heaven! It was only a dream!" Because before he woke me I had been dreaming that I had committed

[a] Hugh Nibley was not a large man and it seems strange that he constantly refers to Bernay as "little." But he's not the only one. In *Rendezvous with Destiny*, Sergeant (later Lt.) Thomas B. Buff, who jumped from the same plane with Bernay, uses the same term as he describes Bernay's coolness under pressure: "My little friend, Dave Bernay, fell asleep as soon as he was seated and continued so almost all the way from there on out" (Rapport and Northwood, *Rendezvous with Destiny*, 83).

THE SS

The *Schutzstaffel* (defense unit) or SS was an organization within the National Socialist party. It began as Hitler's personal guard and eventually expanded into a huge organization with its own large business operations and its own elite army of forty divisions. It included factories and the dreaded *Gestapo* secret police; and it was the SS that owned and operated the concentration camps.

The SS was essentially a Nazi version of priesthood. Candidates for membership had to prove racial purity, undergo training and indoctrination, and swear personal allegiance to Hitler. The organization also staged the party's large pageants and rallies and performed numerous rites and ceremonies that gave a mystical aura to membership. Toward the end of the war, however, many non-Germans were recruited into SS army units because of a shortage of pure Germans.

One of Hitler's supermen

a rather serious crime—I think I committed a murder—and I was terrified by the dream. When I woke in the foxhole with the guns firing and noise and shouting all around and the dense smoke of rifle fire, I was so happy I could sing because I hadn't committed that crime. When I found it wasn't true, it was as if I'd found myself in my bed in a palace. "How happy I am! Everything is all right! The world is lovely and right because I have not sinned!"

I had my other dreams too, my five o'clock impressions. There was the one about the ship, and then I had one where I was in a foxhole and two tanks started coming across the field. That's where the dream stopped. I never knew how it turned out. Then, near Carentan, I found myself in a foxhole looking out at a field and the scene looked very familiar. I remembered the dream of the two tanks coming, and I realized I was looking at the same field I had seen in my dream. There was a reporter from *The Stars and Stripes* in the next foxhole, and I called over to him and said, "Well, this is the end of it. In a minute you're going to see two tanks come across that field, and that's going to decide it for us." Sure enough, here came the two tanks. I had dreamed about them right up to that minute, but I didn't know what was going to happen next. Fortunately, they turned out to be our tanks from Omaha Beach. They'd been put on the wrong beach, and they were wandering around lost. As it turned out, they showed up just in time to save us from a bad situation.

We had one little plane, one of these Piper Cubs that they use for artillery spotting, and Captain Mann, a fat, jolly undertaker from Philadelphia, went up in it just for the ride. From the plane he could see a German battalion marching along the road toward us, protected by a Mark IV tank preceding them. It was quite an impressive sight, and Captain Mann radioed back to warn us. Naturally we built what kind of a barricade we could: a couple of trucks at the end of the road, some dry-goods boxes and stuff like that, a lot of baggage and crates—that was all the defense we had. We also had the two tanks, but one of them had run out of gas and had only one round of ammunition for its gun. The other had run out of ammunition completely. Captain Mann gave the coordinates, and they fired the last shot of ammunition they had left, and it made a direct hit on the German tank. It started flaming furiously and blew up, and that stopped the attack. The battalion turned back and disappeared.

It was purely accidental that Captain Mann should go up and see the approaching battalion and the tank in front, and that we had a tank with only one shell left and a tank that couldn't move because it didn't have any gas, and that the functioning tank was able to zero in on the front tank and make a direct hit. It's unbelievable, but it really happened. That saved the day.

When Hugh finally wrote his first letter from the battlefield, it was a perfect exercise in how to use many words to say absolutely nothing—certainly not to give any hint of what was going on.

June 11, 1944

Dear mother,

Forgive me if I annoy you with this steady cascade of wit, learning and philosophy. You know nothing can keep me from Telling All, only the censor has first priority and last say. But here goes for running the

Piper Cub spotting plane

American artillerymen fire a howitzer into Carentan.

blockade: I am in utter health and my usual high spirits. It is hard for me to act my age when a lordly box of candy such as the last arrives but I am still as fond of Hieroglyphic as ever. Aware of how perilously near this pointed expression comes to a treasonable divulgence of my present activities I hesitate to add another word. Let us hesitate, for example, to add the word "cabbage." What a world of deep insinuation in the sumptuous imagery of that highly involved (744 ± involutions) vegetable! The *omission* of such a staggering audacity that the mere thought of it forces me to conclude with love to all,

Hugh

The day after he wrote this letter, the 101st finally took Carentan.

HUGH NIBLEY: Because we were in Intelligence we were supposed to set up a camp in the town of Carentan on the other side of the canal. Officers weren't allowed to

Military police direct traffic over the bridge into Carentan.

drive, even in battle, so Major Sommerfield told me I had to drive him through Carentan and set up the camp.[a] But Carentan hadn't been taken yet. Then Colonel Cole ordered them to take the bridge to Carentan—with a bayonet charge yet, in this day and age! Colonel Cole, he was all fire, so he led one of the only bayonet charges in World War II and took the bridge. Right after the bridge was taken we drove our jeep over it into Carentan. I was driving—it was the first jeep to go in there—and they started shooting from windows all around. It was just electric— the bullets flying, just zipping around there; they sounded like bees buzzing. One of the windows they were shooting from was the French hospital full of nuns.

Dave Bernay and I went through Carentan together. In the center of the town

[a] Hugh Nibley many times repeated this statement that officers were prohibited from driving. He found this to be one of the main advantages of remaining a non-com. However, there are many accounts of American officers having driven in the European Theater, which seem to contradict Nibley's memories.

was the graveyard, so we ducked into the cemetery and hid behind the tombstones until we were able to duck into doorways. That was something, going door to door. The Germans repeatedly tried to overrun the very thinly held positions the Americans set up; then came the big storm and we found ourselves cut off from any support. It was what the British call a very sticky time.

DIARY ENTRY, JUNE 12, 1944: Wild ride into Carentan with Maj. Sommerfield through the snipers. Finally ducked behind some gravestones. Finally dig in by the canal bank. Firing increases all through the night. Next day they attack in battalion force.

HUGH NIBLEY: In the morning they came in battalion force, and it was a real fire-fight.[a] It was so thick with smoke you couldn't see your hand in front of your face,

GIs on a captured German jeep move through Carentan.

[a] The counterattack that came was not from the weak German coastal defense units, but from Colonel von der Heydte's crack 6th Parachute Regiment.

and everybody was shooting like mad at nothing. We had to throw up anything we had, old crates, whatever.

Once we were in Carentan, the division set up headquarters by the canal that ran through the town. There was a brick building, a factory, there, and we saw a man looking out of the window. The Germans had cleared out of the building, but there was somebody peeking out the upper window seeing what was going on below. Somebody was observing us. Well, Major Danahy (now Colonel Danahy they'd made him) says, "Go up and see who that is." So Dave Bernay and some others went to look, and they brought a guy down. He was dressed in civilian clothes, but he spoke German, so Colonel Danahy said, "Take that man out and shoot him," and he assigned that to Dave Bernay.

Well, Dave had done plenty of killing and he hated Nazis, so this was not a particularly tough assignment for him. He put his gun over his shoulder and said,

A French resistance worker spells out orders to shoot all prisoners.

COLONEL COLE'S CHARGE

LEONARD RAPPORT AND ARTHUR NORTHWOOD JR.: At 0615, Colonel Cole gave the command. The artillery lifted its fire to the railroad track beyond the house. As soon as Colonel Cole heard the shells come over, he blew his whistle and took off across the ditch. Only about twenty men followed him. There were about fifty more men with Major Stopka over on the left and the major was yelling: "Let's go! Over the hedge!" But it was a little company which bounded forward. Company H and Headquarters Company were hardly represented.

Colonel Cole looked back over his line and what he saw almost stunned him; he thought, "My men have let me down."

. . . Colonel Cole trotted halfway across the field. Then he stopped, knelt on one knee and looked back. Fire was clipping the grass all around him and more of it was passing overhead. He saw that his men were trailing behind him in single file. So he waved both arms at them trying to get them to fan out. Instead, they hit the dirt. He started working on them one man at a time, urging them to go on.

He kept firing his Colt .45 wildly in the general direction of the farmhouse and as he fired he yelled:

". . . I don't know what I'm shooting at, but I gotta keep on." Some of the men who heard him, in spite of the danger all about, couldn't help laughing.[12]

DONALD BURGETT: The field was fairly large and surrounded with high hedges. Short grass about two inches high grew from corner to corner. There were no trees, ditches or gulleys for cover, just flat open ground to cross to the next hedge. Troopers were well scattered through the field, all of them doubled over or crouched as low as possible and running toward the other end of the field as fast as they could. I was crouched so low it seemed that my knees were driving on either side of my head. We all fired from the hip as we ran.

Halfway across, the enemy opened up on us with rifle, machine-gun, mortar and 88 shells. Our artillery, which had been pasting the hedges in front of us, lifted and started falling farther back in enemy territory. It was impossible to go back or to either side. We had to take the shortest

Lt. Colonel Robert G. Cole

Street fighting in Carentan

route, straight into the enemy fire, to try and reach the safety of the hedge in front of us. The one that held the enemy. Men were being killed and wounded in large numbers, some of them horribly maimed, with limbs and parts of their bodies being shredded or shot away. I could feel the muzzle blasts of the men behind me as they fired from the hip. I was nearly as concerned about getting shot in the back by a fellow trooper as I was about the Germans in front.

Mortar shells blanketed the field. At least six machine guns were cross firing on us and that terrible 88 was shredding everything in sight. Bounding Bettys leaped into the air to sow their seeds of death on the ones who disturbed them. These were ingenious little devices of the enemy that were triggered when a man stepped on them. The bombs would spring into the air and explode about belly high. The explosion would send steel balls rocketing out in all directions, like the spokes of a wagon wheel. They were very effective. Men were being torn almost in half by them. We kept running straight at the enemy. It was like a dream—no, more like a nightmare. We were running for all we were worth, but standing still, getting nowhere. The hedge at the far end of the field seemed as far away as before.

We were being annihilated, our ranks disintegrating as we ran. Glancing at my comrades around and behind me to draw courage and strength from their presence, I saw that the field was being littered with dead, our dead. A trooper in front of and to the right of me was hit in the chest by an 88 shell. His body disappeared from the waist up, his legs and hips with belt, canteen and entrenching tool still on taking three more steps, then falling. Another trooper went to his knees, ran a couple of yards in that position, tried to gain his feet, stumbled and went down facefirst.[13]

"Come along, let's get going," and took the prisoner out across the fields. They came to a drainage ditch with a little water in it and Dave says, "Step over the ditch," in German: "*Eibe dein fluss.*"

"Ah, you speak German?" the prisoner says. Obviously the guy wanted to stall as long as possible. He saw this guy was going to shoot him, and he wanted to make friends with him, do something. I would certainly start talking, especially if the soldier spoke German. So they struck up a conversation.

Dave says, "Yes, I speak German."

"Where are you from?"

"I'm from Maxmiliansau," Dave said.

The village of Maxmiliansau was hardly more than one factory on the Rhine where they made celluloid out of pine logs. When I was a missionary you'd find rafts of pine logs floating down the river, and you could get on and paddle across on them. Those came from the celluloid factory at Maxmiliansau. That was all there was to the town—not many people lived there, it was just the factory.

"Maxmiliansau?" the prisoner said. "Did you know Herr Bernay?"

"He was my father," Dave said.

And the man looked at him and he said, "My little David!" and he threw his arms around him and took him in a fond embrace.

It turned out this was the guy who got the Bernay family out of Germany and saved their lives. Dave's father was the one who managed the factory, and this man was the Bernay house-servant. He had helped them escape the Nazis and saved their lives. He had been a laborer in the camp by Carentan, and the reason he had stayed behind to spy was because he wanted to desert to us, he was waiting there to give himself up.

Dave told me about it later and he just wept like a fish. "My little David!" That was a close call. Instead of shooting him, they took the guy and gave him a job working in the kitchen.

After the 101st took Carentan the two American beaches were finally linked up, and the division concentrated on expanding the beachhead inland and up the Cotentin Peninsula to Cherbourg and its large deepwater port facilities.

DIARY ENTRY, JUNE 25, 1944: The foxhole fills with rain.

DIARY ENTRY, JUNE 26: Rain, rain, rain.

DIARY ENTRY, JUNE 27: Moving through enemy territory into St.-Sauveur-le-Vicomte. I tent with Bernay.

HUGH NIBLEY: Throughout the Battle of Normandy I was always observing without participating. I was interested in observing what was happening, but I really wasn't in it. I often wondered why I should find myself in a battle like that. Often I would say with Charles Addams, "What am I doing here?" During the time I was at Claremont I'd been on that "Committee on War Aims and Peace Objectives" to take notes. It was very fancy—financed by Rockefeller—and we'd sit around and wisely discuss war aims and peace objectives with these high-powered intellectuals. Then, all of a sudden—it seemed like just a matter of a few weeks later—here I find myself with my face all blackened and clusters of grenades

A GI carries baggage for French civilians.

on my chest with my trusty carbine, and I say, "How in the hell did I ever get into this?" But I think it was to observe. Because I was in the perfect position to observe. I had to see what was going on, not only in my own position, but on the whole front. I had to be in communication and receive the reports over the radio. Once, right in the middle of the Normandy invasion, I was flown back to England to give a broadcast over BBC on the psychology of the German army, and then I was flown back to the division again.

During the time we were in Normandy, after a day of fighting we'd hear the day's news reports on the BBC, and according to the news it was just British fighting the war. The whole thing was a British enterprise. We'd hear about how a British division had taken this position and that village. We'd hear reports about fighting on all the other beaches, but we'd never hear about the American beaches. The British had taken everything; they were just wiping up on the Germans. But at no time did the British commit more than three divisions to the line, when we'd have as many as thirty or forty.[a] But Churchill said, "History will bear me out, particularly as I shall write that history myself."[14] And he did—but he faked a lot of it.

Churchill observing from a ship off the Normandy coast

[a] Hugh Nibley's statement that they had only three divisions committed is an exaggeration. But it is similar to what General Bradley said about the situation in the following December and January (when Nibley was working for him): "Not only were we as fully competent as the British but by now the U.S. had committed 50 divisions in the ETO in contrast to the 15 of Britain" (Bradley, *Soldier's Story*, 488).

Way back in World War I he definitely falsified the news of the sinking of the *Lusitania* to bring Wilson into the war.[a] He was in the Admiralty then, and he knew that the *Lusitania* was going to be sunk and he knew where and he knew by whom. He knew the whole thing. But he knew that if it sank it would bring America into World War I, so he let it happen.

But there are some awful things that happened in Normandy, things I haven't told anyone. In the beginning there was a certain sense of fun to the invasion. Then it began to hit me what we were really doing. Awful things happened because of the instructions they gave to the fellows in the 101st. You see, many of them were from the slums, rough characters; some of them joined because they got prison sentences shortened under condition that they join the 101st. Their orders were, "Search and destroy, and don't go easy on them, whatever you do!" And they didn't go easy on them. The guys told me about one incident that happened when I was on the boat. Colonel Johnson,[b] commander of the 501st, spoke to the men as they were getting ready to get into the planes for the invasion. He was a typical southerner, and he jumped up on the stage with a trench knife in his mouth and he said, "You see this knife? Before the night is over it will be wet with German blood!" And then he let out a hideous rebel yell that just shook the walls.[c] That was Colonel Johnson. That was the spirit Taylor liked. Well, if that's how you get to be a great general, you're welcome to it.

Even the best of them, like Colonel Danahy, would say, "Don't go easy on them! Don't spare anything, we're out to search and destroy—*and I mean destroy!*" They told us that anything you see is legitimate game. "Destroy anything you see,

---

[a] The *Lusitania* was an ocean liner carrying civilian passengers, largely Americans, as well as munitions bound for England when it was sunk by a German U-boat in 1915. There remains considerable controversy about whether the British—and First Lord of the Admiralty Winston Churchill in particular—allowed the ship to be sunk with little warning in order to inflame Americans against Germany. Many historians hotly dispute the allegation.

[b] Colonel Howard R. Johnson (1903-1944) gained the nickname of "Jumpy" as he made more than 130 parachute jumps before his regiment sailed for England.

[c] Colonel Johnson's speech as remembered by Lt. Carl Cartledge in *D-Day* by Stephen E. Ambrose: "He gave a great battle speech, saying victory and liberation and death to the enemy and some of us would die and peace cost a price and so on. Then he said, 'I want to shake the hand of each one of you tonight, so line up.' And with that, he reached down, pulled his knife from his boot and raised it high above his head, promising us in a battle cry: 'Before the dawn of another day, I'll sink this knife into the heart of the foulest bastard in Nazi land!' A resounding yell burst forth from all 2,000 of us as we raised our knives in response" (Ambrose, *D-Day*, 192).

A GI searches young German prisoner of war.

because that's the only way to make an effect." And of course that was true. The Germans had been having it all their own way before the invasion; then when the 101st landed it was a shock. These were mostly coastal defense units, not your tough Nazi troops; they were little kids from Austria that didn't know what was going on. They weren't Nazis, and they had no love for Hitler. They were fifteen- and sixteen-year-olds, if you can imagine that. Some things were pretty bad. I remember one time when a company of guys came in for mess at noontime. They'd just been out and liquidated a bunch of those kids and described how they took real pleasure in doing it. A horrible thing to do, because they were just little kids.

The Germans got to hate us. They called the paratroopers "devils with baggy pants." When they picked up the 101st they usually didn't spare them. But from the very beginning some of our boys were acting worse than any Germans I ever heard of. The French were soon preferring the Germans to us, as a matter of fact, and they told us that quite frankly. As I said, we were actually having fun, like it was some sort of camping trip. Then something happened that hit me like a hammer blow to the forehead. It happened within the first week in Normandy. There was a wedding going on in this Norman church, and five of our boys went in. They lined up all the wedding guests around the wall in the front room, at

Prisoners of war on Normandy beach wait to be shipped off.

gunpoint, while each of the soldiers took the bride in the back room and raped her, all five of them in order. Nice wedding, huh? These people at the wedding were on *our side.*

That's liberaton for you. Liberal-minded way of seeing things. The reason we found out about it was that one of the paratroopers wore a particularly big, beautiful ivory crucifix, and the French were able to identify them with that.

Enemies in Normandy

General Taylor was very much upset and really raised hell. He said, "Boys, don't you ever do things like that!"

But that's absolutely typical, and I know much worse things than that happened. The American soldiers felt they were out of school, and they could do anything they damn well pleased. This was war, and the last thing they were told was, "Don't be too easy on them."

As far as atrocities are concerned, when you capture eight hundred prisoners and only thirty of them survive, there's something wrong there. I heard it reported the first week there: we had eight hundred prisoners, and just a handful were ever taken to prison in England. It was easier to get rid of them; we couldn't be bothered with them. The Germans were doing it the same way. The rules of civilized warfare didn't apply much, and we were in the search and destroy business. You shot what you could see.

I remember an officer in the Engineers. He'd been very hard on some of his men and got himself a promotion to colonel. Then, on the day he was made a colonel, he was given a mission to blow a bridge—a brand-new colonel going out on his first adventure. But he couldn't enjoy being a colonel very long. Some of the men were greatly amused by the assignment to go blow that bridge, because it was an impossible assignment and they knew he wasn't going to come back. They all said, "Goodbye, Colonel, goodbye." He was furious. He never came back either. They thought it was fun, standing there waving, "Goodbye, Colonel."

By June 26, Hugh's letter of June 11 hadn't reached his mother yet. Sloanie wrote to the mother of her son's best friend.

June 26, 1944

Dear Mrs. Springer,

. . . Hugh has been in England for nearly a year. . . . Sloan is in Washington D.C., Richard in Fort Knox, Kentucky. Reid is going to New York to continue music, the Army discharged him. I am a jittery old woman with worry. Am living too long. My precious Hugh is in the 101st Airborne, not a word from him since the 23rd of May. I have often thought of you, and wondered if Paul was in the war. . . .

Sloanie Nibley

Dead German sniper in Cherbourg

Normandy, June 30, 1944

Dear mother

The "late-great" Justice Holmes called war an "organized bore"; even the fastest-moving situation somehow lacks any sense of freshness or novelty, and the noisiest battles are the stupidest, I am told. . . . I know you would not worry on my behalf: not that there has been no cause for alarm, but rather because of the assurance you mentioned in your last. . . . Rich and his crowd[a] will be most welcome if and when they get here.

Love,

Hugh

---

[a] Hugh's brother Richard was serving in an armored division. It was armored troops under General Patton who eventually broke out of the beachhead and drove the Germans back out of France. But they didn't begin their operations until August. Richard Nibley was not in the initial breakout offensive, but did serve with Patton's army later in the war.

HUGH NIBLEY: The whole time in Normandy one thing kept going through my head: Beethoven's "Kreutzer Sonata." I could think of nothing else but that. And that's Normandy to me—the fall of leaves and the litter on the streets and the shooting going on everywhere and the rifle smoke everywhere, and always the sound of Beethoven going through my head. Karl Maria Remarque wrote about that in *All Quiet on the Western Front.* The soldier boy has one thing going through his head in the end—he's singing the beautiful "Linden Tree" song. It evokes this intense pathos of contradicting images. Here he is walking into the enemy fire—it was a deadly command; they should never have done it—and as he goes forward "Der Lindenbaum" keeps running through his head. The linden tree that stood where he carved his initials. Very moving.[a] One gets sentimental, but that's the sort of nonsense you put up with in war. These crazy things would happen.

It had to be a private war. You did your own thinking. If you hang on, you never know what will happen, so you don't give up. I had my patriarchal blessing, which I valued, and it had been carried out so beautifully up to then, so I said, "Well, just keep going. We have a labor to perform."

German infantrymen advance, World War I

[a] Nibley has confused two books here. Previously, he correctly cited Thomas Mann's *The Magic Mountain* as the novel where the main character sings "Der Lindenbaum" while marching into enemy fire as the men in this World War I photograph are doing. But here he says it was *All Quiet on the Western Front* by Erich Maria Remarque. The endings of the two books do have a remarkable similarity. Both of them include the extreme contrast of peace, serenity, and the horror of the World War I battlefront. Mann's ending is more poetic and beautiful. Remarque's has more of the grit and realism of battle. Both are deeply ironic and focus on the obliteration of a generation of the best and brightest of German youth. It's easy to see how he could mix them up.

"DER LINDENBAUM"

Wilhelm Mueller

The well before the gateway
O'er hangs a linden tree
How oft within its shadow
Fair dreams have haunted me;

And many a time I've graven
Fond lines of love thereon,
For still, in joy or sorrow,
I sought its shelter yon.

Today my fancy led me
Near by at dead of night,
I closed mine eyes in passing
To hide it well from sight:

And then, as if 'twere calling,
A sigh went through the boughs:
Come here to me, old comrade,
'Tis here thou findest repose!

The icy winds of winter
My face did wildly spurn,
They tore my hat away too,
Yet never would I turn.

Now many a mile behind me
I've left the linden tree,
And still I hear it sighing:
Repose were there for thee![15]

VIKTOR FRANKL: I think it was Lessing who once said, "There are things which must cause you to lose your reason or you have none to lose." An abnormal reaction to an abnormal situation is normal behavior. . . . The reaction of a man to his admission to a concentration camp also represents an abnormal state of mind. . . . These reactions . . . began to change in a few days. The prisoner passed from the first to the second phase [of mental reaction to camp life]; the phase of relative apathy in which he achieved a kind of emotional death. . . . The newly arrived prisoner experienced the tortures of other most painful emotions, all of which he tried to deaden.[16]

Dear Mother,

All serene again in my department. After some fuss we are at last able to view this situation again with some measure of detachment. Viewing situations with detachment is my peculiar business, and the only interesting job in the war. Only when the view becomes more important than that detachment, interest tends to give place to alarm and as you know, I scare easily. . . . No reports can exaggerate the merits of the boys of the 101st. That exalted zeal that usually invests a few rare souls in the heat of action seems to hold whole battalions for days on end, so that if just one paratrooper was in a place we could say that position was ours. I am all admiration for these chaps whom you can count on in *every* situation. This emotion I share even with those horribly conceited German officers who when pressed will finally admit our moral superiority.

Love to all
Hugh

HUGH NIBLEY: I remember the dream I had in the foxhole outside Carentan. The one where Dave Bernay woke me up and I felt so happy because it was just a dream and I hadn't actually committed the terrible crime I had dreamed about. There I was in the middle of a battle, and I was completely happy. It was a very strong thing; it came to me very strongly: I shouldn't be *happy* in this circumstance! But it's not what happens to you that matters. It's not what becomes of you, it's what you become that's important. And the tragedy today in America is not what becomes of us, but what we become. As Brigham Young used to say, if you don't deserve hell and you're sent to hell it doesn't bother you. You just say, I'm in the wrong place; there has been a mistake. It'll be corrected, I don't belong here. But if you belong there, that's the sad thing. Then it's what you are. There is the tragedy.

DIARY ENTRY, JULY 10, 1944: Camp in the field behind Utah Beach. We had a quiet night. Will we have ships here? No one knows.

JULY 11: In the fields . . . spend the night on Utah Beach. The doubt rises we float and sail. . . .

Thirteen-year-old German prisoner of war

JULY 13: Landed at Southampton returned by train to Newbury. Strong language about people who give life and death orders.

6

FALSE STARTS

STEPHEN AMBROSE: The Germans had taken four years to build the Atlantic Wall. They had poured thousands of tons of concrete, reinforced by hundreds of thousands of steel rods. They had dug hundreds of kilometers of trenches. They had placed millions of mines and laid down thousands of kilometers of barbed wire. They had erected tens of thousands of beach obstacles. It was a colossal construction feat that had absorbed a large percentage of Germany's material, manpower, and building capacity in Western Europe.

At Utah [Beach], the Atlantic Wall had held up the U.S. 4th Division for less than one hour. At Omaha, it had held up the U.S. 29th and 1st divisions for less than one day. At Gold, Juno, and Sword, it had held up the British 50th, the Canadian 3rd, and the British 3rd divisions for about an hour. As there was absolutely no depth to the Atlantic Wall, once it had been penetrated, even if only by a kilometer, it was useless. Worse than useless, because the Wehrmacht troops manning the Atlantic Wall east and west of the invasion area were immobile, incapable of rushing to the sound of the guns.

The Atlantic Wall must therefore be regarded as one of the greatest blunders in military history.[1]

The 101st Airborne mission in Normandy was a brilliant success. They silenced the German guns aimed at the landing beaches and blocked the Germans from getting

Unloading supplies on Utah Beach

reinforcements to the beachhead. They captured Carentan, the first French town to be freed from German occupation, then worked with other units to seal off the Cotentin Peninsula and take the important port of Cherbourg. Some of this was due to the division's fine training and the fighting spirit of the Screaming Eagles. Some was due to the meticulous planning that prepared the massive offensive. And a great deal of this success must be attributed to either divine intervention or dumb luck.

Airborne troops weren't trained for the regular infantry tasks of holding a line and moving it forward. The airborne trooper was designed to drop behind the lines into the middle of enemy forces and fight on all sides at once in lightning-quick surprise attacks that would last a very short time. They traveled light, were difficult to resupply, and were not prepared to fight in place for long periods of time. In Normandy the job was intended to take seventy-two hours. General Taylor had told the 101st before D-Day,

"Give me three days and nights of hard fighting, then you will be relieved."[2] It took more than five weeks instead.

Scotland, July 26, 1944

Dear Mother,

A heavenly week in the Scottish Highlands. Simply scrambling aimlessly from one mountain-top to the next, miles from any road or habitation. . . . The War is a problem, but it is a problem to which we have the solution—all that remains now is the spade-work of carrying out the operation. How different is the rest of the picture! The Fourth Century all over again, with its desperate yearning for quiet security running against an insuperable and mounting inclination to moral degeneracy. . . .

Thanks endlessly for the candy, a rare treat in these parts. . . .

Love,

Hugh

HUGH NIBLEY: I had a close call in the highlands. I took the walk up the glen and climbed Ben Nevis, the highest mountain in Britain. On the way down the stream was running very strongly, but I could see just a couple of miles down there was Kinlochleven. If I could get across the stream to Kinlochleven and take the bus there, it would save me a fourteen mile walk. So I took off my clothes and wrapped them as tightly as I could and threw them over so that I would have to go over and get them—I'd have no choice. But when they lit on the other side they started rolling down, and I thought they were going to go into the stream and I would have to walk back naked. If the water had carried them off it would have been the end of everything, but I got over in time to rescue them and went down to the village.

Back in Newbury we were no longer living in the house we were in before. We were living in tents, and I was running down to London on various assignments at the War Office or the Admiralty building. Then I'd run to Reading, where several of our battalions had their headquarters, or to Maidenhead. On one of these trips I was in the WC[a] in one of the many Red Cross centers in London (I think it was the Rainbow Club) when it was hit by a V-1 "buzz-bomb." You could hear it

a WC: Short for "water closet," the British term for a restroom

coming in: "BZZZZZZ!" And then it stopped, there was a pause, and then it hit right on the part of the building where I had been having breakfast a few minutes earlier.

Another time I was in another big Red Cross dining room in the Marble Arch district of London, right across from the park near the Intelligence headquarters at Hyde Park Corner where I had worked before I was assigned to the 101st. I went over to have breakfast, and the dining room was full of people. All of a sudden a V-2 rocket hit right across the street by the marble arch, and everything in that dining room was just as if a giant hand swept it gradually, slowly across the room and just crunched it all against the wall. Everything was in a jumble of chairs, tables, people, and everything else, and nobody was hurt! We rushed outside to see what it was, and right outside was this enormous hole, I'd say thirty to forty yards in diameter, perfectly round and the edge cut sheer. There was no debris or anything. The crater was rapidly filling with water from sewers, and it made a marvelous pond, a perfect circle right outside the marble arch, but nobody was hurt from that huge bomb that struck right in front of the dining room. The strangest things can happen. There were plenty of other bombings where people did get hurt.

The V-1 and V-2 were "vengeance weapons" used to terrorize Allied civilian populations in retaliation for the bombing of German cities. The V-1, shown above, was an unmanned jet with a warhead that could destroy a city block; it was the ancestor of the modern cruise missile. The V-2 was a ballistic missile something like the "Scud" missiles of the first Gulf War.

At this point in the war the armies in Western Europe were engaged in a battle that had been going on for well over a year. It was not the battle against the Axis powers; it was the battle between the British and American ways of waging war. Resentment between the countries and their military personnel grew as each felt the other was getting

FDR and Churchill hold a press conference in the White House.

too much credit and too much authority in running the war. The combatants in this battle were generals, politicians, diplomats, journalists, and the public. The weapons were political alliances, memos, backroom chats, and newspapers and radio reports. The mutual resentments between the British and the Americans were understandable. By the time America entered the war, Britain had been slugging it out with the Axis for more than two years. Their army had been on the receiving end of the European blitzkrieg campaign of 1940 that culminated in the devastating withdrawal at Dunkirk. Then they stood alone against the Germans in the Battle of Britain and fought back the Luftwaffe in the air over their home soil as they braced themselves for an expected land invasion that never came. The first major campaign where America fought alongside the British was in North Africa, where the poorly prepared and inexperienced Americans had to play catch-up and Eisenhower got his first experience in running a battle. Africa became, for the Americans, a learning experience rather than glorious history. But they learned fast, faster than either the British or the Germans gave them credit for.

By contrast, Africa was the greatest moment of glory for the greatest British hero of the war, General Sir Bernard Law Montgomery, who was later dubbed by King George VI the Viscount of Alamein in honor of his leadership at the battle of the same name. So the British felt that they, as more experienced and battle-hardened warriors, should be planning and leading the battles. But they didn't have the men or the supplies to do that. They needed all those American soldiers, sailors, and airmen (and their machines and fuel) to move around on their chessboard.

The Americans, on the other hand, figured that despite their slow start they were not only ready but more capable of commanding American troops than the Brits were. Especially since by this time the British had only a fraction as many troops on the front in Western Europe as the Americans had. On top of that, the American number was rapidly growing, while the British were tapped out. If the British lost a division it couldn't be replaced, except by Americans.

In late summer of 1944 the Allied airborne units in Europe included three American divisions, one British division, and the Polish Airborne Brigade. These were among the best-trained troops in all the Allied forces, and they had been combined into the First Allied Airborne Army. In the fast movement that characterized the fighting of that summer, this highly mobile army, which could be virtually anywhere in Europe almost instantly, was seen as an important piece on the chessboard. The brass were looking for ways to get them back into action.

Montgomery addresses Allied troops.

HUGH NIBLEY: A period of frantic preparation followed our return to England. The objective would be chosen, the whole operation rehearsed, everyone resigned to fate and all set for the take-off, and then would come word that Patton had already reached the place, or was so near it that we would not have to go in. This happened again and again and was very trying.

DIARY ENTRY, AUGUST 10, 1944: Classified for the new operation, alas!

AUGUST 11: Swim. Farewell to this.

AUGUST 15: Great preparation.

AUGUST 16: A wild ride into SHAEF[a] and back . . . and for the want of a horse-shoe nail the kingdom was lost.[b]

[a] *SHAEF* (Supreme Headquarters Allied Expeditionary Force): Eisenhower's headquarters and the ultimate authority for all Allied operations in the European Theater

HUGH NIBLEY: We heard that the British had taken some pictures of the exact place we were supposed to land, and there were all these German tanks around the area. We wanted those photographs to see exactly where we should land and what to expect. So the night before we were going to cross the Channel on another invasion, I went with a couple of guys down to Southampton to get those pictures. But when we got down there the man in charge of the photographs was a British don who was very snooty and said, "Well, I can let you see the photographs, but if you want to take them you'll have to make an application first; then they'll have to go through processing, they'll have to be approved, and then, maybe, we can let you have them." While he was talking I snuck into the other room where the photographs were all spread out on a table. Fortunately, it turned out that the guy in charge in there was somebody I'd known at Ritchie, so he just looked the other way while I picked up the photographs, stuck them under my tunic, and walked out with them. This was the highest intelligence, but I just walked out with them and said, "Come on, let's go back to Newbury."

So we started to rush back to get there in time to take off, but right at a crucial moment we had to stop for a little old lady and a little tiny poodle getting off a streetcar. The poodle didn't want to cross the street, and the lady wanted her to cross the street. We waited, and we waited, and we waited in the street. We must have lost ten minutes—ten precious minutes—waiting for

[b] For want of a nail, the shoe was lost;
For want of a shoe, the horse was lost;
For want of a horse, the rider was lost;
For want of a rider, the battle was lost;
For want of the battle, the kingdom was lost;
And all for want of a horseshoe nail.
—Traditional

The coast of Holland as seen from an American plane

this old lady to get her poodle to cross the street. Finally they got out of the way, and we rushed back to join the division just in time to leave that night with the photographs. Then, of course, the operation was cancelled.

DIARY ENTRY, AUGUST 18: The great operation called off.

In the period from D-Day on June 6 to September 3, seventeen airborne operations were planned and cancelled. Meanwhile, the competition between the generals in Europe was getting fierce. There was no longer a question about who would win the war. Now it became a race among generals to see who would get the most credit for having won it. Eisenhower described the situation this way:

DWIGHT D. EISENHOWER: When action is proceeding as rapidly as it did across France during the hectic days of late August and early September every commander from division upward becomes obsessed with the idea that with only a few more tons of supply he could rush right on and win the war. This is the spirit that wins wars and is always to be encouraged. Initiative, confidence, and boldness are among the most admirable traits of the good combat leader. As we dashed across France and Belgium each commander, therefore, begged and demanded priority over all others and it was undeniable that in front of each were opportunities for quick exploitation that make the demands completely logical.[3]

War can get personal, and personal differences of a few men can end up having a huge impact on thousands of people. At this time the conflict between the British and American senior commanders became personified in the persons of General Montgomery and General George S. Patton. The contrasts could hardly have been greater. Montgomery was a careful planner of large-scale operations with meticulous attention to detail, which made him ideal for planning and overseeing the execution of Operation Overlord. But his strength was also his weakness, because he was not quick to exploit a sudden opportunity that didn't lend itself to extensive planning and meticulous execution.

Field Marshal Bernard Law Montgomery

Patton took his motto from the Prussian King Frederick the Great: "L'audace, l'audace, toujours l'audace!" Audacity, audacity, always with audacity! He was possibly the hardest driving and most nimble general in military history. He took instant advantage of any opening. If there was no opening, he'd make one. Monty was known for a cautious approach that protected his soldiers and saved lives. Patton had distinguished himself as a marksman and fencer in the 1912 Olympics, and his nickname "Blood and Guts" illustrated his belief that the best way to save

Lt. General George S. Patton in Sicily

lives was to end the war by defeating the enemy as quickly as possible, even if it meant casualties in the short run. Monty's typical dress was casual corduroy trousers and a turtleneck sweater. Patton had tried his hand at fashion design when he came up with a very dashing ensemble for the American cavalrymen, which was, like many of Patton's other ideas that he thought to be strokes of genius, rejected by the army bureaucracy. He himself wore a nickel-plated battle helmet polished to a high luster and a brace of ivory-handled *revolvers, and he gained a reputation (not entirely based on truth) for demanding that his soldiers wear neckties in battle.*

But in certain respects the generals had much in common. They both had enormous egos and an extraordinary talent for tactless statements that outraged the other's camp. Monty seemed to go out of his way to insult the American military. He said, for example, "As a commander in charge of the land operations, Eisenhower is quite useless. There must be no misconception on this matter; he is completely and utterly useless."[4] And Patton repeatedly made politically inappropriate statements that embarrassed and angered politicians and diplomats on both sides, his most famous being when he slapped and threatened to shoot psychiatric casualties in a military hospital for cowardice.

And, of course, each general had a deep loathing of the other.

So throughout the summer and fall of 1944, Monty moved slowly and kept demanding more Allied resources of manpower, equipment, and the fuel for his great battles in the north of the front. Patton dashed through France and kept demanding men, equipment, and fuel for his southern sweep. The plan for Overlord and Operation Cobra, which followed it, was that Monty would hold down the bulk of the Germans in the east so Patton could build up his forces, break out to the west, and move quickly through less-well-held areas of France. It worked. But the Americans resented what they perceived as Monty's sluggishness, while the British claimed Monty was bearing the brunt of the German forces and deserved more credit and resources.

While some of the criticism of Monty was undeserved, Monty's was a personality that almost deserved undeserved criticism. On May 15, in a meeting about which Eisenhower later said, "During the whole war I attended no other conference so packed with rank," Monty boasted in front of King George VI and Churchill about his expectations for D-Day, as described by Stephen Ambrose:

STEPHEN AMBROSE: Storming the beaches was the least of his problems. He wanted to get well inland on D-Day itself and "*crack about* and force the battle to swing our way." It was possible, he said, that he would get to Falaise, thirty-two miles inland, the first day. He intended to send armored columns quickly toward Caen, for "this will upset the enemy's plans and tend to hold him off while we build up strength. We must gain space rapidly and peg claims well inland." He said he intended to take Caen the first day, break through the German lines on that (left, or eastern) flank, then drive along the coast toward the Seine River.[5]

So the Americans can hardly be blamed when they criticized him for not coming close to doing any of those things. Caen was finally taken thirty-three days after Monty said he would have it in his hands, and then only with the help of an enormous diversion of resources that included the greatest aerial bombardment in history up to that point. But Monty did force the Germans into defending Caen, and this allowed Patton to break through in the west. It was the moment for which Patton had been preparing his whole life. He seized it and showed the Germans what it was like to be on the receiving end of a blitzkrieg. *He swept around behind the Germans, and the Allies were able to surround a large part of their forces in the "Falais Gap," where a huge part of the German army was destroyed. Still, British and American generals blamed each other for failing to take full advantage of the situation, and the rancor increased. As the generals squabbled, the airborne troops kept packing and unpacking their gear.*

DIARY ENTRY, AUGUST 31, 1944: Praise the Lord I am to go, but everyone hates this business. Great preparations. Good morning, but what is the use? The general has his heart set on the hard way.

SEPTEMBER 1: Will we go? Will we not?

SEPTEMBER 2: We are briefed we get ready. Great excitement. In the evening everyone takes off but me then immediately after it is buzz bombs.

SEPTEMBER 3: Fire in the sky.

Patton's reverse blitzkrieg *was exciting and glamorous in the newspapers, and equally galling to Monty, who wasn't getting as much ink. By September, the competition between the generals was reaching a fever pitch, and Eisenhower was bombarded with requests, demands, and thinly veiled threats from generals vying for war resources. Perhaps it was Patton's fame for audacious and bold plans that led Monty to come up with a plan that seemed completely out of character for the careful, calculating field marshal.*

C-47 Dakotas lined up next to the Waco gliders they will be towing into battle

HUGH NIBLEY: One day after some of these false alarms I was up in the top floor of the British War Office, where there were rows of wooden bookshelves. I shouldn't have been there, but I went in to look at some maps. While I was in there looking at the maps, very innocently, I heard some heavy footsteps outside the door and some people came in. I heard more feet, then I heard chairs moving around, and what looked like the whole British general staff moved in and started holding a secret meeting. What was I to do? Was I to reveal myself? I'd get picked up for a spy sure as anything. So I just kept still and waited. They were talking about a new plan, Monty's plan for a "dagger-thrust at the heart of Europe" and crossing the Rhine. It was going to end the war. They were going to carry right on through to Berlin. I just stayed there, very, very quiet, while they talked about how Monty was going to take over. They chuckled; they just thought it was a great old thing. They didn't say anything very important for me to overhear, but boy, I'm glad I wasn't caught in there. I don't know what kind of punishment I would have gotten.

Later we were told about the plan they had been discussing, a fantastic operation. We were going for another invasion, this time to Holland. It was all planned just so Monty could take over control of the Allied armies. He wanted all the gasoline and the supplies and resources for his plan, and Eisenhower gave them to him. That's what stalled the whole Western Front operation, because Monty wanted the glory of leading the "dagger thrust at the heart of Europe." It was called Operation Market-Garden, and it was a fizzle. That's where we got beat.

Hugh Nibley was among the first to hear of Market-Garden. Unofficially, hiding in the map room at the War Office, he heard about it before most of the American high brass. Lieutenant General Omar Bradley, commander of the 12th Army Group (of which Patton's 3rd Army was a part) didn't learn about it until after Nibley did, and he was completely blindsided when he did.

> **OMAR BRADLEY:** Had the pious teetotaling Montgomery wobbled into SHAEF with a hangover, I could not have been more astonished than I was by the daring adventure he proposed. . . .
>
> I had not been brought into the plan. In fact Montgomery had devised it and sold it to Ike several days before I even learned of it from our liaison officer to the 21st Group. Monty's secrecy in

ALLIES AND EGOS

What Eisenhower and Montgomery had was a failure to communicate. In his memoir, *Crusade in Europe,* Eisenhower stated that he had wanted a bridgehead over the Rhine and therefore approved the plan for Market-Garden. But he saw it as a piece of his "broad front" strategy. He says repeatedly that Monty was told of the importance of clearing German troops from the Scheldt Estuary in Belgium so the Allies could use the port of Antwerp, which would greatly ease the Allies' supply problem. Market-Garden was to be only a brief and temporary diversion from that high priority. Monty, who always believed the broad front strategy was idiocy—and was not shy about telling Eisenhower what he thought of it—took the approval for Market-Garden as a sign that Eisenhower was finally seeing it his way. But Ike never thought of Arnhem as opening the way for a "dagger thrust."

Eisenhower and Montgomery

planning confused me, for although the operation was to be confined to his sector, the move would nevertheless cripple the joint offensive we had agreed upon a few days before.[6]

DIARY ENTRY, SEPTEMBER 10, 1944: Lovely sunny day. In the afternoon we . . . eat at the Queen's Hotel. . . . Return to find another silly operation.

SEPTEMBER 11: I am learning Dutch again.

SEPTEMBER 12: Operation called off at noon.

SEPTEMBER 13: To Reading. . . . Return to find the same operation again.

Glidermen and their Waco

SEPTEMBER 15: Cold gray weather. . . . At 8:00 [P.M.] we go to Ramsbury assembly area.

Another person Monty left out of the loop in the planning to invade the Netherlands was Prince Bernhard of the Netherlands, commander in chief of the Netherlands forces and head of the Dutch underground. He and his military staff had lots of information on conditions in his country gathered by a very active underground organization, and his officers had gone to school studying tactics on the exact ground where the operation was going to take place. Once they saw some of the plans for the invasion of their country, they pointed out some rather large problems. Cornelius Ryan interviewed Prince Bernhard and wrote in A Bridge Too Far:

> **CORNELIUS RYAN:** The British, Bernhard says, "were simply not impressed by our negative attitude." Although everyone was "exceptionally polite, the British preferred to do their own planning, and our views were turned down. The prevailing attitude was, 'Don't worry, old boy, we'll get this thing cracking.'"[7]

DIARY ENTRY, SEPTEMBER 16, 1944: A nice morning. . . . Black news. A bad run in a tough situation. We must take off very early in the morning. The rest in the worst possible weather.

7

MARKET-GARDEN

HUGH NIBLEY: The day before we went, pilots who flew over our landing areas came back with the worst possible news: terrible weather, murderous flak, and a division of German tanks waiting for us in the landing zone. We found out later it was a rest area for the German 10th Armored Division, and we were going to land right on top of them. But it was too late to turn back—regardless of weather, we would have to make a try for it at dawn the next day.

This time instead of a big Horsa I was in a Waco glider, which was made out of plumbing pipe and canvas, and that was it. The soldiers who were putting together the gliders were having a party because they didn't have to go. As our boys went to get on the planes, the guys who weren't going lined the passage leading down toward the flying field, and their farewell as the boys went out to get into the planes and the gliders wasn't, "Godspeed!" or, "Good Luck!" It was, "So long, suckers!" They were laughing, drunk, having a grand old time because they didn't have to go, lined

A paratrooper's gear often weighed more than he did.

The 101st on their way to Holland

up yelling, "So long, suckers! You'll be sorry!" But I distinctly detected a note of jealousy in what they were saying. It's really true, they envied those paratroopers. They wished they were in their place. They were celebrating because they weren't going, but they were also jealous because those fellows were real heroes, and they weren't. They were ashamed of themselves, that's why they were so drunk. Then when we went over to Holland we lost a lot of gliders in the Channel. They fell down, numbers of them, just like that. The army never mentioned it publicly; it was a big secret. I don't know whether it's true or not, but I heard twenty-seven of those gliders fell down over the Channel flying over to Holland.[a]

Again I was no. 2 man in no. 1 glider on the right of the formation—the one the Germans always try for. Our glider was named Wambling Wabbit and the tow plane pulling us was the only one with a "bathtub," which was a new and very

[a] "Glider losses were heavy. . . . As these serials began to come in, only 53 of the original 70 would arrive without mishap on the [101st] landing zone near Son. . . . Confusion, abortions and fatal mishaps struck the glider fleets in particular. Long before the second lift reached the drop zones, 54 gliders were downed by structural or human error. Some 26 machines aborted over England and the Channel; two were seen to disintegrate during flight, and 26 more were prematurely released on the 80-mile flight over enemy territory, landing far from their zones in Belgium and Holland and behind the German frontier. . . . Three gliders riddled with bullets crash-landed on the zones with their occupants miraculously untouched" (Ryan, *Bridge Too Far*, 216, 365, 366).

A medic leads prayer before boarding The Leakin' Deacon.

secret device which the enemy was dying to get hold of. It was called a bathtub because it was a huge, bulky under-slung affair that nobody could miss, and the pilot said, "The Jerries would give anything to shoot us down to get this." With this cheering prospect we took to the air and of course I became very sick, as I always did in a glider. There was an old piece of armor plate lying on the floor, and out of curiosity I wondered

Parachutes fall like early snow.

INVASION BY GLIDER

Robert M. Bowen in his memoir Fighting with the Screaming Eagles *describes his experience on a glider going into Holland:*

ROBERT M. BOWEN: The gliders were towed by long ropes hooked to the towplanes, and these ropes were coiled up on the tarmac like rolls of spaghetti so a lot of planes and gliders could occupy a minimum of space. As the tugs moved off the ropes uncoiled, snapping the gliders off with a mighty jerk, which is bone shaking. . . . We reached the coast, flying at more than 100mph. . . . A glider broke loose up ahead, went down in a gentle glide then hit with a tremendous splash, it sank like a stone. . . .

Another glider had broken loose, a huge British Hamilcar, which carried a small tank; it didn't fare any better.

As we neared the coast, I could hear the dull rumble of gunfire. My stomach tensed. . . . We had been in the air for more than three hours and some of the replacements were air sick, puking in their helmets. That odor and the stench from the plane's motors were sickening. I prayed for the LZ no matter what we would encounter there. In the air we were sitting ducks, like clay pigeons at a trap range.

As we continued on we hit a wall of flak, which sent deadly steel fragments hurtling through the formation. Fortunately, most exploded over us. I looked through a porthole and saw German soldiers running from homes and buildings with weapons in their hands. Looking back up at the formation I saw another glider break loose and drift downward. . . .

Then there was a loud crack beside my head. I flinched and looked at Frank McFadden, one of my scouts who was jammed against me. The bullet had

With a glider in the foreground, a Dakota dives into a Dutch field.

torn through the fabric on the side of the glider, whistled between our heads and exited out the roof. It was close. We looked at each other and grinned weakly. Bullets were now ripping through the wings and through the glider's ailerons. The enemy fire also came through the glider's honeycombed wooden floorboard and glanced off the cloverleaves of 81mm mortar ammunition that we were carrying tied down to the flooring. I'm sure everyone was worrying about our pilot. What if he were hit?[1]

how it would be to sit on. Just as I slipped it on my little chair with a characteristically witty remark, it absorbed three machine-gun bullets, while another went between my feet. This particular escape became proverbial in headquarters company.

Wambling Wabbit was the first glider landing, and we came in at about fifteen hundred feet, fifty-five miles an hour—a perfect target, you couldn't miss.[a] So they didn't miss, and we got shot up. But they shot too well, and the bullets marched right down the center aisle between where we were sitting; they shot up the glider but missed us. Wacos had a landing gear with these wooden skis on the bottom. The whole thing was wild; it might have been something out of the Napoleonic wars. When we landed, the right wing tipped down and caught in the sand and we spun around and stopped. The glider was all shot up, but I got the jeep out and everything was lovely.

The plan for Market-Garden was for a quick blow by the airborne troops to capture the roads up the middle of Holland so armored units and regular infantry could

[a] Many C-47 pilots flying paratroopers and towing gliders into Normandy had panicked and taken evasive action to avoid flak, dropping the paratroopers and releasing their gliders too early. Their actions resulted in death for many soldiers and caused others to be miles off target. The pilots were criticized for their actions in Normandy, and in Holland they made amends by staying on their low-speed courses even when they were directly over heavy antiaircraft fire, this time in broad daylight. Many of the C-47 crews were killed delivering the troops in Holland because they refused to repeat the mistakes of Normandy.

Wacos landing in Zon, Holland

dash up from Belgium to the bridge at Arnhem and establish a beachhead on the other side of the Rhine, which would open the door into Germany. The 101st's assignment was the southern sector, including the city of Eindhoven. The 82nd Airborne was in the middle sector with the city of Nijmegen and its bridge, and the task of taking the town of Arnhem was given to the British 1st Airborne Division, reinforced by the Polish Airborne Brigade. The

A Waco out to pasture after a rough landing in Holland

airborne part of the operation was to be over quickly. The 101st went in with enough ammunition and food for three days.

The landing was much easier than Normandy for both the parachute troops and the glider troops, for several reasons. Contrary to the gloomy weather predictions of the night before, the weather was fine. They landed in the day instead of night, and they were in an area that hadn't been prepared for defense the way Normandy had. And the pilots bringing them in, who had been strongly admonished about the pilot mistakes

Dutch citizens greet American GIs in Zon.

in Normandy, were much better about staying on course despite murderous anti-aircraft fire.

HUGH NIBLEY: We landed in the fields in a place called Zon, and everything was quiet. As soon as we got out of the glider I saw a sign that said, "Brueghel two kilometers." So I said to my friend, who was a cultivated guy, "Look, that's where the famous artists, the Brueghel Brothers[a] came from. We'd better walk down there, it's only 2 kilometers. We'll go down and see where they lived." So, since it was quiet, we walked the two kilometers down to Brueghel.

There was a little beer hall that was open, and we went in to get something to drink and started talking to the proprietor. Out in back there was an archery range, so we went out to practice and started shooting bows and arrows. As we were shooting we saw these guys digging in the backyard. I said, "There's a lot of digging in the backyard here. What are they digging?" And the proprietor of the beer hall

[a] The Brueghels (also spelled Brueghel or Breugel) were a family that produced several great painters in the sixteenth and seventeenth centuries.

said, "Well, those are the Germans digging their headquarters." And here we were in the midst of them. We decided we'd better get out of there. We put down our bows and arrows and softly walked across the street to where there was a little high school. We went in, and on the first floor there was a classroom and a desk with a drawer full of paybooks. I stuck them in my jacket, and we went out and walked down the road to the 101st. That was valuable information I got in Brueghel, but what if we'd been caught?

Monty's plan was for the parachute and glider troops to clear the roads and create an "airborne carpet" through Holland for the armored troops to get to Arnhem and cross the Rhine. The 101st's main first task was to capture the southern city of Eindhoven. They took the city, on schedule, on September 18, the day after they landed.

HUGH NIBLEY: In Eindhoven there was a big house, a huge estate with some very rich man living inside. Eindhoven was the headquarters of Philips Radio, and I don't know for sure, but I think this estate belonged to Philips himself. The house had a high brick wall around it, and there was all this bloody fighting going on right around this rich man's estate. At this time the Germans were scraping the bottom of the barrel, and the soldiers we were fighting there were just kids, 15- and 16-year-old Austrians. They didn't know what they were doing, and it was just slaughter.

And here, on the wall around this estate in the middle of the battle, was a sign in German: "The land inside the fence is off-bounds to all German army personnel. You will be court-martialed if you go in here." Right next to it was another sign in English: "This is off-bounds to all American and British personnel. We do not go in here." So the man inside was getting rich on the war going on all around him and living in peace, because the armies on both sides had forbidden their men to lay a finger on him, and he was the one who was profiting by the whole thing. It was so symbolic! So symbolic it was just cruel. It was a symbol of what was going on in the world at that time. Satan is like the spider who sits in his web at the center and lets everybody else fight it out.

The whole Dutch campaign was touch and go, with our people scattered all over the land and surrounded and outnumbered most of the time. But there was a good deal of idealism among the Allies, especially when we'd meet up with the

Lt. General Miles C. Dempsey, commander of the British Second Army, with his driver

villagers and other civilians. We got a big reception from the Dutch people, and we felt as if we'd come as liberators and we had to act like it. It wasn't the carnival rampage of the first days at Normandy when they went and did the things they did.

It's strange what sticks in your mind after so many years. I remember a Dutchman, a peasant, who came up to us just after we'd landed, pale as a sheet, and said, "Bee-ware! Bee-ware, bee-ware!" He said it in English. He was calling attention to a battalion of tanks that was down the road coming toward us. So we bee-wared, all right. It was a strange moment that stays in my mind.

There were two new guys in OB Team 5 now, Kipnes and Berger, who came to replace the team members who were killed in Normandy. Kipnes was the nephew of the great Russian basso, Aleksander Kipnes, and he was a nice guy. Berger was a very jolly fellow, very good-natured and that rarity, a blond Jew. So the plan was for Kipnes and me to land from the air, and Berger was to bring in the jeep from Belgium with the armor of the British XXX [Thirty] Corps to where we were in Zon. After we arrived I went out with Captain Mann and hid in some woods and tried to get in contact with Berger by short-wave on the road up from Belgium.

But Market-Garden was the silliest thing you ever saw. It was insane, that operation. I'll show you how insane it was: General Sir Miles Dempsey was commanding the operation because we were attached to the British army, and before we took off he came down to give us a talk and brief us on what we were supposed to do. Everybody saw this would be a bust unless the British commander acted his age. He gave a speech that set an all-time high for silliness and failure to grasp the most elementary aspect of the situation. He came in and said, "Now you'll land from the air, and as soon as you land, GET OFF THE ROADS! Clear off the roads because we'll be coming down those roads with our tanks, two abreast, forty miles an hour!" But you could barely get one tank on those roads. This was the Netherlands, after all, and they were just little narrow Dutch brick roads with deep ditches on both sides for drainage. They weren't going to get two tanks abreast on those, not in a million years.

So down in Belgium, Berger and XXX Corps were just starting out. We were up in Zon waiting for them to come up the road just like General Dempsey had said, "Two tanks abreast, forty miles an hour!" The first thing that happened to the guys coming in from Belgium—what would you expect?—an ambush. Those roads were easy to block, and there was nothing you could do once they were blocked because you had to stick to the road. So the Germans set up a roadblock and just smashed them, just blew them to bits. Meanwhile we were hiding out in the little pine forest in Zon, and we finally made radio contact with Berger. You could hear terrible sounds on the short-wave, all this shooting going on; it was a terrible mess. Captain Mann started to laugh. He said, "What's the matter, Berger? You seem to be having some trouble."

And Berger's voice came in, "Oy, oy, oy! Dere damagin' da moichandise!" A typical understated Jewish joke in the middle of a bombardment. All the fellows I worked with in Intelligence were Jewish anti-Nazis, and Berger was a jolly fellow. I mean when you can take it like that and joke in that kind of a situation, that's something! But they caught him there on the road from Belgium while he was bringing in our jeep, and he was run over by a tank and was gone. That's too bad. Just like in Normandy, our three-man team was shrinking fast. And as for "Two tanks abreast, forty miles an hour!" they didn't get down the road at all.

We set up our headquarters in an old castle with a moat and drew up the drawbridge. It was very quaint.

Cornelius Ryan describes what was happening in the area where Hugh Nibley was fighting at this time.

CORNELIUS RYAN: Some forty miles south [of Arnhem] along the highway, General Maxwell Taylor's 101st troopers were now

175

Burned Allied vehicles at the side of a Dutch road

fighting hard to keep the corridor open. But the German Fifteenth Army's fierce defense at Best was draining Taylor's forces. More and more men were being caught up in the bitter engagement that one division intelligence officer wryly termed "a minor error in estimate." Pressure was building all along Taylor's 15-mile sector, which the Screaming Eagles had newly named "Hell's Highway." It was now obvious that the enemy's intent was to cut off [the British] tank spearhead, using Best as the base. . . .

Even as the battle at Best ended, German armor struck out for the newly installed bridge at Son [Zon] in yet another attempt to sever the corridor. Taylor himself, leading his headquarters troops—his only available reinforcements—rushed to the scene. With bazooka fire and a single antitank gun, a German Panther tank was knocked out almost as it reached the bridge.[2]

DIARY ENTRY, SEPTEMBER 20, 1944: A sticky time. [German] tanks turning up everywhere. Our line is very thin in the 327 [Glider Infantry Regiment] C[ommand] P[ost].

SEPTEMBER 21: We forage eggs in farms. Germans trying a big attack on our castle. Much shelling and small arms fire all about us.

HUGH NIBLEY: We moved from the castle into a big grain elevator in the town of Veghel. It was a pretty sticky time with German tanks all around us, and we still hadn't seen any of the British tanks. One morning, going along a brick road, I turned aside to headquarters. There was a little brick house by the road, and the whole headquarters, the general and his staff, were down on their knees praying. We were surrounded at that time.

DIARY ENTRY, SEPTEMBER 25: The road is still cut. We are being heavily shelled. Small arms fire very close on all sides.

SEPTEMBER 26: What a night. Much air activity during the day. Work with PWs. A lot of running around.

Tech Sergeant Robert Bowen was fighting nearby and wrote about it in his memoir, Fighting with the Screaming Eagles:

> **ROBERT BOWEN:** As we neared Veghel, the sound of a major battle greeted us.
> We rushed into town among screaming shell bursts which rocked the ground under us, unloading and taking cover on a street of row houses, in doorways or alleys. . . . The artillery fire was deafening, as bad or worse than in Normandy. Several houses in the town were aflame and a great pall of smoke was gathering above. The shells were falling fast and close, no more than 100 yards away. Startled, we huddled against the buildings, waiting for a shell to drop in our midst. It was one of the most terrifying moments of my life. . . .
> I crouched in the foxhole watching the German shellfire tear

The Dutch greet British armored troops.

Veghel to pieces, fascinated in a morbid way by the brilliant shell bursts, great palls of smoke, and the raging fires as houses burned. There were people in there, Dutch civilians, American and British troops, paying the price for liberation. I thought about our price so far, the deaths of O'Melia and Mazur, both young and eager. . . . O'Melia had been reading his Catholic prayer book minutes before he had been blown apart. It made me wonder. Was it a failed answer to his prayers or a belief in nonsense? I couldn't get it out of my mind as I watched the city burning.[3]

DIARY ENTRY, SEPTEMBER 27: British units coming up at last. Much air activity and German ground activity in the evening.

SEPTEMBER 28: Two years in the army. A quiet day. The British units coming up at last.

The British tanks were supposed to reach Eindhoven in two to three hours from the start of the attack. They got there eighteen hours late. By the time they reached Nijmegen in the north they were two days behind schedule. And Arnhem, the objective of the whole battle, where Monty had promised the tanks would be in two days? The tanks never got that far. Prince Bernhard could have predicted it.

CORNELIUS RYAN: From the moment Dutch generals learned of the route that Horrocks' XXX Corps columns proposed to take, they had anxiously tried to dissuade anyone who would listen, warning of the dangers of using exposed dike roads. "In our military staff colleges," Bernhard says, "we had run countless studies on the problem. We knew tanks simply could not operate along these roads without infantry." Again and again Dutch officers had told Montgomery's staff that the Market-Garden schedule could not be maintained unless infantry accompanied the tanks.[4]

Later in A Bridge Too Far, *Ryan reports what the British General Allen Adair thought when he found himself on the road to Arnhem, which to him looked like a long, straight island.*

CORNELIUS RYAN: "When I saw that island my heart sank," Adair later recalled. "You can't imagine anything more unsuitable for tanks: steep banks with

Dutch roads were not made for tanks.

General Urquhart and the Red Devils on their way to Arnhem

ditches on each side that could be easily covered by German guns."[5]

A week later the Brits were still stalled.

LEONARD RAPPORT AND ARTHUR NORTHWOOD JR.: The road, raised several feet above the surrounding countryside, was ideally suited to antitank defense. . . . [The Germans] had the entire road enfiladed with 88s. British progress was expensive and slow.[6]

HUGH NIBLEY: When the first British tanks finally came clanking in, they were perfectly harmless; their guns were all full of sand; they were all bedraggled. It was the silliest operation you ever heard of, planned by these arrogant British officers. This was how they showed how good they were. This silly operation was what they called "the dagger thrust at the heart of Europe"! It finally came to be known as the "Bridge Too Far."

After the 101st in the south, the 82nd were the next stretch of the "airborne carpet" the British were moving over. They were slightly more delayed than the 101st. They took the Nijmegen bridge on September 20 and captured the bridge with a daring attack over the river in broad daylight in flimsy boats under heavy fire. The airborne carpet was now an open corridor to the outskirts of Arnhem. In Arnhem itself, things had not gone so well. The Red Devils of the British 1st Airborne had been dropped eight miles from the bridge they were assigned to take because the RAF hadn't wanted to risk too much antiaircraft. The special jeeps that were to rush them from the landing site to the bridge didn't arrive, and they had to walk. Any chance of the lightning-quick shock of surprise that airborne troops are designed for was lost. And they had been dropped not on weak troops, as they had been told they would, but on the resting place of the 10th SS Panzer Division. Their communications were broken down because their radios didn't work. Their commanding general got separated from the division and was completely out of touch for almost thirty-nine critical hours. The Polish Brigade was delayed because of fog on British airfields. One British battalion under Lieutenant Colonel John D. Frost did make it to the bridge and managed to capture one end of it. They held out there hoping for reinforcements for four days before they were forced to surrender. And there was more. The catalog of woes that plagued the British at Arnhem is long and bitter. And mostly preventable.

A Dutch telephone worker helps American soldiers set up communications.

CORNELIUS RYAN: The Dutch resistance ranked among the most dedicated and disciplined underground units in all of occupied Europe. In the 101st and 82nd sectors Dutchmen were fighting alongside the American paratroopers. One of the first orders Generals Taylor and Gavin had given on landing was that arms and explosives be issued to the underground groups. But in Arnhem the British virtually ignored the presence of these spirited, brave civilians. Armed and poised to give immediate help to Frost at the bridge, the Arnhem groups were largely unheeded, and their assistance was politely rejected.[7]

One valuable lesson the Americans got from their native collaborators was that when they had trouble with their radios, they could simply use the public telephone system. The British at Arnhem didn't learn that trick, and the result was a near complete communications breakdown. Ryan shows the British attitude, even after the plans were running into trouble:

Dutch resistance fighters help an American locate positions on a map.

CORNELIUS RYAN: Even now, Bernhard noted, "everything was being blamed on the weather. The general impression among my staff was that the British considered us a bunch of idiots for daring to question their military tactics." With the exception of a few senior officers, Bernhard knew that he was "not particularly loved at Montgomery's headquarters, because I was saying things that now unfortunately were turning out to be true—and the average Englishman doesn't like being told by a bloody foreigner that he's wrong."[8]

HUGH NIBLEY: A lot of my work in Holland was with the Dutch underground, who knew a lot of what was going on. In Eindhoven the underground put us on to where Philips' private car was hidden under a haystack. It was custom-made, brilliant red, and had real onyx trimmings and front-wheel drive, which was really something at that time. It was the very latest thing. Naturally Kipnes coveted it and took it over just like that. It was faster than anything in Holland, and it was to be our car. We had a big white star painted on the hood and we called it the Red Devil.[a]

One day we went down in the Red Devil to visit some artillery. We couldn't find them for a while, and we drove around looking for them. Then we came to this place where the road went up, and there was a nice swell, and there was the artillery. We could see the guns very nicely arranged in the swell, exactly as they

---

[a] "Red Devils" was also the name given to the paratroopers of the British 1st Airborne Division who were fighting in Arnhem and wore red berets into battle.

should be, and the gun crews methodically operating them as they banged away—they're so systematic in artillery. I was driving, and as we were going down to the guns I said, "Wait a minute, Kipnes, this isn't *our* artillery. It's *their* artillery!" And it was. We were right in the middle of it. We caught them completely by surprise too; so we turned around as fast as we could and went down the road in the Red Devil about a hundred miles an hour, and they didn't catch us.

That car would go so fast the Germans couldn't hit it. Everybody was impressed by the Red Devil. The general coveted it too, and he finally got it—but by that time we were glad to let him have it because it had become a favorite target for German gunners, this bright red car with the big white star on it going all over, and everybody seeing it from miles away, spotting it from the air, and shooting at us all the time.

At Veghel there was a rather nice school-house run by the church there, and we set up our headquarters in the schoolyard. Across the street from it was a nunnery, a redbrick Catholic church. Right outside the school-house was a fairly broad canal with a wood behind it, and in the woods, unbeknownst to us, were four Mark IV German tanks. There was a good piano on the stage in the school-house, so I went and started playing the Ghost Trio of Beethoven. Then BAM! BAM! BAM! those tanks in the woods started shooting at the building. We scampered out the other side and stood in front of the door. General Taylor and some of the other commanders were standing there absolutely amazed because we were caught completely by surprise. Then suddenly a shell hit the brick wall just above General Taylor's head and showered us all with red dust. We were covered from head to foot.

This Dutch resistance member's house had a secret hiding place built under its cabinets.

It was very amusing, the general standing there, covered with red dust, and looking surprised.

There was a grain elevator in Veghel that was so big that we set up in one end while the Germans were occupying the opposite end of the same building. Down the road was a little jam factory where on Monday, Wednesday, and Friday we'd get jam, and the other days of the week the Germans would get jam. We agreed to do that—no hard feelings or anything like that. But that homely feeling you get from things like jam is a very necessary thing. In battle you numb your senses; you dull them; you want to be as local as you can. For example, if you're in the headquarters and you're under fire and they're counterattacking on the flank right outside the door, when they're sending in a company in strength and they're really shooting away at each other—well, then is the time to have your coffee and rolls and enjoy it. That's when you want something homely, common, and everyday to

The 101st in Holland

calm you down and make you feel there's something in life that's normal. Of course, the British had to have their tea. Every day they'd pull off the road and make tea. The German planes would come over and strafe and the British soldiers would hide under their tanks and when the planes were gone they'd come out again, still drinking their tea. They said, "It's going to be a long war, might as well enjoy it." You have to admire that kind of cool.

Anyway, there we were in this huge grain elevator, but we didn't have any lights in our part of the building. The general told me to see if we could get lights in there, so I went to *Meinherr* Walters, who was the manager, the custodian of the building, and I said, "Could we get some lights here? Do you have some generators?"

"Well, the only power we have is from the Germans' generators way down in the other end of the building," he said.

"So give us that."

So *Meinherr* Walters hooked us up so we were getting our light from the Germans' generators. We felt good about it, didn't feel guilty that we were stealing. They were the Dutchman's lights anyway.

Several attempts were made to get to Arnhem and rescue the Red Devils of the British 1st Airborne Division. The British tried to get there, but the German Panzers that weren't supposed to be there stopped them. The Poles were finally landed days late and on the other side of the river. They tried a river crossing to reach the British, but they were only supplied with small rubber boats and the mission failed, with heavy Polish casualties. Finally everybody admitted that Arnhem Bridge was not going to fall to the Allies and the bridgehead over the Rhine, the purpose for the whole operation, was not going to happen.

As it became clear that Market-Garden was not going to work out according to plan, the 1st Airborne Army shifted to a battle more reminiscent of World War I than the high speed hit-and-run tactics it had trained for. They had taken a lot of ground and now, even though its purpose as a causeway to a bridgehead over the Rhine was no longer valid, they had to defend that ground or give it back to the Germans. Like dog-faces of the Great War, the troops dug in while big guns dueled back and forth and heavy rain and heavy artillery fell on the soggy paratroopers. On October 4 the 101st was moved to an area known to the Allies as "The Island," which was actually a narrow piece of land almost completely surrounded by the Waal and Rhine rivers.

DONALD BURGETT: The Island was long, narrow, low, and flat. Most of it was below river level, and the German-held side of the Neder Rijn [Lower Rhine] was hilly and much higher. They could therefore look down on us from their higher vantage points and zero their guns in, allowing them to bring heavy artillery fire down on us no matter where we went or what precautions we took. We were never out of their sight or range, so we were compelled to move at night. The enemy also had heavy armored and infantry units dug in along most of the length of the Neder Rijn dike opposite from us. This was not the best military position to be in. Why the hell had the English taken this part of Holland when their original mission was to get to Arnhem? Now that it had become a killing field, Monty pulled his own troops out and ordered us to occupy The Island.[9]

A shower station where American soldiers could remove some Dutch mud

HUGH NIBLEY: Headquarters Company got stuck at a place called Slijk-Ewijk on the muddy island between two rivers that come down there, the Lower Rhine River on the one side and the Waal River on the other side. We were there for a long time just opposite Nijmegen, and we had to go several miles down the dirt road along the Waal to the old bridge that the British were keeping there; then you had to hurry across that bridge as fast as you could go to the headquarters of the 82nd to take a shower. We spent weeks there going through that routine.

Headquarters Company were camped out in a pear orchard and our protection,

GIs under artillery attack

of course, was the orchard. We were only planning to be in our positions there a few days, but as it turned out I actually lived for seventy days in foxholes there in Holland. The weeks dragged on and it was autumn, and pretty soon the leaves starting falling off the trees in our orchard. Then all of a sudden one night all the leaves fell down and there we were, exposed. It was like we were naked, the Germans could look down and see everything we were doing.

DIARY ENTRY, NOVEMBER 9, 1944: A black day in the rear base. Snow and rain. Return to find a sea of mud with all the leaves off the trees.

NOVEMBER 10: The Germans become very active. What mud. I sleep in the IPW [Interrogation Prisoner of War] shed.

NOVEMBER 12: Saw *Double Indemnity*, very good. Bad cold. Very wet weather. No leaves.

A giant railway gun left over from World War I

HUGH NIBLEY: Sometimes they would bring in movies, and we could go watch them in this big tent. They brought in a film with Fred MacMurray, *Double Indemnity,* a very dark story about betrayal. And as we're sitting in this big tent watching the movie, we hear an artillery bombardment beginning, and it was moving. The noise was getting louder and louder, and you could tell it was coming in our direction. Pretty soon shells were landing twenty, then fifteen yards away. But nobody would get up and leave the movie. We wanted to see how it all turned out, what happened to Fred MacMurray in the end, even if meant risking getting shelled.[a]

The German 88s were awfully good guns and they kept us jumping all the time, but they weren't what was shooting at us there in the orchard at Slijk-Ewijk; it was heavier stuff that came our way. They had a big railroad gun up on the other side of the Waal, across the river from Nijmegen, and when the leaves fell down and they found out that our headquarters was in this orchard they started shooting at the orchard. I had this little tiny tent where I was keeping position maps, and one of those 16-inch railway gun shells hit the mud at one end of the orchard and slithered a hundred yards or so through the mud to my foxhole, stopped with its nose right up against the tent, and didn't go off. Just stopped there. I looked out and there was this shell. Everybody came to see it, General Taylor and General Higgins, they all came out and stood around and watched it. It would have made a big crater if it had gone off, but of course it was a dud.

[a] Corporal Glen A. Derber was also serving with the 101st on the island near Nijmegen. "[T]hey showed us a movie and I don't believe I will ever quite appreciate another movie as well as I did that one. As I sat there fresh off the lines with my rifle between my knees watching the scenes which were so much like home, it suddenly dawned on me what a huge gap there was between my two lives. Looking at that show was like looking back into another world" (Rapport and Northwood, *Rendezvous with Destiny,* 417).

DUDS

Hugh Nibley was not the only one to report German artillery duds.

ROBERT BOWEN: The Germans were using their big railroad gun and tossed a few shells at us each night. When the shells went over they made the noise of a passing freight train. One just missed the building my platoon was in, crashing in one across the street where the company CP was located. Fortunately the shell was a dud, smashing through three walls to fall in a room of sleeping men. However, PFC J.B. Roberts, a driver, was crushed to death and several others were badly injured.[10]

STEPHEN AMBROSE: Over four decades of interviewing former GIs, I've been struck by how often they tell stories about duds, generally about shells falling near their foxholes and failing to explode. Lt. George Wilson of the 4th Division said that after one shelling near St.-Lô, "I counted eight duds sticking in the ground within thirty yards of my foxhole." There are no statistics available on this phenomenon, nor is there any evidence on why, but I've never heard a German talk about American duds. . . . The shells fired by the Wehrmacht were made by slave labor from Poland, France, and throughout the German empire. And at least some of the slaves must have mastered the art of turning out shells that passed examination but were nevertheless sabotaged effectively.

   (In 1998, I received a letter from a man who identified himself as a Jewish slave laborer in a German factory making panzerfaust shells. He said he and his fellow slaves had discovered that if they mixed sand in with the sulfur they could render the explosive inoperable, and that they could do it when the German inspectors' heads were turned. He said only German soldiers put on the final touch, the trigger mechanism. But those German soldiers liked to take breaks. When they did, the slaves speeded up their output but in the process screwed up the mechanism. The German soldiers were glad to have a higher output and never inspected the shells that had been produced while they were on break. That, he said proudly, was his contribution, and he was glad to see from the story about German duds in *Citizen Soldiers* that the GIs had noticed and lives had been saved.)[11]

Albert Speer offers another explanation for the high rate of duds in the German artillery.

ALBERT SPEER: The [Allied air] attacks on the hydrogenation plants had indirectly affected the entire chemical industry. I was forced to inform Hitler that "the supply of salt has to be stretched in order to fill the existing shells with explosives. This process has already reached the limit of acceptability." Actually, from October 1944 on our explosives consisted of 20 percent rock salt, which reduced their effectiveness correspondingly.[12]

A dud artillery shell

Explosives behave in strange ways. One day another dud landed and ended up across the top of my foxhole. That one wasn't so big, but when they land right across your foxhole these things are like bad dreams or something. Another time, near our camp at a crossroads, the Germans zeroed in their guns on the crossroads and twelve rounds of 150mm, 175mm came in all at once and the fuses were bad in all of them, none of them went off. And then another time, right across the road, one of these big boys, these large artillery shells, hit a big redbrick Dutch barn, and in the attic were stored all the spools of wire that were used by our Signal Corps. They ran these wires from headquarters to headquarters from these drums, and that's the way we communicated.[a] And when that shell hit the barn where the wire was stored the force of the explosion blew those drums straight up—they went clear out of sight—and wire showered down in all directions. It was spectacular. But this is the joke: the Signal Corps guys were sleeping upstairs in the barn, and not one of them was hurt. They didn't even hear it go off; they were still asleep in the barn. All the force of the explosion had gone straight up.

Colonel Howard Johnson was a sort of a favorite of Maxwell Taylor. I didn't know him very well because he was a regimental commander and I worked for the division commander, but General Taylor was very fond of Johnson and pushed his career along. He was the commander of the 501st PIR, the regiment that did fabulous marches covering something like a hundred miles a day, marching along the whole length of Britain with heavy packs on their backs. The training they did was astonishing, and the 501st was one of best crack regiments we had.

Well, Colonel Johnson was too gung-ho and got himself knocked off. I wasn't there personally; the person who told me about it was my friend Harmon,[b] who had gone along as a bodyguard. Colonel Johnson stood on the canal embankment with General Taylor when the Germans started shooting at them because there were these two high-ranking officers standing boldly on the canal. A shell came over and everybody ducked. General Taylor fell on his face. Not Colonel Johnson;

---

[a] Rapport and Northwood note the 101st Airborne used a total of 4,800 miles of wire during the Holland operation (Rapport and Northwood, *Rendezvous with Destiny*, 377).

[b] Master Sergeant David C. Harmon.

THE ILIAD

"The son of Thetis of the Lovely Locks, Achilles, is not fighting. He is sulking by the ships. . . ."

"'Then *let* me die forthwith,' Achilles said with passion, 'since I have failed to save my friend from death. He has fallen, far from his motherland, wanting my help in his extremity. So now, since I shall never see my home again, since I have proved a broken reed to Patroclus and all my other comrades whom Prince Hector killed, and have sat here by my ships, an idle burden on the earth, I, the best man in all the Achaean force, the best in battle.'"[13]

he was too proud to duck. He was like Stonewall Jackson;[a] he wasn't going to duck; so he got it. That was the end; he was killed.[b]

And boy, talk about Achilles in his tent! General Taylor wasn't fit to live with then because he thought Johnson was really going places. The rest of day he was completely unapproachable. Just like Achilles, he sat in the door of his tent and sulked while I sat nearby and ate a pear and dumped the peelings in a foxhole. He was a genius, the colonel, but if you don't duck when they're shooting at you because you're a colonel and you're too dignified, it seems rather foolish.

[a] Thomas Jonathan "Stonewall" Jackson, the Confederate general, got his nickname at the first battle of Bull Run (or Manassas, as it was known in the South). Confederate Lieutenant William Robbins reported that the remnants of an Alabama regiment that had been badly mauled had retreated and were aimlessly waiting for orders when General Barnard E. Bee rode up. "Bee pointed to the conflict going on up on the elevated ground to our left and said: 'Yonder stands Jackson like a stone wall; let's go to his assistance'" (Imboden, "The Confederate Side at Bull Run," 31).

[b] Other accounts do not show Taylor as having been present at Johnson's death, but other details match Hugh Nibley's account. Rapport and Northwood write, "Colonel Johnson went out inspecting front-line positions in the 2d Battalion area, accompanied by Lt. Richard O. Snodgrass, commander of Company D. As a heavy-caliber German shell gave its characteristic whistle, everyone ducked but the colonel. With his usual disdain for danger he walked on. The shell exploded practically at his feet. Fragments penetrated his arm, his neck, and the base of his spine. Capt. Louis Axelrod, 2d Battalion surgeon, was hurried to the scene and the colonel was shortly started on his way to the Nijmegen Hospital. But he died before he got there, breathing out his last words, 'Take care of my boys'" (Rapport and Northwood, *Rendezvous with Destiny*, 399).

"GERONIMO IS DEAD" (EXCERPT)

The Chaplain has said his word, the volley is fired, the generals file past his grave.

Now the three ranks file off slowly.

They pass among the rows, careful not to disturb the sleeping:

Case, Baldwin, Serawatka, Kane, Parrish, McMorries;

Each pauses at his grave, gazes in at the camouflaged parachute the king sleeps in.

It looks cold down there, wonder if he'll keep warm.

Slowly, the moving-picture camera clicks away, recording the procedure;

But never could it record the feelings of the tough men who pass the grave.

No pity, no tears.

They had lived too long for that, saw death too often,

Three of the men who pass that way, their guns have killed over thirty in one day.

Somehow it's wrong.

Maybe a year ago it would have been easy to figure;

But now it's too late, you only know that as soon as the last man of the honor guard files past you will go
back to the line and the only life you do understand, war.

No, he is not going back.

Propeller blasts have died away.

His parachute days are through.

Yes, there will be a telegram;

Oh! but if she only knew.

The sun is getting lower, the words they
speak are few,

Yet each trooper's thought lingers on
Geronimo,

King of the parachute crew.[14]

Colonel Howard "Jumpy" Johnson straps on a parachute.

Kipnes, my lieutenant, was wounded, shot in the leg as he was jumping across a ditch; so he went back to the hospital and that left me alone again. He eventually came back, but once again I was the only one left in OBT #5, and I had to do everything single-handed as I did in Normandy. I was pretty good at Dutch too, which meant a lot of extra work and extra excitement, of course.

For me it was still a private war, and I would meet others who were fighting the same kind of private war, but differently. We weren't in the same category with the others. All the people I became friends with were that kind, men like George Bailey (you would never tie *him* down!) and Lucien Goldschmidt. If ever there were individualists, if ever there were people who could never be soldiers, it was these men. And it was a nice thing, to have these irregular people around. But the point is, there's such a thing as having private wars. I was in special circumstances as a soldier. To begin with, I went in when I was thirty-two years old and had a PhD. Then the first rule in the army is never volunteer for anything, and I was a sucker because I volunteered for everything. And there I was, always observing, as if I wasn't in it. Always observing without participating. I was interested in seeing what would happen, but I really wasn't in it. Crazy things would happen, but for me and for some others, it had to be a private war. You did your own thinking.

There was one occasion when we were at the battle zone and a British major came by and said, "Come with me, Sergeant!" Now what are you supposed to do? You have an assignment to do for your own unit, and someone from another army says, "There's an emergency! You must come with me!" You have conflicting orders. Well, I went back with him. It seems that there were some gliders landing British troops, and I had to go with this British officer and show him the landing site. I went up there and they were all ready to receive the gliders, but they were in a very touchy position. It turned out to be a good thing I was there to show them around. I was able to do things like that because I was free to move around, and I had the opportunity to go see things, like when I went into Brueghel and looked around.

In war the normal becomes strange and the strange is normal. A new guy came down to join us, a lieutenant who'd never been in any action at all, and the first thing he did when he became part of the 101st, he spent the whole day knocking holes in his helmet to make it look like he was a real old-timer. It wasn't easy—you had to hit those helmets awfully hard because that was tough metal. There was a photographer that we'd see around the battlefield. All he was interested in was taking pictures. The war didn't concern him at all; he just wanted to get good pictures. He was innocent; he wasn't participating. So he could go and shoot pictures on either side; it was all the same to him.

One time I was walking through the woods and walked right through the middle of a German battalion. I was going down to visit a historic village of some sort or other, and here this German outfit comes along, walking down the road and infiltrating through the woods. So I just lay low and let them pass by in the woods, and that was all there was to it. But they could very easily have seen me. One Dutchman, a mean old farmer, wouldn't let us in his barn, so we let him have it to himself, and it blew up. You saw lives ending all around you, and you always knew your own life could abruptly end too. One night a British tank came in and parked all night right on my foxhole so I couldn't get out; I was trapped under it. The regular first sergeant of the Headquarters Company of the 101st, Zilske, used to say, "Everything happens to Nibley, and nothing ever happens to him."

GIs and a Dutch woman in a vegetable garden

The general had an aide named Smith, a tough guy who was a professional boxer but also a nice guy. He heard a report about a place where there was some fresh lettuce. The general wanted the fresh lettuce, so we had to go get it. We got in my jeep and went quite a ways out behind the enemy lines to a brick farmhouse that was all overgrown with ivy—it had grown inside and out and covered the house so it looked like some primitive place. The garden had grown wild too; that's why it was still there and everything hadn't been taken. There were sheep there that were wild—the sheep would attack you. It was the strangest thing you ever saw. Everything had gone back to wilderness just like that.

Sure enough, there was a lettuce patch in the garden, but the place was covered by the Germans. They wanted the lettuce too, and they had a mortar zeroed in on it. Every time we popped out to get a head of lettuce, the Germans across the canal would land a small mortar shell in the lettuce patch: ka-BLAM! We did get the lettuce finally, but the interesting thing was this: while this sparring was going on and they were shooting at us and we were trying to get the lettuce for the general, right across the embankment not fifty yards away all these little Dutch kids were playing soldier—bang, bang, bang, shooting each other with toy guns. And they paid no attention to us. We didn't interest them at all because they were busy playing soldier. How they got there or where they came from I don't know, but they were having fun and they didn't want us to interrupt their game or bother them by bringing mortar fire over while they were playing soldier. The real war was going on all around them, but they weren't interested in *our* war; they were interested in *their* war, playing soldier and shooting each other. It had a

A Dutch boy watches GI activity in Zon, Holland.

very interesting psychological effect. It made me think of the play by Calderon, *Life Is a Dream.*

At Slijk-Ewijk there was a Dutch farm where the barn had been blown up by a shell. They had a lot of turkeys in the yard in back of it, and any time there was to be a serious shelling, about ten or fifteen minutes before it came the turkeys would all hunch together in one corner of the yard there and wait for it. And it would always come; they never missed it; they always sensed it. I've heard that the dogs in San Francisco, at the time of the big earthquake of 1904, all started howling before the earthquake. Animals have those senses. I noticed it and I pointed it out to people. "Now look how they're all hunched together. We're going to get some shells pretty soon." This wasn't an earthquake; this wasn't a natural disaster; but they knew it was coming. Now what instinct was that? I don't know, but they would do it.[a]

There were a lot of heroic doings, and I'm afraid many people didn't get recognized for what they did. I knew many boys that did marvelous things. One of the most striking things happened at two o'clock in the morning. I had a little foxhole right on the edge of the canal covered with a small pup tent, and I would mark the war map there. The general wanted me to make a general map of the front, so I would mark the daily front in my foxhole and then take it over to headquarters. I was fairly cozy there on the bank, and one night I was busily marking the map in the middle of the night, very late, when I heard a terrific lot of shooting just a little ways down the bank. I could hear the British Bren guns going off, then the Tommy guns, and then German Schmeisers, all sorts of things firing away. Everybody was shooting like crazy. I thought, what in heaven's name is going on there? And then, finally, silence.

I waited a while, and then all of a sudden the tent flap parts and a kid dressed in a Dutch farm boy's outfit bursts through the door of the tent and throws himself down into the straw on the bottom of the foxhole. For a minute or two all he could do was say, "There *is* a God! There *is* a God! There *is* a God! There *is* a God!"

---

[a] "We soon noticed that the dog would perk up his ears and run to the shelter just before we heard the incoming rounds. After that, whenever we saw the dog's ears go up and he would start to run for shelter, we would drop whatever we were doing and run, too. This gave us a two- or three-second edge over what we'd had before—seconds that may have saved someone's life" (Burgett, *Road to Arnhem*, 155).

He's crying, sopping wet. He'd just swum the canal with all those people shooting at him. He was a medic, and he'd been on the other side and had gotten lost and was taken prisoner. Then he escaped from the Germans, and a Dutch farm couple took him in and gave him this outfit, and he dressed as a Dutch peasant boy and pretended to be deaf and dumb. He'd point to his mouth wherever he went so he wouldn't give away his language. When he started to swim the canal to make a crossing over to our lines, everybody started shooting at him. They shot everything they could at him, machine guns, rifles—a whole company shooting at him like crazy mad. But they didn't hit him, so he got to the other side and fell into my fox-hole crying, "There *is* a God! There *is* a God!"

He'd been taken all over that region and had carefully watched everything that was going on. He'd been very observant; he'd seen what was going on behind the lines, where the Germans were, what they were doing. He told me where he'd been and what he'd seen. This was priceless information, so immediately I got on the horn to General Higgins and said, "Look, we've got a guy here who knows everything that's going on back behind the German lines."

He said, "Well, let's get him back to Brussels as fast as we can."

I promised the kid, "Well, with this you're going to get promoted or something. You'll at least get a three-day pass for this information."

They took him to Brussels, and I heard a number of Intelligence officers got promotions on the strength of the information he had. Then I saw him about four or five months later in Namur. I said, "Did you ever get your three-day pass?"

He said, "I didn't get a one-day pass. I had to go right back to the line the next day."

They didn't care about him; he didn't get anything. He was caught behind the lines, escaped, pretended to be deaf and dumb, got through enemy lines, swam the canal under heavy fire, and came back with a gold mine of information that caused all sorts of excitement. You would think he should have gotten at least a three-day pass for giving them all that information. Everything they'd been looking for was just handed to them and got promotions for all these other people. But he didn't get a medal or even a three-day pass. He was a medic and he had to go right back into the line. That's the way you get rewarded sometimes in this life. So is this

Clipping from the Cardston News, *Cardston, Alberta, Canada*

heroic? Can you get sentimental about this? If you get sentimental, you can get bitter.

I woke up one morning very early, and there was my grandmother standing right at the head of my foxhole looking down at me. She was there all right. Just as plain as anything I saw her looking at me, and I looked at her and waved.

When the mail came through, it brought word that explained what the image he had seen of his grandmother standing by his foxhole had meant. Margaret Reid Sloan died on October 22, 1944.

Nov. 5, 1944

Dear Mother:

Grandma's departure marks the end of a lot of good things. For us she is the last of the pioneers, living clear through the soft, spoiled second generation, she survived to see the third moving into another time of restless motion like her own—a restlessness which she never outgrew. . . . There is something in Grandma's free and open-hearted spirit that speaks to us as if from some Age of the Gods. . . . In the times of total confusion which lie ahead let us not forget how clearly our own behavior has foreshadowed the horrible commotion of the earth and the elements. I speak in the prophetic vein, because the signs of an impending readjustment in the face of the whole earth are fairly clear.

Ecclesiastes says there is a time to mourn, but Hugh Nibley and the Screaming Eagles were a generation too early for terms like "stages of grief" and "closure." And there was just too much to do. Too many shell bursts. Too many bullets to dodge. Too many prisoners to process. Too much war to fight. Take time to mourn for your grandmother? Not the men of the 101st at the Battle of Holland.

"SAFELY OUT OF THE WORLD"

This letter, which Hugh Nibley wrote to his grandmother in 1938, seems to foretell the coming of the war as well as the time when they would be permanently parted by death.

October 4, 1938

Dear Grandma,

It is always very hard to write to you. My feelings are such as cannot be expressed with restraint and yet would only be misinterpreted by a show of emotion. Do you know it has been almost a year since we saw each other last? What difference between a year and a week? I always find you just as I so often think of you, and at this moment you are as near as if you were in the next room. When we meet we talk about trivial and common-place things, and never exchange more than a few words at a time. Why should we meet at all then? There

Margaret Violet Reid Sloan

is a never-expressed understanding between us upon which distance has no effect. I don't think it would make the slightest difference if we were in different worlds. . . .

You from whom comfort and joy flow to many and distant souls as from a strong untiring fountain-head are less an object of sympathy than of inexpressible envy. There is nothing about you I don't envy; as I have said before, I know of but one person who is just what we should all be, whose soul from the beginning was as clear and noble and magnanimous as my kind can hope to be only after endless years of painful discipline and ceaseless correction. I find it very hard to feel sorry for one whose light has burned so long and so clear and even yet grows brighter every day.

Our sincerest congratulations are due those who are safely out of the world at this time. They will be saved much pain. . . . All the worthy ones who leave us now are those whose condition has so overshadowed their abilities, whose great usefulness has been so vitiated by the exigencies of a profoundly corrupt system, that their lives had become virtually a bondage. . . . If there is any subject for tears it is not these fortunate ones. It is rather those successful ones among us who have found their heaven in rewards of a base conformity, who seek their strength and solace in the buying-power of fellows like themselves, whose possessions alone justify them in all things and whose property is their whole sanctification and authority. These will not have to wait to a hereafter to learn their folly; we are soon to see them giving their lives (and especially, where they can, other people's lives) to save their treasures, which for all that will vanish like smoke. . . .

Love,

Hugh

HUGH NIBLEY: The Germans finally started opening up the dams and dikes and flooding us out. My foxhole was half full of water the last few days I was there. It was a mess, so we had to get out. General Taylor said I was to be the last one to leave our headquarters at Slijk-Ewijk. "Nibley will stay until the last dog is hung," he said. So after everyone else had gone I had to drive out alone in the middle of the night. The British had artificial moonlight, fortunately.[a] There were always great clouds and fog, so they would shine bright searchlights on the fog and it would make this eerie blue light and you could see everything.

To make it more interesting, the Germans had a thousand guns on the other side of the river, and they would all shoot at once, BLAM! The whole lot of them, all that artillery firing at once. Gosh, they thought that was great. But when I started to leave, the road was flooded. I couldn't see where it was. It was a little dirt road just along the bank of the Rhine, and the water was up over the road and over the hubs of the jeep, so I had no idea where it was. If I was just a little bit off I could drive right into the river. So I drove around feeling for the road, sliding and slipping all over, following the ruts till I finally got up to the bridge and made it back to Nijmegen and the 82nd.

[a] Artificial moonlight was created by taking the large searchlights used for spotting enemy planes and shining them into banks of fog to create a glow that would illuminate a large area.

American jeep versus Dutch mud

The saddest moments in the war were watching a village when the planes would fly down the main street and drop their red flares on either side preparatory to wiping it out. It was all so scientific, so systematic. So planned. So ingenious. This was commented on by many people, especially General Bradley and General Eisenhower. They used to weep about it, actually, that all these brains, all this intelligence, all this ingenuity and dedication was only devoted to killing each other. It was utter waste. I remember General Bradley said, "War is waste!" And that's what it is. The utter wastefulness of the thing, the *wrongness* of what we were doing was so strong that everybody would cry. People would cry; they would weep; tears would stream down. The wrongness—it was so utterly, unspeakably sad. During a battle in a firefight it wasn't terrifying—no one was terrified anymore when it started—but it was so sad you could hardly stand it, that people would do such things to each other. The sorrow was just heartbreaking, and everybody felt it that way—the *wrongness* of it. Like what those paratroopers did at the wedding on Normandy. It just hit me like a hammerblow to the forehead. The wrongness of it.

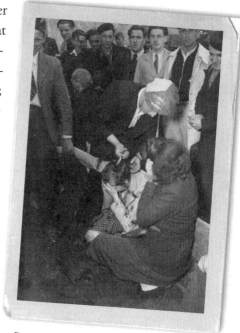

Dutch women who had consorted with the Germans had their heads shaved after the Allies arrived.

VIKTOR FRANKL: Apathy, the main symptom of the second phase [of mental reaction to concentration camp life], was a necessary mechanism of self-defense. Reality dimmed, and all efforts and all emotions were centered on one task: preserving one's own life and that of the other fellow.[15]

HUGH NIBLEY: It was very sad, but this is an interesting thing that was very noticeable there: you feel that the whole thing is being watched over and directed. It's a very interesting thing. Some of the boys in the 101st were pretty rough; in fact, they were recruited from criminals. They were given the choice of going to the pen or joining the 101st, and they chose the 101st. They were pretty rough and tough characters, most of them from the East; and this is the thing I noticed: the tough guys were the first ones to crack. With the Germans the same thing was true too: the rough, tough, really hard-boiled SS men—they would always be the first to crack under questioning. And you'd get some Austrian farm boy who didn't know Hitler from a hole in the ground, and he would not crack. He was very naïve, but

German POWs get a smoke from the Americans.

he would not give up; he would not tell anything. But you'd get an SS man, or somebody that is sworn to the Führer and all this sort of thing, and it was fun. He'd come in and spill his guts, and we'd say, "We don't want to know; we don't need to know; you don't need to tell us this!" He'd say, "No, but I must tell you this!" These were the ones who would crack every time.

And it was so with our people, too. Our boys that were the really tough, roughnecks were the ones that would crack up. And the others? We had a lot of very nice farm boys and so forth; they weathered it out. They got through it all right; they were fine; they could take it.

You didn't hear a lot of profanity, and you never heard dirty stories or anything like that from them, not like the movies. We'd come together in a tent at night, for example, when shells would start coming in right and left, and nobody felt inclined to tell scatological tales or things like that. I had the feeling that everything was being presided over. Then afterwards it's all made into heroics. That's why they have to build up to it with all the trumpets, drums, bugles, flags, and the sort of thing that Reagan liked so much.

The failure of Market-Garden and the diversion of resources to Holland stalled the drive to Germany by Patton and other generals. Still, there were those who worked hard to put a positive spin on the battle for Arnhem. Field Marshal Montgomery declared the operation "90-percent successful."[16] To him the glass was nine-tenths full because the plan had fallen just a little short of its objective. But what is the success of a man who leaps most *of the way across a chasm? Eisenhower stood by his decision to let Monty's plan go forward.*

STEPHEN AMBROSE: In his own defense, Eisenhower wrote, long after the war, "I not only approved Market-Garden, I insisted upon it.

GI with machine gun

What we needed was a *bridgehead* over the Rhine. If that could be accomplished, I was quite willing to wait on all other operations. What this action proved was that the idea of 'one full-blooded thrust' to Berlin was silly." But of all the factors that influenced Eisenhower's decisions . . . the one that stands out is his desire to appease Montgomery. At no other point in the war did Eisenhower's tendency toward compromise and his desire to keep his subordinates happy exact a higher price.[17]

Churchill, as he said he would, wrote a version of the history of the battle that was kind to him.

WINSTON CHURCHILL: Heavy risks were taken in the Battle of Arnhem, but they were justified by the great prize so nearly in our grasp. Had we been more fortunate in the weather, which turned against us at critical moments and restricted our mastery in the air, it is probable that we should have succeeded. No risks daunted the brave men, including the Dutch Resistance, who fought for Arnhem, and it was not till I returned from Canada, where the glorious reports had flowed in, that I was able to understand all that had happened. General Smuts was grieved at what seemed to be a failure, and I telegraphed: "As regards Arnhem, I think you have got the position a little out of focus. The battle was a decided victory, but the leading division, asking, quite rightly, for more, was given a chop. I have not been afflicted by any feeling of disappointment over this and am glad our commanders are capable of running this kind of risk."[18]

That "leading division" was the British 1st Airborne. They went into battle with some ten thousand men, fought brilliantly and courageously, but failed to achieve their objective because poor planning left them with more challenges than their training, experience, dedication, and sheer guts could make up for. When the Red Devils limped out of Arnhem eight days after they came to do a job predicted to last thirty-six hours, there were only 2,400 members left of the 10,000 who had landed. Yet Churchill was not "afflicted by any feeling of disappointment." General Bradley offers an explanation:

OMAR BRADLEY: There is a quality to adversity that summons the noblest in British valor and as a result valor often so obscures defeat that a heroic legend is remembered long after the defeat is forgotten. Arnhem followed in that British tradition. Monty had been turned back short of his goal but so valorous was the defeat that the strategic rebuff passed unnoticed.

True, the British had secured a bridgehead across the Waal but it had been won at an incalculable cost. Not until six months later did Monty force the Rhine and then his crossing was made almost 50 miles upstream from the airborne objective at Arnhem. Meanwhile the neglected campaign in the Scheldt was to drag on through October. Not until November 26 would that vital passage be cleared for Allied shipping.[19]

"THE CHARGE OF THE LIGHT BRIGADE"

Bradley's perceptions may be right. Alfred, Lord Tennyson's classic poem, "The Charge of the Light Brigade," which is perhaps the most famous military poem in the English language, glorifies another great military mistake.

Half a league, half a league,
   Half a league onward,
All in the valley of Death
   Rode the six hundred.
"Forward, the Light Brigade!
Charge for the guns!" he said:
Into the valley of Death
   Rode the six hundred.

"Forward, the Light Brigade!"
Was there a man dismay'd?
Not tho' the soldier knew
   Some one had blunder'd:
Their's not to make reply,
Their's not to reason why,
Their's but to do and die:
Into the valley of Death
   Rode the six hundred.

Cannon to right of them,
Cannon to left of them,
Cannon in front of them
   Volley'd and thunder'd;
Storm'd at with shot and shell,
Boldly they rode and well,
Into the jaws of Death,
Into the mouth of Hell
   Rode the six hundred.

Flash'd all their sabres bare,
Flash'd as they turn'd in air,
Sabring the gunners there,
Charging an army, while
   All the world wonder'd:
Plunged in the battery-smoke
Right thro' the line they broke;
Cossack and Russian
Reel'd from the sabre-stroke
   Shatter'd and sunder'd.
Then they rode back, but not
   Not the six hundred.

Cannon to right of them,
Cannon to left of them,
Cannon behind them
   Volley'd and thunder'd;
Storm'd at with shot and shell,
While horse and hero fell,
They that had fought so well
Came thro' the jaws of Death,
Back from the mouth of Hell,
All that was left of them,
   Left of six hundred.

When can their glory fade?
O the wild charge they made!
   All the world wondered.
Honour the charge they made!
Honour the Light Brigade,
   Noble six hundred![20]

Field Marshal Montgomery wrote in his memoir:

BERNARD MONTGOMERY: In my—prejudiced—view, if the operation had been properly backed from its inception, and given the aircraft, ground forces, and administrative resources necessary for the job— it would have succeeded in spite of my mistakes, of the adverse weather, or the presence of the 2nd SS Panzer Corps in the Arnhem area. I remain Market-Garden's unrepentant advocate.[21]

There are a lot of books about most of the battles in World War II, but there are comparatively few written about the Allied defeat at Arnhem. Ryan's powerful history of the battle, A Bridge Too Far, *ends with Montgomery's unrepentant advocacy and one more quote, this one from Bernhard, the Prince of the Netherlands:*

PRINCE BERNHARD: My country can never again afford the luxury of another Montgomery success.[22]

The bridge at Nijmegen

8

THE ARDENNES

In the fall of 1944, the British were desperate to end the war quickly. They were out of money, out of men, and out of patience. They wanted to get to work rebuilding their country. America, on the other hand, was in a unique position: it was actually getting stronger as the war went on. It still had lots of manpower, its industry was producing more and more, and the economy was thriving. Bombs hadn't fallen on American cities as they had in Europe and Asia, and civilian casualties—virtually non-existent in America—numbered in the tens of millions among the other major combatant countries. Despite his upbeat view of the "decided victory" in Holland, Churchill knew the autumn campaign had not accomplished what the Allies were hoping for. He wrote to FDR on December 6 a letter that seems to somewhat contradict his "kind" telling of the history of the Arnhem operation:

WINSTON CHURCHILL: The time has come for me to place before you the serious and disappointing war situation which faces us at the close of this year. Although many fine tactical victories have been gained, . . . the fact remains that we have definitely failed to achieve the strategic object which we gave to our armies five weeks ago. We have not yet reached the Rhine in the northern part and most important sector of the front, and we shall have to continue the great battle for many weeks before we can hope to reach the Rhine and establish our bridgeheads. After that, again, we have to advance through Germany.[1]

HUGH NIBLEY: After the dismal failure in Holland of Operation Market-Garden, the 101st was withdrawn, and we fell back through the Ardennes Forest down to the Vosges Mountains in northeast France to a little town called Mourmelon-le-Grand to regroup and rest for a while. It was November, Thanksgiving, when we moved down there, and it was very gloomy. I'd have to go through the country up to Reims to get stuff once in awhile, and the place was very depressing because Mourmelon was right in the middle of the World War I battlefields of the Marne[a] and the area had been made into a sort of war museum. The French had left the area unchanged as a tourist attraction so people could see exactly how it was, with all the World War I battlefields exactly as they had been during the Great War. And we had to live right in that miserable place. It was like going right back to World War I.[b]

[a] The region around the Marne River was the scene of some of the bloodiest battles of World War I.

I remember the day World War I broke out. I was four years old but I remember so well, so vividly, everything that happened that day. We were living in the old house on 18th Street in Irvington, Oregon, just outside Portland. It was about five o'clock in the evening, and I was playing under the big oak table in the dining room. Dad came in the house in a sort of hustle with a newspaper under his arm and said, "Well, it's all done now, they killed the Archduke and the war is begun." He sat down and he and my mother started to talk about it, and I was under the table listening. He could see that it was going to be a long, terrible war. I also remember the day that war ended. Meantime, an interesting thing happened. It was the first time there had been a world war and everyone was fascinated; they thought it was great stuff; everybody was enthusiastic about it. So for the next four years in Portland, we played soldier in muddy lots exactly as it was played in France. We dug regular trenches and dugouts and things like that in back lots all over town, just like they had in France, and we played soldier in them. Of course, being Portland, it rained all the time; and I remembered the dismal mud and rain

---

[b] "Mourmelon had been a garrison town for at least 1,998 years—Julius Caesar and his Roman legions had used it as a campground in 54 B.C. The French Army had had barracks there for hundreds of years, and still does in the 1990s. Located on the plain between the Marne River to the south and the Aisne River to the north, on the traditional invasion route toward Paris (or toward the Rhine, depending on who was on the offensive), Mourmelon was in an area that had witnessed many battles through the centuries. Most recently the area had been torn up between 1914 and 1918. The artillery craters and trenches from the last world war were everywhere. American Doughboys had fought in the vicinity in 1918, at Château-Thierry and Belleau Wood" (Ambrose, *Band of Brothers*, 168).

of those trenches thirty years later when I found myself on D-Day in the mud in Normandy with big red poppies growing in the field by my foxhole just like "In Flanders Fields." Then when we got to Mourmelon we moved in among those trenches that had been used in World War I and I thought, "Now this is it, just as I remember; I've already gone through this whole thing in World War I." They had left the barbed wire and all these shell holes around there. It was pouring rain, and there was mud everywhere—and there I was back in my childhood again, camped in the middle of the trenches of World War I. We were in the same trenches and the same dugouts filled with the same mud. And I thought, "What progress we've made! Here I am right back where we started." The "war to end all wars" hadn't ended anything.

By now, with winter moving in and the Allied armies spread out over a front more than a thousand miles long, the rapid advances of the summer had slowed to a crawl. Rather than leapfrogging forward, the troops were digging in and taking up positions they intended to hold for some time, possibly until spring. The hope of ending the war by Christmas was gone, and the grim reality that they would have to fight through the winter settled over the Allied soldiers.

DIARY ENTRY, DECEMBER 10, 1944: Harmon committed suicide an hour ago.

HUGH NIBLEY: I've carried till quite recently a very good German briefcase made of very fine leather on which the locks had been broken. I got it from Harmon when we were still back in Holland. He had been standing out on an embankment with Colonel Johnson when a car went by very fast, a German military car. I remember Harmon told me about it afterwards. The car was going down the road, and the colonel told him to shoot the fellow who was driving the car. It was a German major with his mistress. So Harmon shot that major through the head. They got a briefcase full of pretty good

The briefcase Harmon took from the dead German officer and gave to Hugh Nibley

PERSONAL KILLS

Grossman's research shows that the fear of being killed is less likely to create "psychiatric casualties" in a war than the act of killing. Contrary to common wisdom and Hollywood's portrayal of killing, those who kill in battle tend to suffer for it unless they are among those who are mentally ill to begin with and enjoy killing. Having a clear reason to kill doesn't seem to make this psychological response disappear.

DAVE GROSSMAN: Close range involves any kill with a projectile weapon from point-blank range, extending to midrange. The key factor in close range is the undeniable certainty of responsibility on the part of the killer. In Vietnam the term "personal kill" was used to distinguish the act of killing a specific individual with a direct-fire weapon and being absolutely sure of having done it oneself. The vast majority of personal kills and the resultant trauma occur at this range. . . .

At close range the euphoria stage, although brief, fleeting, and not often mentioned, still appears to be experienced in some form by most soldiers. Upon being asked, most of the combat veterans whom I have interviewed will admit to having experienced a brief feeling of elation upon succeeding in killing the enemy. Usually this euphoria stage is almost instantly overwhelmed by the guilt stage as the soldier is faced with the undeniable evidence of what he has done, and the guilt stage is often so strong as to result in physical revulsion and vomiting.

When the soldier kills at close range, it is by its very nature an intensely vivid and personal matter. . . .

Author and World War II marine veteran William Manchester vividly described the . . . psychological responses to his own close-range kill:

"I was utterly terrified—petrified—but I knew there had to be a Japanese sniper in a small fishing shack near the shore. He was firing in the other direction at Marines in another battalion, but I knew as soon as he picked off the people there—there was a window on our side—that he would start picking us off. And there was nobody else to go . . . and so I ran towards the shack and broke in and found myself in an empty room.

"There was a door which meant there was another room and the sniper was in that— and I just broke that down. I was just absolutely gripped by the fear that this man would expect me and would shoot me. But as it turned out he was in a sniper harness and he couldn't turn around fast enough. He was entangled in the harness so I shot him with a .45 and I felt remorse and shame. I can remember whispering foolishly, 'I'm sorry' and then just throwing up. . . . I threw up all over myself. It was a betrayal of what I'd been taught since a child."[2]

Grossman gives several other examples of similar responses to "personal kills" by even the most battle-hardened special forces veterans.

information off him, and I inherited the briefcase with the broken locks, which I still have—a yellow-brown one, a very elegant briefcase. Of course Harmon had done a lot of shooting, and when the colonel said, "Shoot the driver," Harmon sure enough shot and killed him. But it preyed on his mind. There were other things, too, but that killing particularly did. He talked to me about it; he felt he shouldn't have done

Dead paratroopers

that. And so one night in Mourmelon he came in and sat down on the bunk beside me, and he said, "Nibley, if I want to kill myself, it's my own [profane expletive] business, isn't it?" I said, "No, it will concern other people, too." Suddenly he whipped out a little automatic he had in his pocket, a little Italian Beretta, and shot himself right through the head. Blood splattered all over the place. I immediately put towels around his head, because head wounds bleed like crazy. Then I ran across to get the medics; but he was dead before they got there. He just couldn't stand living with it. The next afternoon we drove through the cold, dark country ten miles and held a funeral. Naturally I had to testify about the suicide, because you have to have a report when somebody gets killed.

Then another thing happened. It seemed I was going to be transferred out of the division at that time, and I had just had an interview with the chief of staff, Colonel Raymond Milliner. He had been living with the stress of the war too. While we're talking there he said, "Do you think this will be the end of everything?" I didn't know what he was talking about, and I left after a while. I hadn't been gone but a few minutes before he put a Colt .45 in his mouth and pulled the trigger and blew his brains out. He was chief of staff for the division. Apparently the strain was too much.

George Allen, whom Hugh Nibley met at Ritchie, was a prisoner of war interrogator with the 101st, and since the division was resting and not in a position to be taking prisoners, he had nothing to do in Mourmelon. In his memoir, To Bastogne for the Christmas Holidays 1944, *Allen recalls Mourmelon.*

GEORGE ALLEN: I soon looked around for something to do since I am constitutionally incapable of doing nothing. Trips to the Rheims Cathedral weren't enough. In a short time I found Hugh Nibley, a devout Mormon and a peacetime professor of Classics at Brigham Young University[a] in Provo, Utah, who ran the Order of Battle section with the aid of a captain and a staff sergeant. The captain had apparently found the "Tarnkappe" or "cap of concealment" which was once owned by a figure in German medieval legend since I saw him only a few times.[b] The staff sergeant had been injured while bringing in the jeep and trailer seaborne to Holland, having unsuccessfully disputed a small portion of the road with a tank at nighttime and he never returned from the hospital. So Nibley said he'd be glad to have me help him.

We took an area of about fifteen feet square at the end of one of the barracks, the remainder of which was occupied by other groups and set to work putting up an Order of Battle section. We found a large piece of plywood or similar material to hold the maps at the end of the building which we fastened to the wall, then we acquired a group of sectional maps of the entire front from Holland down to Switzerland which we mounted on the wood, over which we mounted a large piece of transparent plastic. On this overlay we then plotted with crayon the location of the Allied and German troops with the frontage they covered. Each day we would receive by way of the communications truck a decoded telegram (TWX)[c] which gave the troop positions and any changes that had just occurred. We could thus identify our own and any divisions of the enemy as long as their locations were known. The idea was apparently that the General and

---

[a] Actually, at that time, Nibley had not yet taught at BYU.

[b] This was probably Kipnes, who had been wounded in Holland and may have still been in the hospital or not fully recovered at this time. It may also be that Nibley remembers Kipnes more charitably than Allen does.

[c] *TWX:* Teletypewriter exchange

Reims Cathedral, Reims, France

his staff would come and see what the whole front looked like in relation to our own division. In the period of two weeks I recall seeing only one officer come to check our handiwork, not unusual since we were in reserve and some of the officers were on furlough.[3]

HUGH NIBLEY: When you're in Intelligence and trying to predict what the enemy's up to and what they're going to do, you look for signs, and some are very subtle. That's why in May of 1944 I predicted the war would end in Europe on the 7th of May, 1945, which is when the peace was signed in Reims. Well, that was just intuitive, but it was a pretty good guess. Really it was like those turkeys in Holland who knew when the shells would start falling ten minutes before they came. Don't ask me how they did it; the scientists say it can't be done.

In the same way I was able to predict the breakthrough at the Bulge. I put all sorts of subtle things together and it worked out. There have been a lot of books written about how at the Battle of the Bulge our commanders were taken completely off-guard and it was a total surprise. But it shouldn't have been, because I had it all plotted out. Here's what was happening: All day long the Germans would move on the roads from the Schnee Eifel in the south and Hollerath in the north. They were obviously gathering forces, but they didn't build their defense lines parallel to the Allied lines as they should to strengthen a defensive line. They built them perpendicular to our lines, piling up behind one certain spot. You could see they were going to guard their flanks and punch through our lines, and that's where they were coming through. The peasants, the farmers, and the people were all aware of it. They said, "They're all moving at night and moving in horse-drawn wagons, not making any motor noises, and they're ganging up there and bringing in all sorts of heavy equipment." And our commanders wouldn't believe it at all.

Hitler was getting desperate, but he was still unable to admit the possibility of failure. His "will" and his "fanaticism" stayed focused on his delusions.

ALBERT SPEER: Around the end of November, Hitler said once again that he was staking everything on this offensive. Since he was sure of its success, he added nonchalantly that it was his last effort: "If it does not succeed, I no longer see any possibility for ending the war well. . . . But we will come through," he added, and promptly strayed

Hitler with German military brass

off into more and more expansive and fantastic notions: "A single breakthrough on the western front! You'll see! It will lead to collapse and panic among the Americans. We'll drive right through their middle and take Antwerp. Then they'll have lost their supply port. And a tremendous pocket will encircle the entire English army, with hundreds of thousands of prisoners. As we used to do in Russia!"[4]

HUGH NIBLEY: We sent some boys down from Corps there, some friends of mine from Ritchie, to ask at the new headquarters why the American Lion Head Division,[a] a brand-new division that had never seen battle and had just been in Europe a couple of weeks, had been placed right in that dangerous spot where the Germans were building their forces. But headquarters didn't take it seriously. Why? Because there wasn't going to be any action there. "That's the safe place!" they said. And that's the very place where there actually was going to be action. That was where they were going to break through, and it was very obvious.

We wanted to go down and get the maps of the layout around that area. But the guys there said, "Well, there's nothing happening here; we have no maps for the area." And then they said, "We can't give you anything now anyway because we've got all our stuff packed up. We're moving it to headquarters tomorrow, and we can't unpack any of it." So the fellows didn't get any information or maps because the commanders were sure there wasn't going to be any action on that front. They said, "There are no Germans in the area, and we're not doing anything. We were sent here to rest. Everything's going to be safe here." The high command believed that, and everybody else believed that.

But I didn't believe it. Not me.

It was obvious exactly where that breakthrough would come. I knew who would be there and how strong their force was. We had every indication of it. We'd been getting information all the time. I remember there were armored divisions and the 6th *Fallschermjeager* [paratroops] I had faced in Normandy and Holland. I predicted when it would happen too. I said it would be the seventeenth of December;[b] I was

[a] The 106th Infantry Division

[b] Hugh Nibley consistently refers to the Ardennes Breakthrough as occurring on the 17th of December. In reality it happened early on the morning of the preceding day, December 16th. It's clear from his diary and from other accounts, including George Allen's, that he did not hear any news of the breakthrough until the morning of the 17th. The error of memory may be due to his placing the memory on the day he heard of the breakthrough rather than the day it occurred. His having predicted the breakthrough on the 17th may also help fix that date in his mind. The difference is probably not due to time-dimmed memory, since he also mentions his prediction of the Bulge breakthrough in a letter in August 1945.

convinced that was when it was going to be. I couldn't really prove it or anything, but I used some certain patterns that had been followed. I knew Hitler followed astrology, and the seventeenth of December had always been a special day with Hitler. As far as the time of day was concerned, you would always attack at dawn so there's enough light to see by but not enough to see clearly, and you can spread confusion among your enemy. During the hours of confusion, that's when you strike, so dawn on the seventeenth of December would be the time to attack, and we could tell where it would come because of the way they were lined up, and we knew what units would attack. It was all very obvious. Everything was set up. So when they say the Battle of the Bulge was a complete and total 100 percent surprise, there's no excuse for it. We knew exactly what was going to happen. I told them and told them, and they wouldn't listen.

Max Oppenheimer also claims to have seen the Ardennes attack coming.

> **MAX OPPENHEIMER:** During the early days of December 1944, Fred and I in the OB section, as well as enlisted G-2 map Sergeant Harper, had gathered from many IPW reports that there were ten Panzer divisions—a very unusual concentration—in the enemy sector across the Rhine River. We naturally reported this to First Army, who disregarded the warning. We thought they should have taken it seriously and at least looked into it more closely, possibly having the 9th Air Force bomb the area. On December 17, our concern proved to have been justified.[5]

At the time of the Ardennes breakthrough, Nibley's Ritchie pal Lucien Goldschmidt was with Patton's 3rd Army not too far from Mourmelon.

LUCIEN GOLDSCHMIDT: Although Eisenhower in his memoirs tried to make us believe that [the thin deployment of troops against the Germans in December of 1944] had been a known risk and that he had sort of "played dead," we ourselves in 3rd Army, those who had a little [firsthand] knowledge, think that it is untrue. While Eisenhower's memoirs on the whole seemed to us quite authentic from what we know, we were briefed, ourselves, by air force officers on the invasion of Germany through the Zweibuten Gap, which was going to take place just about the time the

Germans delivered their punch against the Bulge. It is inconceivable to me that had they considered the [Ardennes offensive] possible they would have acted the way they did, that they would have brought so much of the American forces farther south.

a MI5: British Military Intelligence

DIARY ENTRY, DECEMBER 17, 1944: Another sad Sunday waiting for the boys from Paris. The Germans launch their big attack today. I am ready to move to MI5.*a*

HUGH NIBLEY: On the night of December 16th to 17th I was in headquarters and sure enough, very early in the morning here came a captain of engineers. He was all dirty and bloody and messed up and he told us the Germans had broken through. He said he was in charge of a colored company of engineers and they'd captured his whole unit.

When we started marking the information we were getting on the situation map, I noticed things that were happening. We could see here and here and here, the places they'd broken through, places like Malmedy and other places where they never should be. They were flanking us and going right through the Ardennes there. Then General MacAuliffe came in and started sizing up the situation. It was very serious. We thought that the Germans had nothing to go on, and they had everything. They had the whole works back there, more stuff than we ever dreamed they had. Boy, they came rushing through exactly as I predicted weeks ahead. Later, General Taylor congratulated me on it. "You told it right! That's the way it happened."

GEORGE ALLEN: The seventeenth of December was to be our last day together, as replacements were coming for Nibley and his injured colleague and we awaited them. As we were chatting, a messenger came in with a TWX with a new group of changes, and we began to plot them. Nibley changed the disposition as I called out the coordinates. In a minute or two we realized that a serious breakthrough had been made in the Allied lines in the area known as the Eifel on the eastern edge of the Ardennes, crossing the Ourthe River, and two regiments of the 106th Infantry Division and one of the 28th Infantry Division were shown as being encircled with arrows pointing to a German advance on a large front of undetermined depth. According to the TWX the Germans called the operation "Greif" or "Griffin." (This was incorrect. That was an operation within the larger one, which was called

JIM CROW IN THE AMERICAN ARMY

STEPHEN AMBROSE: Old Jim Crow ruled in the Army as much as in the South. Blacks had their own units, mess halls, barracks, bars—State-side, England, France, Belgium, it didn't matter. There were no black infantry units in the ETO [European Theater of Operations]. There were nine Negro field artillery battalions, a few anti-aircraft battalions, and a half dozen tank and tank destroyer battalions. Some did well, some were average, some were poor.[6]

THE MALMEDY MASSACRE

The little Belgian village of Malmedy also became the site of what is now known as the "Malmedy Massacre." All parties agree that German troops machine-gunned American prisoners in a snowy field outside Malmedy, but there is a lot of dispute about how it happened. Were the prisoners trying to escape? Did German replacements mistake them for armed troops? Was it cold-blooded savagery, or expediency by Germans who didn't have enough men to guard the prisoners and believed they were about to come under attack from other American forces?

The Germans had been given the same order for the Ardennes thrust as the 101st had been given for Normandy: "No prisoners." But the Germans had already violated that order and sent many prisoners back before the shootings at Malmedy. Once the American press got ahold of the story it became an outrage. After the war an American tribunal tried the Germans involved and sentenced forty-three to death, twenty-two to life in prison, and others to between ten and twenty years. None of the men were executed and all were released within eleven years, thanks in part to the intervention on their behalf by U.S. Senator Joseph McCarthy.

A German prisoner points out which of his comrades were responsible for shooting prisoners at Malmedy.

"Herbstnebel" or "Autumn Fog"). The attack had begun about 0400 on the morning of Saturday, 16 December, but this was our first knowledge of what was taking place.

* Interrogation Prisoner of War: The intelligence task to which Allen was assigned.

At this point our replacements turned up: Benoit, a French Canadian from Maine, and Herren, from New York City. I had known them at Camp Ritchie and immediately called in [my IPW[a] team members] Schlesinger and Harvey to show them their barracks and other details of our life. . . . Benoit and Herren were extremely excited and happy at being assigned to an airborne division, having wandered about in the Army Wilderness [sic] since July, taking extra training to the extent of parachuting, and we gladly took them under hand. . . . As we were discussing their arrival and the news at the front, General Anthony McAuliffe . . . came in and wanted to know why so many men were in an area called "Top Secret." It was too involved to explain, but fortunately he then turned to the map. Regular army procedure would have had him stop the war long enough to take our names and provide suitable punishment, but he wasn't that sort of general. He knew Nibley, and Nibley may have explained our presence there. Nibley then showed him the situation as well as he could from the knowledge we had from the map, and McAuliffe left. He knew that we and the 82nd Airborne Division were the only reserve divisions in the whole theater, and that we would probably be called to active duty. He went to find out more about the breakthrough and also round up members of the division who were in England or Paris on furlough. . . .

All that gloomy afternoon the news of the breakthrough got around, and by evening it was the only topic of discussion. Few of the men knew where the Ardennes or Eifel were, but they sensed that we would see action soon and were nervous at the same time that they were acting noncommittal. Finally just about lights-out time an officer stood at one end of the barracks, called for attention and announced that we were alerted, we were to remain in the company area, we were to prepare to depart for combat, and we would cross the line of departure at 1300 hours on the following day, Monday, 18 December. This started a hubbub which didn't end until about midnight, when the men realized that they had better get their sleep then as they couldn't know when they would get it later.

HUGH NIBLEY: We were told that the very next morning the division would have to go up and try to do what they could to stop the German advance. I thought I would have to go up with the division but I didn't. During the night there came a call from Paris: "You'll have to go to Paris. We have to meet you down here to be reassigned, quick!" So I had to go back to Paris. Two other fellows took our places there, Benoit and Herren, two very nice boys. They were the ones going to Bastogne. They were awfully well prepared and they were smart kids. I liked them very much. I taught them the ropes and I gave a briefing that morning, as much as I could as fast as I could.

GEORGE ALLEN: The next day we got our equipment together and at 1300 hours we all assembled and formed part of a train of jeeps, trucks and 10-ton trailers which extended for miles. Three hundred eighty of the latter had been assembled on a moment's notice, told to dump their loads, and proceed to Mourmelon, where they picked up 11,000 soldiers and carried them to the front in the same night.

HUGH NIBLEY: All the men had to hustle out and jump into these big gondolas full of troops that were going to pull these troops up to Bastogne; so they packed the boys in and got them up and off. I had to go back to Paris, so I handed over everything to Benoit and Herren. They got into my place and it was goodbye. That's when I was taken out of the 101st Airborne Division.

DIARY ENTRY, DECEMBER 18, 1944: The entire division pulls out at 3:00. A sad day. Finish reading Marquand "Weakest Point." In the evening rest. The post is absolutely deserted.

The soldiers in the trucks and trailers that left Mourmelon had no idea where they were going, although those who worked in the map room—Benoit, Herren, George Allen, and Hugh Nibley—might have known. A common memory for soldiers who fought the Battle of the Bulge is that they rarely knew what country they were in. The destination of the convoy that took Benoit and Herren away was, of course, the small Belgian town of Bastogne, a name now remembered for one of the greatest military engagements of all time. It was where the 101st became known as the "Battered Bastards of the Bastion of Bastogne," and it remains to this day the most legendary battle of the most famous unit of the American military.

As the 101st made its way to Bastogne, it moved against a tide of Americans

The 101st at Bastogne

fleeing in outright panic from the German forces that had punched through the lines, scattering wholesale death and confusion. The 101st hadn't had time to fully equip its men before heading out, but they were able to get a lot of weapons and ammunition from the fleeing soldiers coming down the road to Bastogne. Men trained to fight handed their grenades and ammunition away to other soldiers who would now have to face what they were running from. It was not a pretty sight.

While in Bastogne George Allen took on himself the responsibility of feeding the German prisoners who otherwise would have starved, since there was little food even for the Americans.

GEORGE ALLEN: As soon as day began to break on Friday, 22 December, I called out my cooks and we began the day's work of again preparing food we had brought out of the empty houses for our guests. It was about this time that an officer from division headquarters came in and, seeing me, said, "Allen, I thought you were dead." This surprised me since I was sure that I was very much alive. I didn't even pinch myself, I was so sure. Then he explained that a soldier named Allen had been killed along with Benoit and Herren when a flat-trajectory shell from a tank penetrated the building they occupied at headquarters in the Hitler Youth Barracks and exploded, and he assumed I was the person. This immediately made me sadder than I had ever been before. It was the realization of a dream for Benoit and Herren to join an airborne division, and their stay had lasted just four days. They owed their deaths to their enthusiasm to be with a fighting unit, and I owed my life to them for coming when they did. A day later and they wouldn't have been able to join us, and I would most likely have been in that room when the shell hit it. . . . I felt sad all day, and yet I had the soldier's knowledge that the shell that

Members of the 101st lie dead in their room in Bastogne after a German shell hit the building.

killed them could just as well have killed me. Whenever I thought of their deaths, I repeated to myself the verses, "Vain seemed all the strength to him as golden convoys sunk at sea."[7]

HUGH NIBLEY: I heard later it was the first day or second day at Bastogne as Benoit and Herren were setting up the headquarters an 88 shell came smack right in the door of the headquarters and blew everybody to mincemeat. They were both killed. So that was that.

One of the most remarkable aspects of war and of battle is the selective survival, how often people know that they are not going to be spared or that they will be. We'd sit around and talk about that, and our intuitions were right. My companion in our first team, Weigner, was absolutely convinced that he would die. He was a very rich, spoiled, only child, and he dragged me around to half the fortune tellers in London to get some sort of assurance from them. I kept telling him to forget about it, but that's the way he felt about it. He felt fated. I wasn't with Weigner when he was killed; he wasn't in the team anymore. He went into a house to get some silverware, and he was going up the stairs and a sniper at the top of the stairs shot him through the top of the head and killed him. He shouldn't have gone after the silverware. It was the same way with Braun. He was the lieutenant at

A paratrooper in the snow of Bastogne waits with his bazooka for German tanks.

Normandy and was killed on D-Day. But they both felt very strongly that they would be killed, and of course I knew I wouldn't. But this idea, the selectiveness of survival, makes you think.

Now, once again, the death of Benoit and Herren left me the only uninjured survivor from OB Team 5. Time and again, the same thing. It makes you think of the famous phrase of the last survivor from Job who says, "And I alone escape to tell thee."[a] Or Moroni, the last survivor in the Book of Mormon.[b] I imagine myself as such a survivor at some future time, long after this in another life or something—how would it be if I was a tour guide or something like that trying to explain all this? But there is a sort of certainty you feel. As Sergeant Zilske used to say, "Everything happens to Nibley, and nothing ever happens to him." And it was so. I would always be there and was completely unaware of what was happening until it was all over. I'd look back and say, "Were we in that?" And another time I would be absolutely scared stiff, and it turned out there was no reason on earth to be. Remember, as the Lord says in Matthew 24, "There are two in the field, one is taken, one is spared. There are two

[a] "And there was a day when his sons and his daughters were eating and drinking wine in their eldest brother's house: and there came a messenger unto Job, and said, The oxen were plowing, and the asses feeding beside them: and the Sabeans fell upon them, and took them away; yea, they have slain the servants with the edge of the sword; and I only am escaped alone to tell thee.

"While he was yet speaking, there came also another, and said, The fire of God is fallen from heaven, and hath burned up the sheep, and the servants, and consumed them; and I only am escaped alone to tell thee. . . .

"While he was yet speaking, there came also another, and said, Thy sons and thy daughters were eating and drinking wine in their eldest brother's house: and, behold, there came a great wind from the wilderness, and smote the four corners of the house, and it fell upon the young men, and they are dead; and I only am escaped alone to tell thee" (Job 1:13–16, 18–19).

[b] "And now it came to pass that after the great and tremendous battle at Cumorah, behold, the Nephites who had escaped into the country southward were hunted by the Lamanites, until they were all destroyed. . . . I even remain alone to write the sad tale of the destruction of my people. But behold, they are gone. . . . Therefore I will write and hide up the records in the earth; and whither I go it mattereth not. . . . My father hath been slain in battle, and all my kinsfolk, and I have not friends nor whither to go; and how long the Lord will suffer that I may live I know not" (Mormon 8:2–5).

women working in the kitchen, one is taken . . ."[a] You can't plan for that sort of thing.

The 101st held out in that place for a long time, and it was not a fortunate thing that happened there. The guys always remembered that; they hated Bastogne. At the end of the fighting I wrote up the only report they could have on the activities of OB Team Number 5, and it got us the presidential citation for the smallest unit in the army, but I wasn't in it then

GIs hold church services in Bastogne.

because I'd been transferred. So the later guys that succeeded us after the shooting had stopped, they were wearing presidential citations for OB Team 5. Typical army.

By December 22 the Germans had entirely encircled Bastogne with three Panzer divisions and two infantry divisions, which led some Screaming Eagles to comment, "They've got us surrounded, poor bastards." The fighting was intense, food was scarce, and the troops were not equipped for winter fighting. The freezing weather was punctuated by constant artillery bombardments with sudden flashes of hellish heat and white-hot shrapnel that sizzled when it struck flesh. The commander of the German forces surrounding Bastogne demanded a surrender:

December 22nd 1944

To the U.S.A. Commander of the encircled town of Bastogne.

The fortune of war is changing. This time the U.S.A. forces in and near Bastogne have been encircled by strong German armored units. More

---

[a] "Then shall two be in the field; the one shall be taken, and the other left. Two women shall be grinding at the mill; the one shall be taken, and the other left" (Matthew 24:40, 41).

German armored units have crossed the river Ourthe near Ortheuville, have taken Marche and reached St. Hubert by passing through Hompré-Sibret-Tillet. Libramont is in German hands.

There is only one possibility to save the encircled U.S.A. troops from total annihilation: that is the honorable surrender of the encircled town. In order to think it over a term of two hours will be granted beginning with the presentation of this note.

If this proposal should be rejected one German Artillery Corps and six heavy A.A.[a] Battalions are ready to annihilate the U.S.A. troops in and near Bastogne. The order for firing will be given immediately after this two hours' term.

All the serious civilian losses caused by this artillery fire would not correspond with the wellknown American humanity.

The German Commander.[8]

McAuliffe's answer was succinct.

December 22nd 1944

To the German Commander at Bastogne

Nuts!

The American Commander

On December 19 Eisenhower had called a meeting of his commanders at Verdun, the site of the greatest battle of World War I. They discussed how to get help up to the 101st in Bastogne.

OMAR BRADLEY: "How soon will you be able to go, George?"[b] I asked, knowing how difficult his movement would be over the limited roadnet that connected Luxembourg with his Alsatian front. George estimated 48 hours; any other commander would have held his breath and believed himself taking a chance on 98. . . .

"Brad," he exclaimed, "this time the Kraut's stuck his head in a meatgrinder." With a turn of his fist he added, "And this time I've got hold of the handle." . . .

Even before he left Verdun for Nancy on December 19, George

[a] *Antiaircraft: These units included the dreaded 88s.*

[b] Bradley is addressing General George Patton.

Patton, right, after awarding General McAuliffe, left, and Lt. Colonel Steve Chapruis the Distinguished Service Cross for the defense of Bastogne

had touched off the movement by phone. Two days later, on December 21, he was attacking toward Bastogne with an armored and infantry division. By Christmas those original two had been joined by four more. Within less than a week Patton had switched the bulk of his Third Army, with its guns, supply, and equipment, from 50 to 70 miles north into the new offensive. More than 133,000 tanks and trucks joined that round-the-clock trek over the icy roads.[9]

LUCIEN GOLDSCHMIDT: Patton had gained great prominence by being able, from his knowledge of the First World War, to give orders to his individual regimental commanders from memory, village by village, as to where they would have to move. I know from another member of the Order of Battle section, a fellow called Arcadi from Connecticut, who was also friendly with Hugh Nibley but who was not in our class [at Ritchie], that that is indeed what happened, and Patton was thereby able to reach the outskirts of Bastogne in time, before the Germans had managed to slice through to the Channel, which was the great fear at the moment.

While the Ardennes offensive hit the Allied front lines hard, it also brought the stewing competition between the Allied generals to a boil. Montgomery was commanding the 21st Army Group in the north and Bradley's 12th Army Group held the area where the breakthrough occurred. The German attack cut through Bradley's forces and made it difficult to communicate with his two northern armies. Eisenhower decided to temporarily transfer command of the American armies to the north of the bulge to Monty, which annoyed the Americans a lot.

NIGEL HAMILTON: An hour and a half later, with the Union Jack flying on the hood of his Rolls-Royce and a cavalcade of outriders, Monty arrived at First U.S. Army's new Verviers headquarters, "like Christ come to cleanse the Temple," as his ADC recalled.[10]

True to his nature, Monty began once again to lecture Eisenhower on how to run the battle. Eisenhower began early on to describe the situation as an opportunity and that he wanted rapid counter attacks, which U. S. commanders like Patton delivered.

Monty

Monty's plan was to wait on the defensive until the Germans had exhausted all their aggressive strength before attacking. Ike kept urging attack, while Monty spent valuable days "tidying up" his lines, waiting for the Germans to attack, and—once again and with new energy—demanding he be given command of all the Allied ground forces. It got to the point where Eisenhower was ready to fire Montgomery. When Monty found out his successor had already been chosen, he backed down and promised to do what Ike ordered. The Americans were more disgusted with Monty than ever. What annoyed them even worse was when Monty held a press conference where he claimed credit for winning the battle and made comments that insulted the Americans deeply. "I think [it's] possibly one of the most interesting and tricky battles I have ever handled," he told the papers.[11]

STEPHEN AMBROSE: Bradley, Patton, and nearly every American officer in Europe were furious. As they saw the battle, they had stopped the Germans before Montgomery came onto the scene. Almost no British forces were even engaged in the Bulge. Far from directing the victory, Montgomery had gotten in everyone's way and botched the counterattack.[12]

The British press took up the cry that Monty should be placed in command of all the Allied troops. Bradley and Patton swore they would resign rather than serve under the Brit.

OMAR BRADLEY: By this time I could not have temperamentally subordinated myself to Montgomery's command. Not only were we as fully competent as the British but by now the U.S. had committed 50 divisions in the ETO in contrast to the 15 of Britain. So overwhelming a superiority, I argued, strongly supported our insistence that U.S. troops be fought under a U.S. field command.

On this question of a super ground commander, Eisenhower stood firm and the British press relented. Eventually it remained for Churchill to pour oil on the troubled waters. In a speech before the House of Commons on January 18 he said:

"I have seen it suggested that the terrific battle which has been proceeding since December 16 on the American front is an Anglo-American battle. In fact, however, the United States troops have done almost all the fighting and have suffered almost all the losses. They have suffered losses almost equal to those of both sides at the Battle of Gettysburg. . . . The Americans have engaged thirty or forty men for every one we have engaged and have lost sixty to eighty men to every one of ours. That is a point I wish to make.

"Care must be taken in telling our proud tale not to claim for the British armies undue share of what is undoubtedly the greatest American battle of the war and will, I believe, be regarded as an ever-famous American victory. I have never hesitated to stand up for our own soldiers when their achievements have been cold-shouldered or neglected or over-shadowed, as they sometimes are, but we must not forget that it is to American homes that telegrams

GIs in a jeep guard a German in American uniform, who rides on the hood.

of personal loss and anxiety have been coming during the past month and that there has been a hard and severe ordeal during these weeks for our brave and cherished ally. . . .

"All these [British and American] troops fought in magnificent fashion and General Eisenhower, balancing the situation between his two commanders, gave them both the fairest opportunity to realize their full strength and qualities.

"Let no one lend themselves to the shouting of mischief makers when issues of this momentous consequence are being successfully decided by sword."[13]

a CIC:
Counter
Intelligence
Corps

HUGH NIBLEY: I was rushed back to Paris, where I was assigned to British CIC[a] at the military Intelligence headquarters in Le Vesigne in the suburbs of Paris. At that time a lot of the U.S. forces were temporarily attached to the British Second Army, so I was working with two guys from British CIC. We were supposed to go around to various towns and places in the Ardennes woods of France, Luxembourg, and Belgium, and look for fifth-columnists,[b] because there were a lot of those in the Battle of the Bulge. They had whole German units dressed in American uniforms, and that's what we were after, those sorts of guys. The two CIC guys were doing most of the work; I was along for the ride because I spoke French, German, Russian, and Dutch, and that helped them. There was a war of rumors; we were hearing reports of all kinds of things, including a plot to assassinate General Eisenhower.

---

b *Fifth column:* A term coined during the Spanish Civil War when a general laying siege to Madrid with four columns of soldiers said he would take the city with his "fifth column," meaning those non-uniformed citizens inside the city who were working for his cause.

DIARY ENTRY, CHRISTMAS EVE, 1944: No pass.

CHRISTMAS DAY, 1944: Very clear with heavy frost. A wonderful dinner, walked to St. Germain du Laye.

The Allies had been able to deceive and confuse the Germans on D-Day, now the Germans were playing their own deceptions and it was the Americans' turn to be confused.

German POW in American uniform

OMAR BRADLEY: English-speaking Germans in captured American OD's[a] had infiltrated our lines in a brash attempt to panic our rear areas. . . . Volunteers were . . . selected and trained by the notorious [German] Lieutenant Colonel Otto Skorzeny, the airborne privateer who the year before had snatched Mussolini out of the Italian hotel in which he had been imprisoned following his fall from power. Most of these GI-uniformed enemy troops were cut down before they reached the Meuse but not until a half-million GI's played cat and mouse with each other each time they met on the road. Neither rank nor credentials nor protests spared the traveler an inquisition at each intersection he passed. Three times I was ordered to prove my identity by cautious GI's. The first time by identifying Springfield as the capital of Illinois (my questioner held out for Chicago); the second time by locating the guard between the center and tackle on a line of scrimmage; the third time by naming the then current spouse of a blonde named Betty Grable. Grable stopped me but the sentry did not. Pleased at having stumped me, he nevertheless passed me on.[14]

[a] *ODs:* Olive Drabs, common term for American battle fatigues

SLAVERY IN THE REICH

ALBERT SHIRER: By the end of September 1944, some seven and a half million civilian foreigners were toiling for the Third Reich. Nearly all of them had been rounded up by force, deported to Germany in boxcars, usually without food or water or any sanitary facilities, and there put to work in the factories, fields and mines. They were not only put to work but degraded, beaten and starved and often left to die for lack of food, clothing and shelter. . . .

In the massive deportations of slave labor to the Reich, wives were torn away from their husbands, and children from their parents, and assigned to widely separated parts of Germany. The young, if they were old enough to work at all, were not spared. Even top generals of the Army cooperated in the kidnaping of children, who were carted off to the homeland to perform slave labor. A memorandum from [East-European Commissioner Alfred] Rosenberg's files of June 12, 1944, reveals this practice in occupied Russia.

"Army Group Center intends to apprehend forty to fifty thousand youths from the age of 10 to 14 . . . and transport them to the Reich. The measure was originally proposed by the Ninth Army. . . . It is intended to allot these juveniles primarily to the German trades as apprentices. . . . This action is being greatly welcomed by the German trade since it represents a decisive measure for the alleviation of the shortage of apprentices.

"This action is not only aimed at preventing a direct reinforcement of the enemy's strength but also as a reduction of his biological potentialities." . . .

But rounding up the slave workers was only the first step. The condition of their transport to Germany left something to be desired. A certain Dr. Gutkelch described one instance in a report to Rosenberg's ministry on September 30, 1942. Recounting how a train packed with returning worked-out Eastern laborers met a train at a siding near Brest Litovsk full of "newly recruited" Russian workers bound for Germany, he wrote:

"Because of the corpses in the trainload of returning laborers a catastrophe might have occurred. . . . In this train women gave birth to babies who were thrown out of the windows during the journey. Persons having tuberculosis and venereal diseases rode in the same car. Dying people lay in freight cars without straw, and one of the dead was thrown on the railway embankment. The same must have occurred in other returning transports."[15]

Displaced persons on rail cars

Hugh Nibley could have quoted long passages from Thucydides in the original Greek, but it's lucky he wasn't given too many questions like these or he might have been taken for a German infiltrator and shared the fate of those that were caught—immediate execution by firing squad. His new assignment was to go out and find the infiltrators who were causing the trouble.

HUGH NIBLEY: The settings were like a spy thriller. We'd meet contacts in certain arranged places, we'd find things in caves where they'd been hidden, and so forth. On the twenty-seventh [of December] I went up with the CIC guys to visit the ruins of a dump that had blown up near Reims. The place was a madhouse. All over France there were a lot of displaced persons wandering around because of the slave laborers that had been liberated or were escaping from German-held areas. We talked with two wild young Russians, but we let them go on their way.

DIARY ENTRY, DECEMBER 29, 1944: A madhouse. Visit the castle by night.

JANUARY 2, 1945: Searched for the fallen plane. Very cold night in the woods.

HUGH NIBLEY: On the third of January we picked up a German girl in a paratrooper uniform. She was all dressed up fit to kill in a brand new store-bought parachuting outfit. She had gone into it for the romantic thrill of it or something. She wasn't carrying any weapons or anything, and she wanted to be captured. She just wanted some romance. She didn't belong to the German army or anything, she just went out on her own to join the war.

French resistance fighters and police work with GIs.

A GI near Luxembourg during the Battle of the Bulge

We spent January 6 and 7 searching caves in the area around Soissons with French soldiers, and we found some supplies the Germans had hidden. The next day we went to a large farm that was being run by Poles who seemed very slippery. We couldn't tell whose side they were on; it could have been either one. The Polish guy running the place was sullen and uncooperative, and he had two sneering, strutting sons who seemed pretty suspicious. We didn't find out much there and went on to search more caves. On the ninth I went to St. Quentin with a CIC guy named Steve Jurcko to interview a Dutchman who we thought might have information. He was weak and foolish and obviously being manipulated by his wife who didn't want him to talk, so he wasn't very helpful. We were always dealing with these kinds of odd characters and getting into petty quarrels with the mayors of small towns and things like that. A lot of that was sort of political business, since we were in border areas that had changed back and forth from being German and French many times in the preceding centuries, depending on who had won the last war, and it was hard to tell where peoples' loyalties lay. The French were on our side, we'd work with them most of all, and they knew what was going on in the villages and so forth, but the French were the French. They were very stubborn, very proud, and didn't want anybody to tell them what to do or anything else. So they made more trouble than the Germans did a lot of the time. In fact they'd sometimes tell us, "We like the Germans better than we like you. It was better when the Boshe were here." Priests were a particular problem because you never knew which side they were on.

Hitler's great Ardennes offensive was a massive failure. The Americans took an initial shock that stunned them, but they quickly pulled themselves together. Eisenhower moved to take advantage of the German gamble, and the German forces never got the gasoline and oil they had planned to capture from the Americans to fuel their attack. The drive for Antwerp was stopped, and the "bulge" turned into a noose around the German army's neck.

DIARY ENTRY, JANUARY 12, 1945: Arrive 3:20 in Paris. Walk through very cold dismal absolutely deserted streets. Ride back to Le Vesigne in a jeep and get a little sleep. It snows all day. In the evening a GI show *Alice in Wonderland.*

9

ENDGAME

ALBERT SPEER: All that was involved by now was empty talk. The failure of the Ardennes offensive meant that the war was over. What followed was only the occupation of Germany, delayed somewhat by a confused and impotent resistance.[1]

Shirer records how Hitler put his own spin on the German defeat at the Bulge:

WILLIAM SHIRER: Although he admitted that the Ardennes offensive had not "resulted in the decisive success which might have been expected," he claimed that it had brought about "a transformation of the entire situation such as nobody would have believed possible a fortnight ago."

"The enemy has had to abandon all his plans for attack. . . . He has had to throw in units that were fatigued. His operational plans have been completely upset. He is enormously criticized at home. It is a bad psychological moment for him. Already he has had to admit that there is no chance of the war being decided before August, perhaps not before the end of next year."[2]

Another "ninety percent success."

As surely as power corrupts, failures will be spun into triumphs as those responsible write "kind" versions of their own histories. But for Germany the war had been lost long before the Battle of the Bulge. Goebbels' propaganda machine fed false hopes to the

Hitler and his mistress, Eva Braun, at The Eagle's Nest, Hitler's retreat in the Alps

German people, and there were still soldiers assigned to carry out the hopeless and increasingly bizarre orders of a Führer who clung to the hope that new miracle weapons would save the country. Even Hitler, though he denied it, knew the game was up. His was a life based on spite, rage, bitterness, and death. Like the heroes of the Teutonic myths, he gloried in slaughter. Over and over he made his claim that loss of the war would mean the annihilation of the German race. As the end approached, his narcissistic obsession with himself as the soul of the German people led him to a conscious decision to destroy himself and the country that he believed took its life from him. Speer recounts what Hitler said as the end approached:

ALBERT SPEER (quoting Hitler): If the war is lost, the people will be lost also. It is not necessary to worry about what the German people will need for elemental survival. On the contrary, it is best for us to destroy even these things. For the nation has proved to be the weaker, and the future belongs solely to the stronger eastern nation. In any case only those who are inferior will remain after this struggle, for the good have already been killed.[3]

Like some cliché plot from an overwrought tragedy, Hitler put out orders to destroy the entire infrastructure of his country so there would be no possibility of rebuilding. The German approach to national suicide was to be, of course, systematic and scientific.

ALBERT SPEER: [A] teletype message came from the Chief of Transportation. Dated March 29, 1945, it read: "Aim is creation of a transportation wasteland in abandoned territory. . . . Shortage of explosives demands resourceful utilization of all possibilities for producing lasting destruction." Included in the list of facilities slated for destruction were, once again, all types of bridges, tracks, roundhouses, all technical installations in the freight depots, workshop equipment, and sluices and locks in our canals. Along with this, simultaneously all locomotives, passenger cars, freight cars, cargo vessels, and barges were to be completely destroyed and the canals and rivers blocked by sinking ships in them. Every type of ammunition was to be employed for this task. If such explosives were not available, fires were to be set and important parts smashed. Only the technician can grasp the extent of the calamity that execution of this order would have brought upon Germany. The instructions were also prime evidence of how a general order of Hitler's was translated into terrifyingly thorough terms.[4]

This destruction of Germany was not done in order to stop the invaders—that was impossible. It was done in pure hatred and spite to achieve two objectives: to leave the invaders with no prize to claim, and to punish the German people who had betrayed Hitler by failing to achieve victory through his deranged leadership. When Hitler made his last flailing offensive move at the Bulge, many of the German soldiers who went into the fight—the ones who were not completely deluded—knew full well they were helping their country commit suicide. They recognized the only real hope for the future of Germany was to make peace with the western Allies and throw their country on the mercy of the democracies, because there would be no mercy from the Russians, not with

Frankfurt, Germany, early 1945

Stalin in charge and not after the German genocide in the Soviet territories and the
abduction of millions of Soviets for slave labor. As they moved into position in the west
for the offensive through the Ardennes, the German soldiers knew that they were

Ike, right, and King George VI, left, with General Bradley in the background

leaving the eastern door weakly guarded and that the Russians would be coming through. Hitler's gamble at the Bulge helped set the stage for a half century of Soviet domination of Central Europe.

HUGH NIBLEY: On the thirteenth of January I was ordered to move from British CIC to 12th Army Group in Luxembourg, and I would be with a guy named Martin and an old friend named Seigfried Kramer. It took me three days to get there. I went up through the bright snow in a truck to Reims, which was now a world of blue and white. I stayed at the transit barracks there, then had a very cold ride to Vouziers, where we got an American-style lunch at the roadhouse at Château-Thierry, the site of the famous World War I battle.[a] I drove the jeep from there to Luxembourg, where I got a place to sleep at the 3rd Army. The next day I went to work in the big warehouse across the tracks there, analyzing captured documents and keeping up on the strength and location of enemy units.

Patton's trucks and tanks were stopped on the street for breakfast, and while I'm looking for the headquarters, I bump into my brother Richard on the sidewalk. We exchanged some classified information—casually, then Richard's unit had to move on. I wondered, when will we meet again? Were we there, chatting on the street in Europe, because of an insane Austrian painter turned politician? What

[a] The battle for Château-Thierry was a critical part of the Second Battle of the Marne and a defining event for the American military. The United States entered World War I late, and there was doubt among the Europeans as to the quality of the American fighting men. When the Germans launched an offensive in the summer of 1918, French Field Marshal Foch sent the fresh American troops to block the spearhead of the attack. In a counterattack, the Americans were able to achieve surprise and stop the German advance. The Americans proved themselves by making a significant contribution to the battle that ended German hopes of winning World War I.

THE SLAVS

Martin Bormann, Hitler's political secretary and the highest ranking Nazi Party official next to the Führer, wrote a letter on July 23, 1942, stating the party's views on the Slavic peoples:

MARTIN BORMANN: The Slavs are to work for us. In so far as we don't need them, they may die. Therefore compulsory vaccination and German health service are superfluous. The fertility of the Slavs is undesirable. They may use contraceptives or practice abortion—the more the better. Education is dangerous. It is enough if they can count up to 100. . . . Every educated person is a future enemy. Religion we leave to them as a means of diversion. As for food they won't get any more than is absolutely necessary. We are the masters. We come first.[5]

Cologne Cathedral, 1945

had produced this vast insanity? My meeting with my brother in Luxembourg is like an episode in a novel—a happening without significance. If Richard had been doing his thing as a tank soldier or I had been doing mine, there would be something to report. But we were just in the army doing the army's thing in a Beetle Bailey world. Neither of us was doing anything. Soldiers must have medals to show that their time has not been wasted. It was worse on the officers, and they tended to hit the bottle.

An army group usually contains several armies, each of which would have several divisions. The 12th Army Group under command of Lieutenant General Omar Bradley had three armies until the Germans pushed their bulge into the Allied lines and made it hard for the 12th AG to communicate with the two armies north of the bulge. This is why Eisenhower had temporarily given command of the two armies north of the bulge to Monty, leaving Bradley with only one—Patton's 3rd Army. So when Hugh Nibley went to work for the 12th AG, he was essentially in Patton's outfit.

LUCIEN GOLDSCHMIDT: I remember seeing him shortly after the Battle of the Bulge. Probably the units were shifted around and he came say, half an hour away from 3rd Army Headquarters [where I was]. That is when I saw Hugh Nibley and he described some of his adventures, although he underplayed it always. He never wanted to seem to be heroic.

It was January 28 before the Allies had recaptured all the land lost in the German offensive and the Battle of the Bulge was officially over. The final curtain was falling, but there was still a very big mess to clean up, including tens of millions of Germans who were not going to sit by as the Allies invaded their homeland. Albert Speer tried to convince Hitler to give up his plan to destroy the country and take some action to ensure that even in defeat the German people would survive. In many cases he deliberately disobeyed the Führer and left facilities intact that Hitler wanted to destroy. That may explain this diary entry by Hugh Nibley.

DIARY ENTRY, JANUARY 23, 1945: German government orders mines to be given over intact. Why?

Through the fog of war it would have been difficult to see at that time, but a strange sort of cooperation was beginning to develop between the Allies, who wanted to defeat the Third Reich but not necessarily to destroy Germany, and the Germans who were convinced the war was lost and were starting to think about how to make sure something—anything—would be left of their country after the smoke cleared.

ALBERT SPEER: On my trip to Upper Silesia, I met General Heinrici, a sensible man with whom I had to collaborate confidentially during the last weeks of the war. At that time, in the middle of February, we decided that the railroad installations which would be needed in the future for distributing coal to southeast Germany were not to be destroyed. Together, we visited a mine near Ribnyk. Although the mine was in the immediate vicinity of the front, the Soviet troops were allowing work to continue there. The enemy, too, seemed to be respecting our policy of nondestruction. The Polish workers had adjusted to the change in the situation. They were working as efficiently as ever, in a sense repaying us for our pledge that we would preserve their place of work if they refrained from sabotage.[6]

Belgium, Feb. 5, 1945

Dear Mother

. . . From Paris I was sent on a safe but quite melodramatic mission to _____, and after a couple of weeks was attached to the present address, first in Luxembourg and now in Belgium. Luxembourg is an unbelievably tidy town, everything so pretty and correct—one is constantly expecting the music (by Lehar) to begin and the lights to go up and a host of blue hussars to begin the opening chorus. The heavenly quiet at nights seems too good to be true. The airborne have been misrepresented, it seems when you are fighting fire with fire a gang of cutthroats can be very useful. . . . You should see the "brass" around here! We are not impressed. Their power-and-authority is a very little thing, if you must take *it* seriously, then the men themselves become ridiculous. . . . As for learning Russian, I think you would do very well to start in on it yourself, and if you know of anything more important please let me know by special delivery. . . . Rich will have it a lot easier pretty soon, but we can expect no security any more—too many people misbehaving.

Love

Hugh

The war was almost over, but if there had ever been any glamour in soldiering it was very dim indeed after the Bulge. Ambrose describes the mood among the 101st in Band of Brothers:

> **STEPHEN AMBROSE:** The veterans resolved not to take any chances. The end of the war was in sight, and they now believed what they could not believe at Bastogne, that they were going to make it. Safe. More or less intact. They wanted to escape the boredom of garrison, they knew how to take care of themselves, they were ready to do their job, but not to be heroes.[7]

The Americans who had faced the Austrian farm boys and unwilling Russian conscripts in Normandy were mostly inexperienced kids with high morale. But a few days in heavy combat ages men years. Now they were seasoned veterans, more experienced and more cautious, moving onto the Reich homeland.

C. P. STACEY: In this, the twilight of their gods, the defenders of the Reich displayed the recklessness of fanaticism and the courage of despair. In the contests west of the Rhine, in particular, they fought with special ferocity and resolution.[8]

DIARY ENTRY, FEBRUARY 16, 1945: Why do not we do anything? The Germans gang up on the southwest and we do nothing.

Frankfurt, 1945

FEBRUARY 18: Sickening the way we do nothing. Why do not you attack? There's nothing there! What a night. What a strange unleashing of power.

FEBRUARY 19: Our generals are still waiting.

Nibley was not alone in his feeling that they should be doing more. At this time General Patton had been ordered to go on the defensive, but he defied his orders and kept attacking. On the day Nibley worried that the generals were still waiting, Patton was writing on the same subject.

> **GEORGE PATTON:** On the nineteenth [of February 1945], I wrote General Bradley a letter saying that all the United States troops except the Third Army were doing nothing at all, and that while I was still attacking, I could do better with more divisions. I asked for from one to three additional. I believe this is the only letter I ever wrote for the record, but I felt very keenly at that time that history would criticize us for not having been more energetic. . . . It always made me mad to have to beg for opportunities to win battles.[9]

As Nibley looked at the top secret Order of Battle maps, he could see what most American soldiers couldn't. American forces were building up in preparation for Operation Grenade, an attack from the southwest that was delayed because the Germans had flooded the Roer Valley to slow down the Allies. This was also another case in which General Montgomery was in command of the operation and once again Americans (at least this one American master sergeant) found reason to chafe at what they saw as the British general's slowness in taking action. Montgomery finally unleashed Operation Grenade on February 23, almost two weeks after it had been scheduled. Monty had another plan in the works as well. It was classic Monty, an enormous set-piece battle that included an amphibious assault across the Rhine as well as the biggest airborne operation of the war—bigger than Normandy, bigger than Arnhem. In Monty style, it took weeks of preparation and enormous masses of men and material.

HUGH NIBLEY: Once we had Antwerp and the harbors and we could take in all the supplies we needed, the object became the Rhine, and that's where they were going

Frankfurt Cathedral, 1945

Young Germans carry their wounded mother.

to use this 17th Airborne Division to which I was to be attached. Among the OB guys I was supposed to be some sort of expert in airborne operations because of my experience with the 101st, but I wasn't looking forward to this one.

DIARY ENTRY, FEBRUARY 20, 1945: Struck again! We are going to go to a new airborne division.

FEBRUARY 22: Or will we?

FEBRUARY 23: Yes.

FEBRUARY 24: No.

FEBRUARY 25: " [ditto marks]

FEBRUARY 26: Now it's for certain.

HUGH NIBLEY: It wasn't certain after all. I was taken off the assignment to the 17th, which didn't break my heart at all. I didn't want another airborne division. I was feeling very low at this time and when we drove down to Paris on some business or other, who should I find there but a man I thought was dead—Berger! The last I'd heard from him had been "Oy, oy oy! De're damagin' da moichendise!" as he was being shelled on his way into Holland. Now he was the acting chief clerk for the Intelligence operations there in Paris, and he was able to catch Major Choos in the right mood and got me a furlough to England.

Maybe what Berger recognized in Hugh Nibley was that he really needed a break. His diary around this time begins to mention depression repeatedly—strange for a man who very rarely mentions any negative feelings of his own. He had come a long way since his basic training, where he found the army fun and relaxing. It seemed the attitude that infected Ambrose's Band of Brothers *was in Nibley as well. Longing for nature and solitude, he set off for the closest thing he could find to Zion Park.*

Russian soldiers in Germany

March 3, 1945

Dear mother,

. . . All of a sudden I get a week's leave for England, so I'm off for the Highlands [censored]—I am almost tempted to call them "my" Highlands, I know them so well, though there is certainly nothing cozy or intimate about them. But they do have a spirit of thoughtful solitude about them which is the most restful thing in the world. And whether it rains or snows the whole time is all the same to me, just so I can have a couple of days alone. Much dashing around recently with frequent changes of scene and language. . . . I have never told you about some of the men I have come to know in the last year. A fantastically large proportion . . . of our soldiers are surprisingly high-minded and well-behaved. It is a sort of army within an army, living in a world of their own but a world in common with many of their fellows. A person of sense or sensibility need never feel himself lost—as seems to have been the case in the last war—men of superior part . . . [censored] are found everywhere in this morass, and waste no time in stating their case. So far as I have been able to make out, this is not the case with the British army, in fact the only Europeans that evince a spark of life today are the Russians. Most of the Russians I have talked to are simply bursting with energy and good spirits and an honest desire to better themselves—there is nothing "negative" about them; the salt of the earth, I say, and the complete antithesis of the contemporary Frenchman. . . . I will try to write you from Scotland.

Love

Hugh

Having lost all faith in the Germans, he begins to mention the Russians more and more and to envision the mantle of cultural leadership falling on the Slavs. Hugh Nibley's belief in the Russians is another thing he had in common with the Führer. Hitler always saw World War II as a great struggle between the Aryan Germanic race and other races, including the inferior Slavs. He dismissed the Western democracies as weak and spoiled, incapable of the great sacrifice necessary for world domination. The Russians were more willing to wage ruthless, all-out war. With repeated defeats, Hitler thought, his people had failed their test and deserved annihilation even if it was at the hands of an inferior race. World leadership would fall to the Russians. Hugh Nibley's reasoning was different, but his conclusion was similar.

ERNIE PYLE: We were sitting in the gun pit one dark morning when word came over the field telephone that a delegation of Russian officers might be around that day on an inspection trip. Whereupon one of the cannoneers said, "Boy, if they show up in a fighting mood I'm taking out of here. They're fighters."

Another one said, "If Uncle Sam ever told me to fight the Russians, I'd just put down my gun and go home. I never could fight people who have done what they have."[10]

Dear Paulus,

. . . Just finished a furlough in my favorite country: there are valleys in the Scottish Highlands which move me almost as deeply as Zion itself. I propose (quite seriously) we walk thru Glen Novis to Loch Leven the next time we get together—it is a weird desolate, volcanic world, savage and primitive in the extreme—wonderfully disquieting. . . .

HUGH NIBLEY: When I got back to Paris I was privileged to have some conversations with "a rose is a rose is a rose" Gertrude Stein. She wanted to be patriotic, you see, and she would give lectures on culture and the war and so forth. So when I got back from Scotland I arranged to meet George Bailey at the Ste. Chapelle and we went and attended one of these lectures. Afterwards she made herself available to American soldiers; she would sit on the window sill there at the club and you could come and talk to her at any time, so we got into a real engaging conversation. She was talking about the French mostly; she was working for them. We discussed their freedom, their independence, their individualism; how they were very private people, very intellectual, and the weaknesses they had were the same. We talked a good deal about it. She was interesting

The next day I was alerted that I was being transferred again, this time to the OB team with the 6th Army Group. My old friend from Ritchize, Oliver Van Patten, was the lieu-

GI Joe meets Ivan in Germany

tenant and Joe Zupsich was the other member. I also knew Zupsich; we had bunked together at Ritchie. He was a good guy. I liked him very much. We were on our way to 6th Army Group headquarters when we stopped in the village of Domrémy where Joan of Arc grew up. While we were there we witnessed a celebration. The children came parading down the street singing, "*Premier, dernier, premier, dernier.*" "Beginning, end, beginning, end."

"*De quoi?*" I said. "Of what?"

"*De l'anée, monsieur!*" It was the beginning and the end of the year that the children were celebrating. It was March 30 when we were in Domrémy, and what I was seeing was actually an ancient Roman rite of spring. At the first of spring all the boys would go around the city and chant in this same way. It was called a "quest song." And when they'd come around and chant the quest song, the people would have to give them a good gift if they wanted to prosper for the year. These are very ancient year rites and I'd written on that subject, so I was enchanted on this beautiful day when the children sang "*premier, dernier.*" So I staged a *sparsio*. I'd published an article on the ancient Roman custom of the *sparsio* where the king goes among the people and disperses gifts. That's what *sparsio* means: "I scatter or disperse." The king throws things to the people as you would scatter grain over the fields, and what he's doing is planting, sowing the

Hitler in the ruins of the "Thousand Year Reich"

seeds of good fortune and prosperity among the people. Well, in Domrémy I had some candy with me, so I sprinkled it to the children like an ancient king performing the *sparsio*. Boy, were they delighted! And this was as it should be, because they had been going around singing the quest song to welcome the first day of spring.

It was an end and a beginning. The eternal cycle was in play, and, like the seasons, Hugh Nibley was returning to where he and Hitler had done their youthful preaching. As Nibley performed his sparsio, *playing the king role in the ancient rite of spring, Hitler removed himself from his public and hid deep underground in a bunker in Berlin. The sound of Russian guns began to be heard in the suburbs of the city. Albert Speer, perhaps the closest thing Hitler ever had to a real friend, described him in the spring of 1945.*

ALBERT SPEER: Now, he was shriveling up like an old man. His limbs trembled; he walked stooped, with dragging footsteps. Even his voice became quavering and lost its old masterfulness. Its force had given way to a faltering, toneless manner of speaking. When he became excited, as he frequently did in a senile way, his voice would start breaking. He still had his fits of obstinacy, but they no longer reminded one of a child's temper tantrums, but of an old man's. His complexion was sallow, his face swollen; his uniform, which in the past he had kept scrupulously neat, was often neglected in this last period of life and stained by the food he had eaten with a shaking hand.

This condition undoubtedly touched his entourage, who had been at his side during the triumphs of his life. I too was constantly tempted to pity him, so reduced was he from the Hitler of the past. Perhaps that was the reason everyone would listen to him in silence when, in the long since hopeless situation, he continued to commit nonexistent divisions or to order units supplied by planes that could no longer fly for lack of fuel. Perhaps that was why no one said a word when he more and more frequently took flight from reality and entered his world of fantasy, when he spoke of the clash between East and West which must be on the point of erupting— when he bade us realize that it was inevitable. Although the

Going house to house through Germany

entourage could scarcely have been blind to the phantasmal character of these ideas, his constant repetitions had some sort of hypnotic effect—as when, for example, he claimed he was now in a position to conquer Bolshevism by the strength of his own personality and in alliance with the West. It sounded believable when he assured us that he was continuing to live only for this turning point, that he personally wished his last hour had come. The very composure with which he looked forward to the end intensified sympathy and commanded respect.[11]

Hugh Nibley's first encounter with Hitler as a young man had revealed the Nazi leader to be human—coming out of a restroom. "Wozelbest der Kaiser muss: The place even the Kaiser must go." Now Nibley was coming back to witness the confirmation of his first impression of the Führer.

HUGH NIBLEY: I was assigned to the 6th Army Group and went into Germany, the same area where I had served as a missionary sixteen years earlier, and it was familiar territory. It struck me that it is infinitely harder to go through a hostile village as a missionary than it is as a soldier. As a missionary it was a clash of minds, because the people were tremendously hostile. When I went through some of the same villages with a carbine, dashing from door to door, I would think time and again, this is so much easier than trying to confront these people eye to eye. Shooting at a distance was much nicer and much safer.

DAVE GROSSMAN: The *potential* of close-up, inescapable, *inter*personal hatred and aggression is more effective and has greater impact on the morale of the soldier than the *presence* of inescapable, *im*personal death and destruction.[12]

The once orderly Germans loot wagons for food.

As the war wound down, the pace of the Allied advance sped up, with units moving toward the heart of the Reich from all directions at once, like a boa constrictor tightening its grip. But as the physical momentum increased, the moral focus of the fight blurred. Soldiers lost the vision that had made their jobs so clear in Normandy. Their belief in what they were doing became clouded with cynicism. Evil was rampant in the war from the start on both sides: the malicious officer who ordered Nibley to use a toilet brush to prepare the officers' mess; the colonel who would give a man ten years hard labor because he asked him for the password; the rapists at the Norman church wedding; the industrialist in Holland, protected by both sides, who profited from the death surrounding his luxurious home.

But there was great goodness too: men who did their dangerous jobs in spite of the fear and the pain, because they knew it was right; the "suckers" who jumped from planes and rode fragile gliders into Normandy and Holland; the medic who swam the canal under fire from both sides, then went back into the lines without even a three-day pass. As the pressure lessened, the human greatness that emerges under great stress receded and stripped bare the naked tawdriness that lies underneath the heroic armor of war. The warriors' virtues dissolved into a sea of pettiness, into the surreal world of Catch-22,[a] with a dose

---

[a] Hugh Nibley claimed *Catch-22* was the most accurate book he ever read on the military. I took that as possible hyperbole until I mentioned it to a retired air force colonel who told me he had been assigned the book in the Air Force Academy where the professor had pointed out that *Catch-22* has been compared to *Alice through the Looking Glass* by literary critics.

of Alice through the Looking Glass *thrown in. Once the moral certainty that drove men on all sides of the conflict was gone, they were adrift. There was still much to do, but less to believe in. Except getting home. There were very few idealists in Europe in the spring of 1945.*

HUGH NIBLEY: I ended up in Heidelberg at the headquarters for General Devers[a] and the 6th Army Group. That's where all the fancy people were, and they kept giving each other medals every Thursday and this, that, and the other. General Devers liked comfort, and he wanted everybody to be comfortable. We enjoyed ourselves in Heidelberg. This was the center of German education, and when I had been a missionary in that region I had seriously considered returning to go to school in Heidelberg. Also, the city had not been touched by the war and stood all intact.[b] The first thing after we got there, some old friends of mine from Ritchie went to look for a good respectable frat house for the non-coms, because we wanted our own club. Heidelberg is of course where the tradition of university fraternities reached its zenith and the city was full of wonderful mansions used by the fraternities, so our guys went to this very elegant one, the Germania House. I wasn't there, but they told me about it. They said, "We went up and knocked on the door and a butler in full-dress livery—everything but a powdered wig—came to the door and looked at us in surprise and said, 'Well, you people were here yesterday. We don't have any of the records any more. They're all gone.'

"'What records? What happened?' we said.

"'Well, they had these big trucks, and we took all the records out and put them in the trucks and they took them away.'

"We said, 'What records?'

"'Your Standard Oil records. We had all your Standard Oil Company records here,' the butler said."

It seems there was an agreement that we wouldn't bomb Heidelberg if they

[a] General Jacob L. Devers (1887-1979) was an expert on tank warfare and had previously served as Deputy Commander-in-Chief, Allied Force Headquarters, and Deputy Supreme Allied Commander, Mediterranean Theater of Operations. After the war he was named Commander of the Army Ground Forces.

[b] There were reasons Heidelberg had not been destroyed. One was that it was the hometown of Albert Speer, the Reich's Minister for Armament and War Production. He visited the city in late March 1945. "The Americans had already taken Mannheim, only twelve miles away, and were slowly advancing toward Heidelberg. After a nocturnal discussion with Mayor Neinhaus of Heidelberg, I offered a last service to my native city—by writing to SS General Hausser, whom I already knew from my work in the Saar, and asking him to declare Heidelberg a hospital city to be surrendered without a fight" (Speer, *Inside the Third Reich*, 449).

wouldn't bomb Oxford, so they had all the Standard Oil records there in Heidelberg. Of course, Standard Oil had been hand-in-glove with the German Bayer concern that was famous for making aspirin but also made a lot of other things. Joseph Borkin wrote a book about that, *The Crime and Punishment of I. G. Farben.* They built Auschwitz, for example, and they were so bad that the SS—mind you, the SS!—pleaded with them to let up on the poor prisoners because they couldn't produce unless they got something to eat, and they were just dying like flies. When I first went on my mission in the late twenties, I was sent to Ludwigshafen for the first few months, and everybody there was talking about the greatest explosion in

Hugh Nibley in Germany, 1945

German history that had taken place at the Oppau factory, the I. G. Farben factory at Ludwigshafen, this sordid industrial town.

At this time the Germans were very restricted in what military materials they could produce, and they were supposed to be producing fertilizer in this plant, but they'd been making high explosives. They took us through the factory and showed us the processes that the chemicals would go through, and at the end out comes ammonium nitrate for fertilizer, and they had these little bags of fertilizer they were filling. But of course ammonium nitrate can also be used for explosives, so a little trickle of fertilizer would flow from this huge factory, but everybody knew that what they were doing was making munitions. And I. G. Farben was hand-in-glove with Standard Oil. The companies were in partnership, and they protected each others' patents and they exchanged their knowledge and formulas during the war. Bayer aspirin, Hoechst, BASF—they're still among the biggest corporations in the world, and they were all parts of I. G. Farben. And all this was going on, and we'd

I.G. FARBEN: STANDARD OIL, PART II

The company that got Standard Oil to help protect its technological secrets from the U.S. went on to be a major force in the Nazi war machine. After the company built the concentration camp at Auschwitz, it operated a large plant there using slave labor, making synthetic rubber with the technology they had kept from Americans. I.G. was also the company that manufactured Zyclon-B, which was the gas pumped through showerheads in gas chambers to kill large numbers of undesirable people such as Jews.

Although the gas was considered a marvelous piece of efficiency—far faster and more economical than shooting people—I.G. discovered an even more efficient way of killing people at its labor camp in Auschwitz. Unlike other slave-based economies, such as that in pre-Civil War America, where slaves were viewed as valuable livestock to be bred and fed to get the most work out of them, the Nazis' slaves were meant to work toward the complete annihilation of their own races. So, with a simple formula of extracting more calories of work from inmates than the amount of calories they were fed, the Nazis found they could simply work people to death.

JOSEPH BORKIN: Conditions were such that sickness was a pervasive fact of life among the inhabitants of Monowitz [the I.G. slave labor camp at Auschwitz]. The hospital wards built by I.G. were so inadequate that even the S.S. suggested additional wards be built. I.G. refused because of the cost. . . .

Starvation was a permanent guest at Auschwitz. The diet fed to I.G. Auschwitz inmates . . . resulted in an average weight loss for each individual of about six and a half to nine pounds a week. At the end of a month, the change in the prisoner's appearance was marked; at the end of two months, the inmates were not recognizable except as caricatures formed of skin, bones, and practically no flesh; after three months, they were either dead or so unfit for work that they were marked for release to the gas chambers at Birkenau. Two physicians who studied the effect of the I.G. diet on the inmates noticed that "the normally nourished prisoner at Buna could make up the deficiency by his own body for a period of three months. . . . The prisoners were condemned to burn up their own body weight while working and, providing no infections occurred, finally died of exhaustion."[13]

The factory at Oppau was a technological wonder of its time and the first factory to produce synthetic nitrates, which were critical to the Germans during World War I when their traditional source of nitrates from Chile were cut off. Borkin tells what happened after that war ended.

JOSEPH BORKIN: Within weeks after the armistice, Allied troops poured into the Rhineland. No sooner had the occupying forces settled down than the infant chemical warfare services of the Allied armies began to press for the disclosure of the secret processes and production methods in use at the various I.G. plants turning out poison gases, explosives, dyestuffs, and nitrates. The I.G. companies resisted on the ground that such disclosure would adversely affect their commercial position in the postwar world. Unlike the French, the Americans and the British were careful not unduly to upset the I.G. officials. Assurances were given that the investigators would not "pry into secrets of commercial value in times of peace." No technology would have to be revealed nor questions answered unless they concerned weapons or military applications. . . .

The investigators soon became aware that [the nitrate plant at Oppau] represented a fundamental scientific breakthrough as well as a triumph of ingenuity and skill without which Germany could not have continued to fight as long as it did. . . .

However, when the French members of the investigating team demanded that the plant be started up so that it could be observed in operation, Bosch stubbornly refused. All attempts to move him, including threats of severe consequences, proved futile. The outraged French petitioned the Allied commission to force Bosch to operate the equipment and reveal the know-how and basic elements of the process of nitrate synthesis. To the disgust of the French, the commission ruled in support of Bosch, holding that the process was a commercial, not a military, affair.[14]

Hugh Nibley's statement that there was a deal to spare certain cities from bombing for commercial reasons may sound extreme, but Speer also mentions a deal that was made to spare at least one other I.G. Farben facility.

ALBERT SPEER: [Field Marshal] Model decided not to use the largest pharmaceutical plant in Germany, Bayer-Leverkusen [an I.G. Farben concern], as an artillery base. He agreed to inform the enemy and request him to spare the factory.[15]

bumbled onto it in Heidelberg. The place we were trying to get for an NCO club was full of Standard Oil records.

On April 16 Marshal Zhukov[a] was in the outskirts of Berlin, and his First Byelorussian Front began their assault on the city. In the first few days of the battle they fired 27,000 tons of artillery shells into the city.

Germany, April 17, 1945

Dear Mother,

. . . This unstable life is a delight after the hard grind of the 101st. This is high tide for the opportunists, among them Springer: one would like to ignore them, but they are going to wreck everything, just wait and see. Aunt Clara's honey is a tower of refuge in a world without sweets. The Germans have changed—much for the worst—after their intensive course in autoinfatuation. . . . Glad you are not here. . . .

Heidelberg, April, 1945

Dear Mother

. . . At last it seems that I have been *paid*—the first time since November! The Army with its matchless ingenuity misplaced my records (that is why you got no bonds) but now they have been found everything is just too lovely. . . . The Army is no more incompetent than it ever was, only during operations its blunders are strict military secrets: oy! I should write a book, me with my grandstand seat—always the hotly detached observer. You mentioned something about the British—what they did, or didn't do, was shocking, but the blame was all with their commanders. . . . I wonder about the Germans. Other people have their vices as opposed to their virtues, but the Germans' vices *are* their virtues and vice versa; by an act of that *Will* they are forever talking about, they turn good qualities into vicious ones or clothe any crime that suits them in moral garments. They remain, after

[a] Soviet Marshal Georgi Konstantinovich Zhukov (1896-1974) commanded the final offensive against Germany and is considered by many to be the greatest general of World War II. He is certainly recognized as one of the greatest heroes of the eastern European war where the fighting was much worse than in the West and where the Soviets gave the German army 80 percent of its casualties.

all, still the most dangerous people in the world—unwilling to distinguish good from bad. . . . The atmosphere here is quite interesting though it is portentous with future ills. The God of Battles has become the God of Brothels, and those whom I know for the best of Saints*a* have given up their good works in weary disgust and turned to the ways of the world in the worst possible sense. I don't know a single exception. The Army is exacting a frightful toll for its noisy services.

Love
Hugh

a Saints: Short for Latter-day Saints or Mormons

On April 25 American soldiers met Russian soldiers at the Elbe River and shook hands and traded cigarettes and vodka. Five days later, as Russian shells exploded on the streets above his underground bunker in Berlin, Adolf Hitler married his longtime mistress, Eva Braun.

WILLIAM SHIRER: They finished their farewells and retired to their rooms. Outside in the passageway, Dr. Goebbels, Bormann and a few others waited. In a few moments a revolver shot was heard. They waited for a second one, but there was only silence. After a decent interval they quietly entered the Fuehrer's quarters. They found the body of Adolf Hitler sprawled on the sofa dripping blood. He had shot himself in the mouth. At his side lay Eva Braun. Two revolvers had tumbled to the floor, but the bride had not used hers. She had swallowed poison.[16]

Then came May 7, the day Hugh Nibley had predicted the war would end. Shirer describes it in The Rise and Fall of the Third Reich:

WILLIAM SHIRER: In a little red schoolhouse at Reims, where Eisenhower had made his headquarters, Germany surrendered unconditionally at 2:41 on the morning of May 7, 1945. . . . [Gen.] Jodl asked permission to say a word and it was granted.

"With this signature the German people and the German Armed Forces are, for better or worse, delivered into the hands of the victors. . . . In this hour I can only express the hope that the victor will treat them with generosity."

Looting in Munich

There was no response from the Allied side. But perhaps Jodl recalled another occasion when the roles were reversed just five years before. Then a French general, in signing France's unconditional surrender at Compiègne, had made a similar plea—in vain, as it turned out.[17]

ª Bauern:
Peasants

DIARY ENTRY, MAY 7, 1945: P.M. off to Koenigstohl and then down the Neckar talking with *Bauern.*[ª] Still the same good, uninterested Germans.

HUGH NIBLEY: It was so ridiculous! One minute you were shooting madly at somebody, trying to kill him, the next minute—because somebody signed a piece of paper—you were the best of friends. It was the funniest thing you ever heard of. In Reims they signed the agreement, and the war was over. All of a sudden we said, "Isn't that great!" and we all ran out and embraced each other. It was so ridiculous!

WILLIAM SHIRER: The guns in Europe ceased firing and the bombs ceased dropping at midnight on May 8–9, 1945, and a strange but welcome silence settled over the Continent for the first time since September 1, 1939. In the intervening five years, eight months and seven days millions of men and women had been slaughtered on a hundred battlefields and in a thousand bombed towns, and millions more done to death in the Nazi gas chambers or on the edge of the S.S. Einsatzgruppen pits in Russia and Poland—as the result of Adolf Hitler's lust for German conquest. A greater part of most of Europe's ancient cities lay in ruins, and from their rubble, as the weather warmed, there was the stench of the countless unburied dead.

No more would the streets of Germany echo to the jack boot of the goose-stepping storm troopers or the lusty yells of the brown-shirted masses or the shouts of the Fuehrer blaring from the loudspeakers.

After twelve years, four months and eight days, an Age of Darkness to all but a multitude of Germans and now ending in a bleak night for them too, the Thousand-Year Reich had come to an end. It had raised, as we have seen, this great nation and this resourceful but so easily misled people to heights of power and con-quest they had never before experienced and now it had dissolved with a suddenness and a completeness that had few, if any, parallels in history.[18]

DIARY ENTRY, MAY 9, 1945: Ridiculous lecture on non-fraternizing. The neurotic Rosenbaum has moved on to my balcony.

STEPHEN AMBROSE: It should have been the most perfect summer ever for the men of E Company. In fact, after the first couple of weeks,

GIs and German girls at a hotel in Germany

GIs throw snowballs from Hitler's private getaway.

most of them hated it. They were frustrated by the Army bureaucracy, they were bored, they were drinking far too much, and they wanted to go home.

Getting home depended on points, which became virtually the sole topic of conversation and led to much bad feeling. The point system set up by the Army gave a man points for each active duty service month, points for campaigns, points for medals, points for being married. The magic number was 85 points. Those with that many or more were eligible for immediate shipment home and discharge. Those with fewer points were doomed to stay with the division, presumably right on through to the Big Jump in China or Japan.[19]

HUGH NIBLEY: It was at this time, after the war ended, that I really had a chance to see things. We had the jeep and we could go pretty much where we wanted to go, so we went all over. We drove down into Austria and everywhere else, going to various places that had been involved in the war and asking what had been going on in those areas. I got an earful on that trip. We drove in two jeeps with Van Patten, another guy named Wooten, and a third called Vincent via the Autobahn to Munich, where we stayed at the hideout of some bigwig. Then we went around seeing all the sights in Munich, which was nothing but ruins. The next day we stopped off at Chiemsee, a lake outside of Munich, had lunch in Heisendorf in the Tyrol, then went to Salzburg and Ober Salzburg to Berchtesgaden. The 101st was everywhere up there because that's where they had ended the war, up there in Hitler's old hideout.

As the Allies had been closing in on the Reich, there were a lot of rumors of "were-wolves" hiding in the mountains of southern Germany. This was the name supposedly given to secret SS forces that remained loyal to Hitler, who were to hide out in the mountains and continue to wage a guerilla insurgency against the Allies after Germany collapsed. Hitler would lead them from his mountain hideaway at Berchtesgaden, and there they would hold out for years until the Third Reich could rebuild and make a comeback. Allied commanders took the rumors seriously, particularly when their Intelligence reports showed a disproportionate number of elite SS units transferred to southern regions. As it turned out, the werewolves were another of Goebbels' propaganda fairytales. Resistance was light, and the 101st easily captured Hitler's Eagle's Nest.

HUGH NIBLEY: It was a bright morning in Berchtesgaden so I said, let's go up to the Eagle's Nest, up there where Hitler had his headquarters. So we drove right up

The Eagle's Nest in the hands of the Allies

the road. There was nobody up there. There was the balustrade where Hitler had his picture taken with Eva Braun overlooking the mountains, and that's where we parked the jeep and went in. When we got in the door we heard a lot of scuffling of feet and banging of doors and so forth, and we looked around. There was nobody in there but you could smell cigarette smoke quite strongly, and there was a cup of coffee on the table. I went over to it, and the coffee was still warm. Apparently a caretaker or somebody had just been there. We didn't know who, but whoever it was had scampered out of there in a hurry. And then I saw an interesting thing: there was a nice pile of the most beautiful stationery you ever saw. It seemed to be on real vellum with pure gold stamped on it: *Führer Haupt Quartier*—"Headquarters of the Führer." I got a bundle of that stuff and took it home with me. Dad wanted to show it to some of his friends, so he took it. I think he sold it; I don't know. I never saw it again, but it was elegant stuff.

Then we went down to the village, and the guys wanted to go and get a beer. We stopped and I waited out with the jeep while they drank their beer. While I was waiting I looked up at this big old timbered house, and on the top floor I saw a face looking very intensely at me, with this very fierce expression. The look he gave me! And I looked at him and by George, it was Martin Bormann!

Martin Bormann, center, with German officers

He was the man the Allies were trying to get, the highest ranking Nazi after Hitler that hadn't yet been caught or killed. I was absolutely sure it was him, because I'd seen lots of pictures of him and they told us to be looking out for him, and when I saw him I said, "That's the guy!" The Allies were trying hard to get him, so I went inside and got the guys away from their beer so we could go up and see what was what up there. But by the time I got back he was gone, of course. He really got out in a hurry. The other guys wouldn't believe it was Bormann. I couldn't make them believe it, so we just left. We didn't bother to search for him. We said, "Well, if he gets away they'll just get him somewhere else, I suppose." But they never did get him. Years later I wrote a report on that to a friend of mine who was working with the military. It was taken seriously and published. They had traced Martin Bormann, and the Berchtesgaden area is where they believe he was at that time. I'm quite sure that it was him I was looking at that day in the Bavarian Alps. As far as I know I may have been the last person to see and recognize Secretary to the Führer Martin Bormann.[a]

After Bertesgaden it was on to Innsbruck, Austria, where we stayed overnight in Mozart's hometown at the guardhouse of the 103rd Division. One of the things you saw a lot of after the war were DPs—displaced persons—because of all the people from all over Eastern Europe the Germans had brought to the Reich to be enforced laborers. While we were there in Innsbruck, three MPs found some Russian girls who were enforced laborers trying to get back home. The Germans called them *Katinka,* Russian girls who were impressed into enforced labor and had to come to Germany to work. We were in a hotel in Innsbruck on the

"Katinkas"

[a] Some sources claim Bormann was killed trying to escape Berlin, others that he committed suicide. In 1973, the German government declared Bormann legally dead, but there is still controversy about his final end. According to *The Penguin Dictionary of the Third Reich,* "Even in Hitler's retreat to the Bunker, Bormann continued his climb to power. He witnessed Hitler's will and marriage, tried to order Göring's execution, saw Göbbels' death and sent Dönitz news of his succession as Führer. When Hitler was dead, he considered trying to treat with the Russians but, realizing this was hopeless, he ordered a mass breakout from the Bunker. He was never seen alive again, although persistent rumours have placed him in several countries, usually in South America. He was tried *in absentia* with the twenty-one other major war criminals at Nuremberg, found guilty and sentenced to death" (Taylor and Shaw, *Penguin Dictionary of the Third Reich,* 48).

top floor, and these three girls came in. These *Katinkas* had served as house servants and were all very capable. They were walking from Germany back to Russia again or to the Ukraine, and they had nothing. It was raining, it was cold, they had nothing but thin linen housedresses, and they were as happy as larks because they were going home. They took the room next to ours, and in the middle of the night these MPs got drunk and tried to get in and take advantage of the girls. A mistake they never should have made. You should have seen them come flying out of there. The girls beat the tar out of them. In the morning at 6 o'clock I could hear singing, and I looked out the window. There were these same girls going down the road, singing in the rain, happy as larks on the way back to Russia. I had to admire them; they showed real spirit. They weren't to be fooled with.[a]

We drove all over Central Europe, through the snow over the Arlberg Pass between Austria and Italy, past castles, falls, and mountains to Bregenz in Lindau, a wonderful plateau through the Schwarzwald to Offenburg. I climbed the Heiligenberg up to the monastery on top of it and went to a lot of other places too. Then we went to see the 9th Division boys at Dachau. They showed us through the concentration camp, which had been liberated by the 101st. This was on May 27, a month after the liberation, and we saw pictures of what had been there. They had cleared out the bones and things like that pretty well by then, though we saw some of them. But it was ghastly enough, even then, Dachau was.

Viktor Frankl had been transferred from Auschwitz to Dachau and was there when the Americans liberated it. He writes:

VIKTOR FRANKL: And now to the last chapter in the psychology of a prison camp—the psychology of the prisoner who has been

[a] Shirer describes the lot of Russian women forced to work in the Reich:
"Even the Slav women seized and shipped to Germany for domestic service were treated as slaves. As early as 1942 Hitler had commanded Sauckel to procure a half million of them 'in order to relieve the German housewife.' The slave labor commissar laid down the conditions of work in German households.
" 'There is no claim to free time. Female domestic workers from the East may leave the household only to take care of domestic tasks. . . . It is prohibited for them to enter restaurants, movies, theaters and similar establishments. Attending church is also prohibited. . . .'
"Women, it is obvious, were almost as necessary as men in the Nazi slave labor program. Of some three million Russian civilians pressed into service by the Germans, more than one half were women. Most of them were assigned to do heavy farm work and to labor in the factories" (Shirer, *Rise and Fall of the Third Reich*, 1239–40).

released. In describing the experiences of liberation, which naturally must be personal, we shall pick up the threads of that part of our narrative which told of the morning when the white flag was hoisted above the camp gates after days of high tension. This state of inner suspense was followed by total relaxation. But it would be quite wrong to think that we went mad with joy. What, then, did happen?

Slaves in layers at Buchenwald

With tired steps we prisoners dragged ourselves to the camp gates. Timidly we looked around and glanced at each other questioningly. Then we ventured a few steps out of camp. This time no orders were shouted at us, nor was there any need to duck quickly to avoid a blow or kick. Oh no! This time the guards offered us cigarettes! We hardly recognized them at first; they had hurriedly changed into civilian clothes. We walked slowly along the road leading from the camp. Soon our legs hurt and threatened to buckle. But we limped on; we wanted to see the camp's surroundings for the first time with the eyes of free men. "Freedom"—we repeated to ourselves, and yet we could not grasp it. We had said this word so often during all the years we dreamed about it, that it had lost its meaning. Its reality did not penetrate into our consciousnesses; we could not grasp the fact that freedom was ours.

We came to meadows full of flowers. We saw and realized that they were there, but we had no feelings about them. The first spark of joy came when we saw a rooster with a tail of multicolored feathers. But it remained only a spark; we did not yet belong to this world.[20]

THE LIBERATION OF DACHAU

WILLIAM COWLING: The first thing we came to were piles and piles of clothing, shoes, pants, shirts, coats, etc. Then we went into a room with a table with flowers on it and some soap and towels. Another door with the word showers led off of this and upon going through this room it appeared to be a shower room but instead of water, gas came out. Next we went next door to four large ovens where they cremated the dead. Then we were taken to piles of dead. There were from two to fifty people in a pile all naked, starved and dead. There must have been about 1,000 dead in all. Then we went through a building where fifty men were guarded in a room the size of your kitchen. There were hundreds of typhus cases and all through the camp men cheered us and tried to touch us. Incidentally many of the dead and living showed signs of horrible beatings and torture. It is unbelievable how any human can treat others as they were treated. One wasted little man came up and touched my sleeve and kissed my hand. He spoke perfect English and I asked him if he were American. He said no, Jewish and that he was one of the very few left, that thousands had been killed. He had been there six years. He was twenty-eight years old and looked to be sixty years old. The Germans I took prisoner are very fortunate they were taken before I saw the camp. I will never take another German prisoner armed or unarmed. How can they expect to do what they have done and simply say I quit and go scot free. They are not fit to live.[21]

The crematorium at Buchenwald

Part of the Dachau complex was liberated by Hugh Nibley's old companions of the 101st Airborne, as Ambrose recounts:

STEPHEN AMBROSE: [Easy Company] was present in the morning when the people of Landsberg turned out, carrying rakes, brooms, shovels, and marched off to the camp [which was part of the Dachau complex]. General Taylor, it turned out, had been so incensed by the sight that he had declared martial law and ordered everyone from fourteen to eighty years of age to be rounded up and sent to the camp, to bury the bodies and clean up the place. That evening the crew came back down the road from the camp. Some were still vomiting.[22]

Even the top brass could get very emotional about what they found in the concentration camps. General Bradley wrote of Eisenhower's reaction:

OMAR BRADLEY: "I can't understand the mentality that would compel these German people to do a thing like that," Ike said. "Why, our soldiers could never mutilate bodies the way the Germans have."

"Not all the Krauts can stomach it," Patton's deputy chief of staff explained. "In one camp we paraded the townspeople through to let them have a look. The mayor and his wife went home and slashed their wrists."

"Well, that's the most encouraging thing I've heard," Ike said slowly. "It may indicate that some of them still have a few sensitivities left."[23]

Germans under American guard unearth a mass grave.

HUGH NIBLEY: I went up into the French Alps, up to Grenoble and Chambéry and Aix-les-Bains. We stayed in a cabin and went out and raided cornfields with some local boys. They had American corn, the only place you could get American corn in all France, I suppose. I told these local boys that it was edible and they got quite excited.

> Dear Mother
>
>   . . . For the past month I have been in Heidelberg, which has not been scratched by the war. Mannheim and Ludwigshafen have simply ceased to exist. The weeks with the 6th Army Group have been delightful: we live in sumptuous quarters and have a club that makes the pavilions of the Golden Horn look like something on the wrong side of the tracks. What the future holds is up to nobody. All I control is my own mental process, which simply ignores the army, and that is all the power I ever want to have. Hereafter when anything important transpires I will be allowed to let you know immediately. Meanwhile we are moving with unerring compliance to prophecy straight into the Next War: nobody seems to believe even half-heartedly that the peace is permanent. We never will learn that there is no point to being clever: every sharp operator in Europe has walked right into his own trap. If we know what's good for us we won't tangle with the Russians—ever: in one week the German break-through in the Ardennes had us scraping the bottom of the barrel, though we were dealing with less than a third of the German Army. Unlike other armies the Russians have an unbelievable capacity for learning; unhampered by pride or tradition they have a positive veneration for truth and never seem to be able to learn enough; their vitality is fabulous, and their birth-rate is simply out of sight. I think the Lord has big things in mind for them.

> **GUSTAVE GILBERT:** It occurred to me why Goering had mentioned to me slyly that the Russians would not let [Admiral] Raeder be executed, and hinted that the Russians had better use for Raeder. [Admiral] Doenitz had apparently decided that his trump card was to show the Americans that they had better use for him. Thus, the game of playing the East against the West continues behind the scenes, with the admirals already choosing up sides for the next

war, before the peace treaty has even been signed for this one.[24]

Suddenly medals were becoming very valuable. The point system gave credit for decorations, and a bronze star was worth five points, which could put a soldier weeks closer to home.

STEPHEN AMBROSE: Inevitably the Army's hierarchical and bureaucratic systems played favorites. Lieutenant Foley recalled "the regimental adjutant who picked up a Bronze Star for—according to rumor—selecting the Hotel Zell for [Colonel] Sink's HQ."[25]

The 101st at Berchtesgaden

HUGH NIBLEY: Every Thursday at 6th AG Headquarters there would be a big formation in the courtyard, and the staff there would give out bronze stars to each other. The army put a quota so it wouldn't get too out of hand: 60 percent of the soldiers getting bronze stars had to be enlisted men, so they couldn't all be officers goofing off.

DIARY ENTRY, JUNE 8, 1945: Captain [name unclear] gets a medal for the African landing, which took place while he was still a civilian in the states.

HUGH NIBLEY: At the end of World War II, the generals were very discouraged. When I was in Heidelberg with the 6th Army Group under General Devers, you could cut the gloom at headquarters with a knife. The war was winding down too fast. It meant the end of quick promotions. It meant the slowing down of careers. The officers were

Frankfurt ruins with Frankfurt Cathedral, 1945

thinking some of them would have to be out of the army altogether and go back to selling washing machines. They were colonels with all this power and privilege, and it had been a lark for most of them; to see it all end was a tragedy.

Then they discovered the concept of brushfire wars. It was General Taylor who burst in one day in high glee. He had been over to Washington and he was back, so excited he could hardly contain himself. They had discovered we could always have these little wars where we can go in and mop up and get our promotions. We can get our practice, we can keep in drill, and we can always keep pressure on Congress for more money because these are going on. It's ideal. We could have these little wars going on continuously with no great risk.

GUSTAVE GILBERT: [Accused (later acquitted) Nazi war criminal Hjalmar Schacht, Reichsbank President and German Minister of Economics said,] "If the military profession is honorable, it is the most self-effacing profession in the world because its duty is to prevent its use." We discussed militarism a little further and agreed that experience had shown that, when German militarism was faced with a showdown between peace and war, the training, obedience, and ambition of the generals swung the decision in favor of war.[26]

DIARY ENTRY, JUNE 18, 1945: To Frankfurt by the Bergstrasses with Zupsich. The vast muni[tions] works at Hoechst have not been camouflaged. No bomb ever found the area in spite of what the BBC said. Returned by autobahn to find the team has been broken up.

HUGH NIBLEY: In mid-June I went to Frankfurt. I'd been there on my mission and knew the area, so I scouted all around on my own and talked to the head man at the vast munitions works at Hoechst, just eight miles from Frankfurt. They called him the custodian, but it was a huge factory, and he was really the manager in charge of the factory. Well, I found out that all during the war they had bombed the devil out of Frankfurt and never touched Hoechst. The munitions plant was never defended; it had no antiaircraft; it never had a blackout. Everybody near there had blackouts every night, but they never had any at the plant in Hoechst; they worked all night with bright lights. The BBC announced repeated bombings, but it was never touched. I heard that was because there was British money in it. Everyone was puzzled at that time why some of these places had never been bombed during the war like Hoechst and Heidelberg. I was finding out things I shouldn't be finding out, I suppose. It looked as though from the beginning the whole thing was operated, controlled, and orchestrated by the same interest on both sides.

Dear Mother,

. . . This place is Gmund, in the heart of Wurttemberg. It is on the edge of what is called the Swabian Jura—a land of sharp little hills and extensive woods, as green as Oregon. It is also rabidly Nazi. The beer is very good, but as usual I stick to stronger stuff, having found that where beer puts you to sleep, water wakes you up. . . . You may wonder what anyone could do now that could be of assured permanent value. With the passing days a thousand petty skills and techniques, once prized above fine gold, turn out to be worse than worthless. Our vast bomber fleets barely got into their stride before they were as obsolete as so many slings and battle axes. . . . Everywhere in Europe they are having bumper crops this year, which is a break if there ever was one. Nobody as yet seems at all interested in the atom bomb, which has already made the next war inevitable and perhaps final—it is a beautifully apt expression of the general sub-conscious and I for one am heartily glad that we are in for a showdown. If we must act with the high-handed immorality of the [Norse] gods it is only right to have our bluff called and the reins thrust into our hands—but of course there can only be one end to the farce. . . .

Love,

Hugh

HUGH NIBLEY: Late one moonlit night I was driving Van Patten down the main street in Karlsruhe past the big church in the bright moonlight. The city was all in ruins; it had all just been wiped out by firebombs from the English planes. They just smashed the whole city. Suddenly I jammed on the brakes and ground to a halt. Van Patten said, "What's wrong?" There was the framework of the door to the

Running from bombs in Germany

FIRESTORMS

GWYNNE DYER: Huge numbers of four-pound incendiaries [were used] to start fires on roofs and thirty-pound ones to penetrate deeper inside buildings, together with four-thousand-pound high-explosive bombs to blow in doors and windows over wide areas and fill the streets with craters and rubble to hinder firefighting equipment. But on a hot, dry summer night with good visibility, the unusually tight concentration of the bombs in a densely populated working-class district created a new phenomenon in history: a firestorm.

Eventually it covered an area of about four square miles, with an air temperature at the centre of eight hundred degrees Celsius and convection winds blowing inward with hurricane force. One survivor said the sound of the wind was "like the Devil laughing." . . . Practically all the apartment blocks in the firestorm area had underground shelters, but nobody who stayed in them survived; those who were not cremated died of carbon monoxide poisoning. But to venture into the streets was to risk being swept by the wind into the very heart of the firestorm.[27]

RAF CREW: It seemed as though the whole of Hamburg was on fire from one end to the other and a huge column of smoke was towering well above us—and we were on 20,000 feet!

Set in the darkness was a turbulent dome of bright red fire, lighted and ignited like the glowing heart of a vast brazier. I saw no streets, no outlines of buildings, only brighter fires which flared like yellow torches against a background of bright red ash. Above the city was a misty red haze. I looked down, fascinated but aghast, satisfied yet horrified.[28]

TRAUTE KOCHE: Mother wrapped me in wet sheets, kissed me, and said, "Run!" I hesitated at the door: In front of me I could see only fire—everything red, like the door to a furnace. An intense heat struck me. A burning beam fell in front of my feet. I shied back but then, when I was ready to jump over it, it was whirled away by a ghostly hand. The sheets around me acted as sails and I had the feeling that I was being carried away by the storm. I reached the front of a five-storey building . . . which . . . had been bombed and burned out in a previous raid and there was not much in it for the fire to get hold of. Someone came out, grabbed me in their arms, and pulled me into the doorway.[29]

butcher shop where I had preached back in 1929. It was the butcher shop where the woman came out raving, waving the cleaver, and yelling, "Don't you tell us we'll be destroyed by fire from heaven!" And all you could see was the framework of the door there. The old butcher shop was in complete ruin. It had been burnt out totally. Fire from heaven destroyed it. We went to Pforzheim, which is nearby, and the whole town had been firebombed; there was nothing left. A town of

U.S. military dentistry

eighty thousand people, and the mayor there told me in the last fire raid there thirty thousand people were burned to death. So they got fire from heaven all right. It was a strange thing—that such things should happen!

DIARY ENTRY, JUNE 28, 1945: Sick. In the P.M. have four teeth filled by a dumb dentist. Very stiff neck. [On a bet] he took one minute per tooth.

JULY 4: At the office and toothache.

JULY 6: My famous 1-min. filling has to be replaced.

HUGH NIBLEY: Van Patten's father had some connections with the Russian royal family, so we ended up with a special assignment. My business was to travel with the Grand Duke Vladimir. The last czar, the one who was killed by the Bolsheviks, was Nicholas II. Then his brother came after him in succession, and this guy Vladimir that I was riding around with was his brother's son, the nephew of Czar Nicholas II. He was the heir to the throne of Russia, the next in line to be czar. When he was introduced to the officers there at Heidelberg, the general would announce him in a very fancy way as the Duke of Finland and Friedland and all the Balkan countries like Estonia and all these other places. He was the czar as far as the brass were concerned, and they were going to see that he got back on the throne. So I had to take him around, which was fine with me because he was a delightful fellow. He had no illusions about himself; he joked about it. The czar of all the Russias.

We'd go around and visit other members of the royal family, retired princesses and such, like the Grand Duchess of Galicia, who was a charming woman. They were royalty, but they were really outcasts, refugees. This grand duchess made her living by doing very fine weaving and selling it in Paris for the latest fashions. I had some nice talks with her. In Heidelberg I took Russian lessons from Madame Yeryevna, who had been the governess to the royal family and teacher to Czar Nicholas II's children. And she would weep; she would talk about the Russian revolution and say, "*Es musste kommen; es musste kommen.* It had to come; it had to come. We were wicked; we exploited those people. We were cruel to them. *Es musste kommen.*"

DIARY ENTRY, JULY 17, 1945: [Study] Russian in the morning. In the P.M. drove the Grand Duke Vladimir[a] and his Colonel to their castle in the Amersdorf. Wonderful ride.

JULY 19: A very hot day. I am getting religion again. Damn!

JULY 20: Everyone living on the moon. That empty feeling.

HUGH NIBLEY: Once Van Patten and I were going down to Paris to visit a grand duchess, and as I was driving and we were going along the road we got into a long parade of North Africans. It turned out the Bey of Tunis[b] himself was in the procession, riding in a car in style. They were just going along at a marching pace, all these Algerian soldiers, but of course we couldn't pass him. He was His Highness,

---

[a] Vladimir Kirillovitch Romanoff (1917–1992) had many titles during his life, including His Highness Prince of Russia, His Imperial Highness Czarevitch and Grand Duke of Russia, and Head of the Imperial Family of Russia. He maintained his right to the throne until his death, at which time his daughter the Grand Duchess Maria Vladimirovna took up the claim of leadership of the Romanoff family. She has reportedly met with the leaders of post-Soviet Russia to assert her right to the monarchy, though other descendants of Russian royalty dispute the claim, and there are those who believe a reestablishment of the monarchy in Russia in some form is a possibility.

[b] The Bey of Tunis, Sidi Lamine, was the hereditary head of state of Tunisia, which was a French protectorate until 1956.

and you don't pass the king, do you? So what were we to do? We finally took a cut-off to Duerkheim, so we didn't pass him but went by another way.

We actually spent some time running around trying to get the family jewels of the Romanoffs. They would have been plenty valuable too, but needless to say, we didn't get them. On one of these trips I went with the Grand Duke to a big, stately brick mansion—it was really a castle but it was more modern—up in northwest Germany. It was a nineteenth century Victorian monstrosity with a huge lawn and woods around it, looking quite British, as a matter of fact, and the grand duke said, "This belongs to a British admiral. We have great parties here." It seems that just a few weeks before, all the Nazi bigwigs had been there. He said Goering was there, and the Nazi brass had a great party in the mansion. And since Vladimir was the next successor to the czar, the Nazis were also talking about pushing his claim to the throne, and he had been invited to this party with all the Nazi bigwigs.

I said, "Well, what did the British admiral have to say about that?" and I laughed. "Of course, he wouldn't know about how the Nazis were using his house for parties."

And the Grand Duke said, "Oh, he was there! He came over for it."[a]

Heidelberg, July, 1945

Dear Lieut. S,

. . . One thing that appears clear above all others is that we are dealing with the same old P.E.S. We would rather not. The major change in my constitution has been the development of a deep and chronic dislike for anything German. After three months in lovely Heidelberg, the only undamaged city in Germany, (whither the remnants of the *gebildete Welt*[b] have foregathered) I am fed up. Let HOELDERLIN speak for me [the following is translated from the German]: *"So I arrived among the Germans. I did not demand much* (by the way, there is a huge, ugly monument to Hoelderlin on the hill above Heidelberg) *and was prepared*

---

[a] Goering liked to party, as Gilbert reported from his trial in Nuremberg: "Goering's reception of officials dressed in a toga and sandals like Nero, with painted face, lipstick and red fingernails, was read, to the amusement of everyone in the court, except Goering" (Gilbert, *Nuremberg Diary,* 314).

[b] *Gebildete Welt:* World of the learned; intellectuals.

Civilians forced to look at the workings of a concentration camp

to find even less. I came there humbly, like homeless, blind Oedipus to the games of Athens, where the sacred grove received him; and fair souls came to greet him—

"How different my experience! . . .

"It is a hard saying, and yet I speak it because it is the truth: I can think of no people more at odds with themselves than the Germans. You see artisans, but no men,[a] thinkers, but no men, priests, but no men, masters and servants, but no men, minors and adults, but no men—is this not like a battlefield on which hacked-off hands and arms and every other member are scattered about, while the life-blood flows from them to vanish in the sand. . . .

"I tell you: there is nothing sacred that is not desecrated, is not debased to a miserable expedient among this people; and what even among savages is usually preserved in sacred purity, these all-calculating barbarians pursue as one pursues any trade, and cannot do otherwise; for where a human being is once conditioned to look, there it serves its end, seeks its profit, it dreams no more—God forbid!—it remains sedate; and when it makes holiday and when it loves and when it prays, and even when spring's lovely festival, when the season of reconciliation for the world dissolves all cares and conjures innocence into a guilty heart, when, intoxicated by the sun's warm rays, the slave in his joy forgets his chains, and the enemies of mankind, softened by the divinely living air, are as peaceable as children—when the caterpillar itself grows wings and bees swarm, even then the German sticks to

[a] Hoelderlin's phrase "aber keine Menchen" translates not only as "but no men" but also as "but no humanity."

Male and female Russian soldiers dance.

his petty tasks and scarcely deigns to notice the weather!"[30] It is a wicked world and one in which there is little to choose between one group and another—but one of the few things that is clear is that the Germans, by their own choice, are a world apart, whose monumental humbug is only equaled by their zeal for dehumanizing everything they touch. Of course we give candy to good German children, but unlike any other kids they NEVER share among themselves *"Geb's dem nicht, geb's mir nur!"* ["Don't give to them, give only to me!"][a] They have shortages and rations but for all their training the grown-ups simply cannot be forced to form a line by anything less than a military order, not, of

[a] Other witnesses of post-war Germany contradict Nibley and give accounts of children making sharing with each other a high priority.

Rechsburg Castle, photographed by Hugh Nibley, 1945

course because they don't like regimentation ("*wir wollen gerne gehorchen*" ["we're eager to obey"] is the slimy phrase you hear a dozen times a day) but simply because they cannot conceive of fair dealing. The town simply swarms with *Gelehrten* [the intelligentsia], the fine old German type—one could forgive their being 96% phony if only they weren't so everlasting . . . dull. But being conscientiously dull is what comprises an important part of being a German. Hard words, but not as hard as Hoelderlin's—and he is not describing the SS heel but the good peace-time German. If these people ever did have anything, their mantle has now fallen upon the Russians, who are everything that the Germans are not. I never saw human beings with such an enormous capacity for enjoyment. The earsplitting laugh, the bearlike hug, the magnificent drinking, above all the fierce insatiable passion for reading mark the healthy barbarian if anything ever did. A really noble and lovable people. We will do wisely not to tangle with them—after all it was they who licked three-fourths of the German army (though unlike the French and British they always give due credit to their allies)—and let us not forget how we were scraping bottom after one week of the Ardennes breakthrough: how far would we get in a protracted struggle in which a united home front would be out of the question?

I was amused by your feverish political activities. Though I have 80 points my chances of returning to the States are not brilliant. There are a good many jobs available over here right now, and if old Hugh were anything of a politician he could have half a dozen commissions by now. But I do nothing because I flatter myself I have other and more important business in hand. Deep and devious thoughts ooze through the dark phantasmagoric caverns of my twisted mind as I explore the twilight zones of subhuman experience. For this sort of thing one has to be let alone, and in the Army the nearest thing to being let alone is to be a M/Sgt. Heidelberg has been heaven, and even in the 101st I went strictly my own way, for my position was unassailable: if they kicked me out they knew jolly well they could never get another sucker to take my place, and moreover everyone in the Div. was simply yearning to get kicked out anyway. I suppose I will end up in the Far East, though I don't relish the prospect. . . . Our author regretfully admits the thoroughly sordid and uninspiring nature of his theme at every period; it is a silly and repetitious story, in which the plot never gets going because all the characters succumb sooner or later to a strange and willful passion for the paradoxical and

German civilian at the site of a mass grave for murdered eastern Europeans

contradictory. . . . I have spent a good deal of time in the Bavarian and Austrian Alps—strangely enough they are rather depressing: you can never escape the atmosphere of exploitation and artificiality—everything is just too picturesque and too tame—none of the fierce free atmosphere, the vast desolation and weird Arctic color (orange skies, black basalt mountains with blinding flashes of snow, coffee-colored lochs, green bays, etc., etc.) of the Highlands. Moreover, in these Alps you find *gute, gediengene Bauerleute* [good, wholesome peasants]—"*aber keine Menschen*" [but no men/humanity], whereas in Scotland you walk all day without seeing so much as a ruined cottage, but when you do meet someone it is a long-lost brother. . . . Having visited all the scenes of my missionary labors by jeep, and beheld the painfully literal justification of the warning word to these foolish people 17 years ago, I speak with confidence of calamities to come. Everything has turned out exactly as I had imagined, so there is no reason to suppose that it won't continue to do so. During the past few months I have had some extremely interesting documents in my hands, for Heidelberg is the official depository of all German war documents; invariably these paper loving boors waited until too late to destroy documents, and the result is that you had better not try to tell little old me who started the war.

Greet Nell and your parents and try to be good *bis auf Wiedersehen.*

Hugh

" bis auf Wiedersehen: Until we meet again

DIARY ENTRY, AUGUST 16, 1945: Pfc. Edinger tells why the gliders fell: they were all drunk at Ramsgate.

HUGH NIBLEY: One night when I was traveling, a group of the men that put the gliders together for the 101st before the invasion of Holland were being retired. They were passing through Schwäbisch-Gmünd and stayed one night in the same barracks where I was sleeping. They started talking about that night at Ramsgate before the takeoff for the Holland invasion. They talked about how they were supposed to assemble the gliders and how they were laughing their heads off. One of them said, "We were as drunk as lords! We did such a sloppy job; we didn't put all the pins on!" And they laughed like it was the biggest joke in the world. "We were having fun! We left out half the pins in the darn things!" They didn't know I'd been in one of those gliders. So that's why so many of them had fallen. Dozens of gliders had just fallen out of the sky because they weren't completely put together because the people who assembled them were drunk.

DIARY ENTRY, SEPTEMBER 3, 1945: 83 points. Evening in the Polish DP [displaced persons] camp. Very sad. Salzburg?

SEPTEMBER 9: Feeling very well.

10

BACK TO ZION

In the late twenties, two preachers in southern Germany were giving speeches on street corners and handing out pamphlets. One became the essence of militarism, challenged the world, and energized his nation with a vision of world dominance. The other, among the least likely soldiers in the world, joined several million other oddballs and military misfits to challenge the dictator and bring his thousand-year Reich to a disgraceful end only twelve years after it had come to power. The war was over. Hitler's Teutonic ideal of discipline, regimentation, and racism had challenged the spoiled, flabby, disorderly democracies—and lost. The strange and indirect association of the two ardent preachers of Bavaria was over.

Hitler didn't die a tragic hero, although he thought he did. The prototypical tragic heroes Hamlet and Oedipus may, like the fallen Führer, have lost everything, including their lives, but they gained wisdom in their defeats and in the end died better than they lived. Not Hitler. There was no catharsis in his ruin. He died a fool, never even recognizing who had defeated him. To the end he believed in the weakness of democracy and in the low quality of the American military. He believed the war was determined not by a triumph of democracy over totalitarianism, but by the defeat of one dictatorship—his own—by another more fanatical, more rigid, and more dedicated to ruthless domination—Stalin and the Soviets.

Stephen Ambrose points out that the Battle of Normandy was not won by the Allies' superior resolve, training, military science, and discipline—the "will" that Hitler found so all-important—but by the culture of democracy:

Mushroom cloud over Nagasaki, Japan

STEPHEN AMBROSE: What Hitler regarded as the greatest German assets—the leadership principle in the Third Reich, the unquestioning obedience expected of Wehrmacht personnel from field marshal down to private—all worked against the Germans on D-Day.

The truth is that despite individual acts of great bravery and the fanaticism of some Wehrmacht troops, the performance of the Wehrmacht's high command, middle-ranking officers, and junior officers was just pathetic. The cause is simply put: they were afraid to take the initiative. They allowed themselves to be paralyzed by stupid orders coming from far away that bore no relation to the situation on the battlefield. Tank commanders who knew where the enemy was and how and when he should be attacked sat in their headquarters through the day, waiting for the high command in Berchtesgaden to tell them what to do.

The contrast between [American officers] in adjusting and reacting to unexpected situations, and their German counterparts could not have been greater. The men fighting for democracy were able to make quick, on-site decisions and act on them; the men fighting for the totalitarian regime were not. Except for Colonel Heydte and a captain here, a lieutenant there, not one German officer reacted appropriately to the challenge of D-Day.[1]

Hitler understood the power of will. What he never learned was the power of free will. You might say Omaha Beach is where the slippery culture of jazz faced the orderly culture of Beethoven—and jazz won. The ability to take the lead and improvise, to play by ear instead of by carefully reading the score, the instinct to follow your gut rather than looking to the conductor, prevailed. These are principles that can be learned only in a society that values freedom over obedience.

The great nations that had held the places of leadership on the world stage all lay in ruin: bankrupt, broken down, and exhausted. America, which had never been a leading player, was left the only world power in good health—and it was thriving. From the day it was born, America had always been an oddball in the community of nations. No other country had ever thought to call such a thing as "the pursuit of happiness" a basic human right. Few countries had ever considered that there was *such a thing as a basic human right. One anonymous veteran put it this way:*

ANONYMOUS VETERAN: Imagine this. In the spring of 1945, around the world, the sight of a twelve-man squad of teenage boys, armed and in uniform, brought terror to people's hearts. Whether it was a Red Army squad in Berlin, Leipzig, or Warsaw, or a German squad in Holland, or a Japanese squad in Manila, Seoul, or Beijing, that squad meant rape, pillage, looting, wanton destruction, senseless killing. But there was an exception: a squad of GIs, a sight that brought the biggest smiles you ever saw to people's lips, and joy to their hearts.

Around the world this was true, even in Germany, even—after September 1945—in Japan. This was because GIs meant candy, cigarettes, C-rations, and freedom. America had sent the best of her young men around the world, not to conquer but to liberate, not to terrorize but to help. This was a great moment in our history.[2]

A French girl gives wine to a GI.

Just as the American generals had refused to bow to supposedly superior British military wisdom and had run their war in their own American way, the country approached the aftermath of war in a way the world had never seen before. Standard wisdom had always been that to the victor go the

French civilians with the 101st

General of the Army George C. Marshall, center, Army Chief of Staff

spoils, to the loser disgrace and punishment. That's certainly the philosophy the French and British had followed at the end of the First World War when they forced the Versailles Treaty down the Germans' throat and planted the seeds of resentment that Hitler harvested in a nation dedicated to hatred. There has been only one great war on American soil where the population smelled the stench of tens of thousands of bodies rotting in the sun and great cities burned as women and children died in the flames. It was the Civil War, and in the middle of it Lincoln had laid out a new American doctrine for treating former foes: "With malice toward none, with charity for all." In this tradition America set to work not to pillage and demean their conquered enemies, but to feed them, rebuild them, and make them whole again.

General George Marshall, Chairman of the Joint Chiefs of Staff and the man who was Eisenhower's boss, had led the American military in its drive to destroy the Axis powers. Yet before the war was over he was already busy creating the organization to rebuild what he was busy breaking down. The Marshall Plan became one of America's proudest achievements. Many countries can boast of their history of destroying their foes, but how many can boast of rebuilding them? Instead of milking their defeated enemies for reparations, how many raised them up not only to be vital and strong, but to become their own fiercest economic competitors?

ALBERT SPEER: Do you know how you could have discredited Nazism once and for all? Just by letting our administration stay and rule Germany. All you had to say was, "Go ahead, try to govern your-selves; you made your bed, now lie in it.—We won't interfere, but it is not our responsibility to feed you. You started it; now finish it."—

A stream of German prisoners walks down the Autobahn.

GIs with enough points to go home

Why, Germans would simply have starved by the million.[3]

Eisenhower oversaw the plan to rebuild Europe with his usual diplomacy and human warmth. In the Pacific, General MacArthur, whose personality was much more imperial than Ike's, played a similar role in a way that was uniquely suited to the Japanese. The Japanese, who had been prepared to protect their emperor and their imperial homeland with the "honorable death of a hundred million," got busy studying western democracy. Big changes. For the GIs who had fought the war there were also big changes. They found there was no real going back; there was only going forward.

HUGH NIBLEY: I continued to do a lot of traveling everywhere, from Holland in the northwest over to Czechoslovakia. I finally ended up in the suburbs of Paris, where I was put in charge of a company of what they called "casuals," which weren't casualties, they were just soldiers passing through. I had enough points to go home, but it had taken years to get all the American military over there and now there was a lot of red tape to go through to get them back. At the end of September my papers finally came through. I moved out to Compiegne near where there was a hideous PW camp. I was camping in the place where the peace of World War I was signed, the Treaty of Versailles. When Hitler invaded France and forced the French to surrender it, he had his day of glory because he had hated the humiliation of the Treaty of Versailles so much. He had forced the French generals to sign the surrender in the same railroad car there in Compiegne. Now I had my sleeping bag right by the car where both documents had been signed. I was made platoon sergeant in charge of a bunch of guys on their way home, and we were busy processing and doing all the paperwork to get home.

DIARY ENTRY, OCTOBER 13, 1945: Usual ground fog. Walk to the train. 40 & 8's. Sleep well on the straw to Le Havre via Noyon!

HUGH NIBLEY: The cars we rode in were boxcars from World War I called 40 and 8's. They got that name because they could take forty men or eight horses. We got into Le Havre in the morning where we stayed with an easy-going outfit, but I was still impatient to get on with it and we kept having to wait.

DIARY ENTRY, OCTOBER 16, 1945: Feeling very vicious.

HUGH NIBLEY: We waited over a week before we finally got assigned to a ship called the *Eleazer Wheelock.*[a] Then our sailing was postponed again several days because of the worst storm they had there in twenty years. We didn't actually cast off until October 27. We had a young, jolly crew out of New England, just out for the first time together, and our destination was Boston. It was one of these liberty boats, a leaky old freighter.[b] One of the ships accompanying it actually sank. The bottom fell out it was so badly made. The liberty ship took

Liberty ship poster

weeks to cross, and we had big storms, and the seas were very high, very rough. I loved to stay on the deck. It was a lot different from the *Queen Mary,* which had

---

[a] The *Eleazer Wheelock* was named for a Revolutionary War hero who was also the founder of Dartmouth College.

[b] *Liberty ship:* Freight ships built under a program Franklin D. Roosevelt launched in 1941 to help get America ready for war. The ships were originally called "emergency ships" but were more commonly known as "ugly ducklings" since they were designed to be cheap and easy to build rather than beautiful. The first ship built under the program was the *SS Patrick Henry,* and FDR said it would bring liberty to their European allies. He quoted Patrick Henry's famous line, "Give me liberty or give me death." From then on they were known as "liberty ships."

taken me over the Atlantic in record time. In the big ocean liner you barely noticed if the seas were rough, but in that liberty ship you felt every wave.

The inevitability of the next war was very clear to me on the way home. I was worried about another war coming because of the way everybody acted on the boat. It was plain that we hadn't learned a thing. The soldiers were so vulgar and so nasty about things; all they could think of was sex and violence, that sort of thing. They had a library up front in the boat, and I was the ship librarian, but nobody ever came for books. You'd think these people, now it was over, would settle down to some quiet reading and patronize the library, but they didn't. All day long they played these records, "Drinking rum and Cokaah Cola . . ." All day long that sort of stuff. We hadn't improved.

DIARY ENTRY, OCTOBER 28, 1945: [drawing of waves]

OCTOBER 29: [drawing of bigger waves]

NOVEMBER 3: Calm

NOVEMBER 4: Calmish

NOVEMBER 5: Bad storm

NOVEMBER 6: Very high seas running from the south

HUGH NIBLEY: As we approached the American coast we had a change in our course. We would not be going to Boston, but to New York instead. I had rushed across the Atlantic to the war two years earlier in only five days. Now, after almost two weeks rolling around stormy seas in the liberty ship, we landed at Staten Island at dusk on November 9. We had a very warm train ride to Camp Kilmer, where they processed all the returning soldiers, and it was the same old red tape mess. Over in Manhattan were my brother Reid (who was there

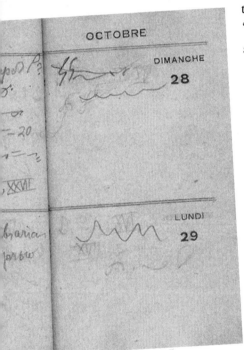

Diary entries for October 28 and 29

studying piano with Andor Foldes), Goldschmidt, and of course his assistant, Anahid Iskian. Another brother, Sloan, was also living nearby with his wife and five-year-old son Philip. Reid had been rejected by the army because of problems with his foot and Sloan was serving in the navy.

DIARY ENTRY, NOVEMBER 10, 1945: Phone A[nahid] Iskian and Reid and talk to Goldschmidt.

HUGH NIBLEY: After two days of sitting in Camp Kilmer I got a pass and went in to New York by train. I went and picked up Anahid and a friend of hers and we all went to Sloan's place and had a big reunion. I didn't get back to Camp Kilmer until 4:30 in the morning. I spent a few days there. When I couldn't get a pass I broke out of camp without one and stayed with Reid anyway. The last day in New York I got back to camp at 4:00 in the afternoon, and that evening we went to an airfield in New Jersey and boarded a C-47 for Nashville and Memphis. At 6:00 the next morning we were on the plane again.

This was my first time flying inside a C-47 rather than being towed behind one in a glider and also my first time flying over the American continent. We went slowly, droning along looking down on the muddy meandering of olive drab rivers of the South and at the woods that would alternately thicken, then thin out again over the light brown earth. We went to Ft. Worth, then El Paso, then on to Phoenix, and finally landed at March Field in San Bernardino, where I got on a bus which got lost but eventually stopped at Ft. MacArthur. It was exactly the same as it had been that day when I had first been inducted into the U.S. Army. The family met me, and we went to the house on Mariposa Street and had a big dinner. But I was still in the army, so in the evening I took a streetcar back to the camp.

DIARY ENTRY, NOVEMBER 19, 1945: Received $367.89. That idiot Andrus walked off with my bag. Drive . . . to Lynwood and back to MacArthur in the evening. A wonderful night. The Glendale Symphony play.

HUGH NIBLEY: At Fort MacArthur I found the same service and supply guys who had been there when I took off for basic training, and they were running a crooked outfit. They had to give you mustering-out money, but the officer in charge

JOSEPH HELLER'S *CATCH-22:* WAR AS GOOD BUSINESS

"It all goes to the syndicate. And everybody has a share. Don't you understand? It's exactly what happens with those plum tomatoes I sell to Colonel Cathcart."

"*Buy,*" Yossarian corrected him. "You don't *sell* plum tomatoes to Colonel Cathcart and Colonel Korn. You *buy* plum tomatoes from them."

"No, *sell,*" Milo corrected Yossarian. "I distribute my plum tomatoes in markets all over Pianosa under an assumed name so that Colonel Cathcart and Colonel Korn can buy them up from me under their assumed names at four cents apiece and sell them back to me the next day for the syndicate at five cents apiece. They make a profit of one cent apiece, I make a profit of three and a half cents apiece, and everybody comes out ahead."

"Everybody but the syndicate," said Yossarian with a snort. "The syndicate is paying five cents apiece for plum tomatoes that cost you only half a cent apiece. How does the syndicate benefit?"

"The syndicate benefits when I benefit," Milo explained, "because everybody has a share."[4]

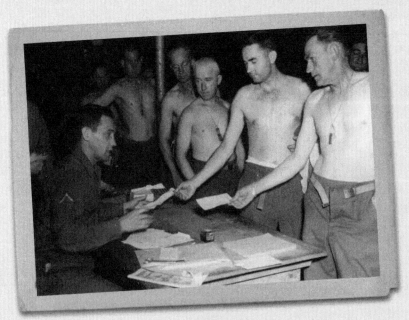

Mustering out

self-righteously said, "Wow, more than $300! You soldiers will just go out and get drunk with all that money, and we don't want *that* to happen! So we'll keep half of it here and give you the other half." Then he said, "Of course, if you don't want to take just half your mustering out pay, you can stay in the army another six weeks." So everyone had to waive half their mustering out pay and let these guys keep it. It would have made Milo Minderbinder proud.

After months and years of anxiously waiting to get back to home and life as normal, World War II veterans often found themselves strangely unable to fit easily back into life at home. Many of them found something fundamental inside them had changed, and in a strange way civilian life and a desk and business suit could be more uncomfortable than a muddy foxhole and wet ODs. And Hugh Nibley? Well, he had never really felt at ease in "normal" American life.

a Ward: A Mormon congregation similar to a parish in Catholicism

HUGH NIBLEY: The next few weeks I tied up loose ends and did this and that. I paid my taxes, went to the bishop of my old ward*a* in Claremont and paid my back tithing. I went swimming at the beach in Santa Monica. I opened a bank account. I never did see the rest of my mustering-out pay.

DIARY ENTRY, DECEMBER 6, 1945: Wrote letter about mustering out pay.

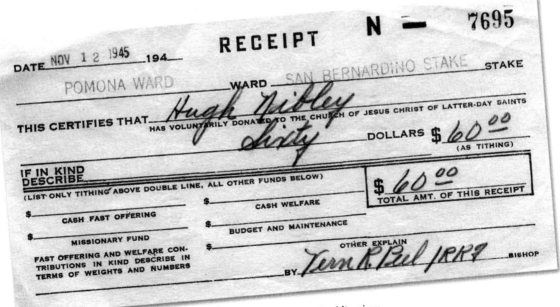

Catching up with stateside obligations

The holidays were approaching, the traditional time of family, good cheer, and contentment. The year before at Christmas the Battle of the Bulge was in full swing and it still looked dicey for the Allies. Nibley hadn't been able to get a pass on Christmas Eve, and he spent the holiday walking alone through Paris. The year before that he spent Christmas with a British family, who had taken him into their home. The year before that he was in weather school on the frozen plains of Illinois. Even if he had ever been a great celebrator of the Yule season, Hugh Nibley was out of practice with Christmas traditions. As always, he was uncomfortable with comfort. And as for peace on earth, he had his doubts about that.

RICHARD GABRIEL: Societies have always recognized that war changes men, that they are not the same after they return. That is why primitive societies often require soldiers to perform purification rites before allowing them to rejoin their communities. These rites often involved washing or other forms of ceremonial cleansing. Psychologically, these rituals provided soldiers with a way of ridding themselves of stress and the terrible guilt that always accompanies the sane after war. It was also a way of treating guilt by providing a mechanism through which fighting men could decompress and relive their terror without feeling weak or exposed. Finally, it was a way of telling the soldier that what he did was right and that the community for which he fought was grateful and that, above all, his community of sane and normal men welcomed him back.[5]

DIARY ENTRY, DECEMBER 13, 1945: Leave 4:40 [A.M.] arrive St. George at 6:00 [p.m]. A very fine day, the entire San Gabriel Range can be seen from Barstow. . . . Coldest weather in ten years.

DECEMBER 14: Car stalling because of bad gas. At 12 go to Zion. Walk from Springdale to the lodge. The clearest sky I've ever seen.

DECEMBER 15: Car stalled again. Get room and board with the Reeve family [in Hurricane] for $10 a week.

DECEMBER 16: With wondering awe! Up the canyon to the narrows great icicles and warm springs.

"WITH WONDERING AWE"

With wond'ring awe the wise men saw
The star in heaven springing,
And with delight, in peaceful night,
They heard the angels singing:
Hosanna, hosanna,
hosanna to his name!

By light of star they traveled far
To seek the lowly manger,
A humble bed wherein was laid
The wondrous little Stranger.
Hosanna, hosanna,
hosanna to his name!

And still is found, the world around,
The old and hallowed story,
And still is sung in ev'ry tongue
The angels' song of glory:
Hosanna, hosanna,
hosanna to his name!

The heav'nly star its rays afar
On ev'ry land is throwing,
And shall not cease till holy peace
In all the earth is growing.
Hosanna, hosanna,
hosanna to his name![6]

Zion Canyon photographed
by Hugh Nibley, circa 1947

Hurricane, January, 1946

Sweet Stuff [aka Paul Springer],

Don't be *boes' auf mich* [angry with me]. I thought I wrote you last week but I guess I didn't—it must have been the week before or something. I am now the complete Zivil—so what did we do first of all and last of all? The only wise thing as long as I have a penny in the bank, which is to consider the lilies of the field and nothing else.[a] In the desert south of Zion on the Arizona border is a place where I hang out, gradually setting up on a spot last occupied by the Pueblos some time in the 10th Century of Our Era. My rear base is near Hurricane. Right now I am celebrating the "Holidays" in the land of Goshen but raring to get as far from the post-war world as circumstances will allow, i.e. back to my softly howling wilderness. Do you know we missed all the best stuff around Zion: it is the neighboring terrain that is really staggering once you get into it. I visited Zion a couple of times when I had the car. Why people go there in summer is beyond me—any other season is better, but especially winter. The air is so clear that you can stand in the shadow of a cliff and pick out Mars and Jupiter shining bravely in the mid-afternoon sky. Not a soul in the park and the animals are having a

---

[a] "No man can serve two masters: for either he will hate the one, and love the other; or else he will hold to the one, and despise the other. Ye cannot serve God and mammon.

"Therefore I say unto you, Take no thought for your life, what ye shall eat, or what ye shall drink; nor yet for your body, what ye shall put on. Is not the life more than meat, and the body than raiment?

"Behold the fowls of the air: for they sow not, neither do they reap, nor gather into barns; yet your heavenly Father feedeth them. Are ye not much better than they?

"Which of you by taking thought can add one cubit unto his stature?

"And why take ye thought for raiment? Consider the lilies of the field, how they grow; they toil not, neither do they spin:

"And yet I say unto you, That even Solomon in all his glory was not arrayed like one of these.

"Wherefore, if God so clothe the grass of the field, which to day is, and to morrow is cast into the oven, shall he not much more clothe you, O ye of little faith?

"Therefore take no thought, saying, What shall we eat? or, What shall we drink? or, Wherewithal shall we be clothed?

"(For after all these things do the Gentiles seek:) for your heavenly Father knoweth that ye have need of all these things.

"But seek ye first the kingdom of God, and his righteousness; and all these things shall be added unto you.

"Take therefore no thought for the morrow: for the morrow shall take thought for the things of itself. Sufficient unto the day is the evil thereof" (Matthew 6:24–34).

field-day; the snow has lain on the trails for three weeks and the only shoe-tracks on it are mine. The water that seeps through the sandstone covers the cliffs with the most fabulous icicles (you can imagine what the Weeping Rock looks like) but the air is warm and dry—you never have to wear a coat. One of the pleasant surprises was to discover that most of the springs are warm-springs—between 70 and 80 degrees (the Ranger wouldn't believe it until he investigated in person) and their green borders and pink sands heighten the sense of magic in that wonderful gorge.

Almost as comforting as the long-delayed joys of solitude is the company of the plain and sober people of the area where I live—quite the best I have found yet. And what a contrast to the Armed Forces of the United States of North America! One of those proverbs in Burckhardt's famous old collection neatly summarizes the military life: Behold the soldier—when he is hungry he steals, and when he is full he fornicates—that covers everything. Only half the books I sent *ex partibus infidelium*[a] ever got here, but that still gives me a noble Arabic collection, from which I daily derive joy and some knowledge. Also we have taken an old love back to our bed, namely Icelandic, and find the reading of the sagas (of which we now possess the whole collection) more exciting than ever. Our poor old noggin is positively churning with ideas, and the siren call of mere *Gelehrsamkeit*[b] has never been so strong. It was to escape this as much as anything that we fled to the red sandy walls of little Tibet, and now, behold, we are slowly but surely moving our entire library in that direction! Our *Weltflucht*[c] seems, in fact, to be taking on suspiciously familiar form, and it may be necessary to break the spell betimes. Among other things I think it would be profitable for us to get together again some time. Should that be possible you would find me in a rather difficult state of mind—the result of trying to do many things at once while really doing nothing at all; in fact I seem to have fallen victim to the well-known American mania that craves to have everything and be everything and do everything immediately and at once. Add to this an enormous impatience with things as they are and a towering disgust for almost everything our age finds desirable and you discover in me a first-class crank. Only in the desert wastes can we collect our "thoughts" and bring ourselves to the essentially animal habit of doing one thing at a time. Another cause of

[a] *ex partibus infidelium:* From the land of the infidels
[b] *Gelehrsamkeit:* Intellectualism
[c] *Weltflucht:* Escape from the world

frustration my dear Lt. (for I have decided to tell all), is the reluctance—to put it mildly—of a certain fair Armenian damsel (I may have told you about her before this) to concur with the most honorable suggestion of which my far from courtly nature is capable. The odd thing about this odious state of mind is that I find it rather interesting. My head is not so empty but what amusing and sometimes edifying intimations are engendered in its dim phantasmagoring chambers. A procession of odd (quite probably pathological) images marches before us across the barren *nejd.*[a] Perhaps the only way to exorcise them is to write them down, since writing is the secret of forgetting—at any rate it would be worth a try. In the Army, as one does, I came to know a number of men remarkable for intellectual, artistic or moral qualities which I greatly admired. Yet at the end of that instructive but unhappy

[a] Nejd: Desert region of central Saudi Arabia

A German general reads the terms of surrender.

philibuster [sic] I must still admit that the world has produced only one to my knowledge whose very vices are as interesting as other men's virtues—meaning you, Snookums. Someday I'll tell you where I'm hiding and then your astral body can pay me a visit. It *is* a weird sort of life, you know, sometimes it presents rather frightening possibilities—what I mean I will tell you later. For the time being try to bear with this irregularity, give a resounding buss to the delectable Nell and a very non-military salute, if you ever see them, to your esteemed ancestry.

Hugh
My desert address is General Delivery, Hurricane, Ut.

Back in Europe Hitler and Goebbels were dead at their own hands, and what was left of the Nazi leadership was brought to trial before judges and prosecutors representing the various countries that had suffered under their Third Reich.

WILLIAM SHIRER: I went down to Nuremberg to see them. I had often watched them in their hour of glory and power at the annual party rallies in this town. In the dock before the International Military Tribunal they looked different. There had been quite a metamorphosis. Attired in rather shabby clothes, slumped in their seats fidgeting nervously, they no longer resembled the arrogant leaders of old. They seemed to be a drab assortment of mediocrities. It seemed difficult to grasp that such men, when last you had seen them, had wielded such monstrous power, that such as they could conquer a great nation and most of Europe.[7]

Gustave Gilbert was a psychologist who ended up as an officer in Intelligence. As the Nuremberg trials got underway he served as the court psychologist, and in that capacity had a unique opportunity to study the psychology of totalitarianism. He kept notes which he later published as Nuremberg Diary, *a book that gives a revealing look at the men who destroyed much of the world, recording not only their intimate conversations, but their body language, vocal inflections, and facial expressions from the careful observations of a psychologist. What is striking in both Gilbert's and Shirer's reports on the great demons of Nazism is the pettiness of the men. Their jealousies, insecurities, spats, tantrums, whining self-pity, and finger-pointing seem more appropriate for*

Over the body of a German sniper, Czechs wave to American soldiers.

school children than masters of the world. Their ordinariness is frightening. These weren't devils; they were just the kind of bureaucrats and ambitious bores you find in any corporation or university or government office. If they were demigods of evil (as the propaganda always tells us our enemies are) they would seem much safer. But the picture we see here could be people we know. They could be us.

"I didn't know what was going on" was one popular defense. It seems these men who a few months before had been passing themselves off as competent to rule the world were not very aware of what was happening in the regions they were governing. The number two man in the Reich was "innocent as a babe."

REICHSMARSCHALL HERMAN GOERING: Do you know, [Hitler] never kept me informed on all the circumstances? Really. Most of those things you are referring to, I am finding out for the first time in the trial. . . . But all the persecution and atrocities are revolting to all of us, I assure you. It just isn't German. Can you conceive of me killing anybody? Now you are a psychologist. Tell me frankly, do any of us look like murderers? I can't conceive of Hitler ordering such things. I can't believe that he knew about it. He had a hard side, I know—but I believed in him with all my heart. He could really be so tender. I was willing to do anything for him. Himmler must have ordered those things. But I doubt if he was a real German. He had a peculiar face. We couldn't get along.[8]

Everyone was just following orders. No one seems to have been responsible for anything.

FIELD MARSHAL WILHELM KEITEL, CHIEF OF STAFF OF THE GERMAN HIGH COMMAND: An officer can't stand right up before the Führer, his Commander in Chief, and object! . . . It's hard for Americans to understand the Prussian code of discipline.[9]

Another common excuse was "Everybody else does it!"

GUSTAVE GILBERT: "What the devil do you mean, morality?—word of honor?" Goering snorted. "Sure, you can talk about word of honor when you promise to deliver goods in business.—But when it is the question of the *interests of the nation!?* Phooey! Then morality stops! That is what England had done for centuries; America has done it; and Russia is still doing it! Why do you suppose Russia won't give up an inch of her territory in the Balkans? because of morality?—" He thrashed around the cell as he changed his uniform. *"Herrgott!* When a state has a chance to improve its position because of the weakness of a neighbor, do you think it will stop at any squeamish consideration of keeping a promise? It is a statesman's *duty* to take advantage of such a situation for the good of his country!"[10]

Nazi literature

Alfred Rosenberg, the philosophical brain behind Nazi racism, claimed to have no idea what impact his words were having. They never meant any real harm, and it was (still) the Jews who really forced *the Nazis to take it to extremes.*

REICHSMINISTER ALFRED ROSENBERG: I don't know. I guess it just ran away with him [Hitler].—We didn't contemplate killing anybody in the beginning; I can assure you of that. I always advocated a peaceful solution. . . . I had no idea that it would lead to extermination in any literal sense. . . . The foreign Jewish-democratic press began hammering against the Party, and they forced the issue. . . . I had nothing actually to do with the Nuremberg Laws. I just read them when proposed in the Reichstag, and naturally I couldn't stand up in the Reichstag and say "I object!" That was out of the question.[11]

Some of the Nazis seem to be sounding a warning voice to us.

HITLER YOUTH LEADER BALDUR VON SCHIRACH: In my youth I moved in aristocratic circles and never even came in contact with Jews. I had no reason to be anti-Semitic, but I did notice a sort of underhanded quiet prejudice against the Jews "in the best circles." This did not impress me, however, until someone made me read the American book, *The International Jew* [by Henry Ford], at the impressionable age of 17. You have no idea what a great influence this book had on the thinking of German Youth, who did not have the maturity to think for themselves. . . . I don't think there will ever be anti-Semitism in the world again, after this horrible example. But people must fight this quiet underhanded social stigmatization which was the breeding ground for the disease.[12]

Another Nazi youth leader was less optimistic about the future.

GUSTAVE GILBERT: [During the Nuremberg trials] I had a long talk with Fritz Wieshofer, 31, one of the chief Austrian Youth leaders. He said he . . . could see something worth living for to spread the word of denunciation of Nazism and anti-Semitism. German Youth, he said, was in such despair, not knowing what to think, that this word from their former leader would have a great effect.

"But how about your country?" he asked. "I am amazed to hear American officers express anti-Semitic sentiments even now! Hasn't the world learned anything from Germany's horrible example? How can there still be anti-Semites after what has happened in Germany? Of course, there are some who may say they never realized before what racial prejudice can lead to. But now?—After Auschwitz . . . ? German Youth certainly learned its lesson. . . . We have learned in bitterness and misery what racial prejudice leads to. But hasn't the rest of the world learned yet?"[13]

Perhaps the most chilling example of the way the poison of prejudice creeps into the mind is Colonel Rudolph Hoess.

RUDOLPH HOESS: After the war started, Hitler explained that World Jewry had started a showdown with National Socialism—that was in a Reichstag speech at the time of the French campaign—and the Jews must be exterminated. Of course, nobody at that time thought that it was meant so literally. . . . It was always stressed that if Germany was to survive then World Jewry must be exterminated and we all accepted it as truth.

An old Italian who fought the Germans in World War I beats a German sniper he found hiding in his house as he leads him to the American MPs.

That was the picture I had in my head, so, when Himmler called me to him, I just accepted it as the realization of something I had already accepted—not only I, but everybody. . . . The problem itself, the extermination of Jewry, was not new—but only that *I* was to be the one to carry it out, frightened me at first. But after getting the clear direct order and even an explanation with it—there was nothing left but to carry it out.

GUSTAVE GILBERT: So that was the background for accepting a mass murder order?

RUDOLPH HOESS: Yes, when I think back on it all, it is hard to figure out—but at that time I didn't think of it at all as propaganda, but something one just had to believe.[14]

Some of the prisoners on trial in Nuremberg. Front row, left to right: Hermann Goering, Hitler's second in command and head of the Luftwaffe; Rudolph Hess, a Nazi party leader; Joachim von Ribbontrop, foreign minister; Wilhelm Keitel, Wermacht chief of staff. Back row: Karl Doenitz, grand admiral of the German navy and Hitler's successor; Erich Raeder, admiral of the German navy; Baldur von Schirach, Hitler Youth leader; Fritz Sauckel, chief of slave labor recruitment.

Hoess described the ultimate result of his unquestioning belief in Nazi doctrine.

GUSTAVE GILBERT: After completing his [psychological] test, we discussed briefly [Colonel Hoess's] activity as the commandant of the Auschwitz concentration camp from May, 1940, to December, 1943, which camp was the central extermination camp for Jews. He readily confirmed that approximately 2½ million Jews had been exterminated under his direction. The exterminations began in the summer of 1941. In compliance with Goering's skepticism, I asked Hoess how it was technically possible to exterminate 2½ million people. "Technically?" he asked. "That wasn't so hard—it would

THE TRIAL

At the opening of the Nuremberg trial, the court was shown a documentary film of atrocities committed by the Third Reich.

GUSTAVE GILBERT: (Kelley and I were posted at either end of the defendants' dock and observed the prisoners during the showing of this film. Following are my notes jotted down during the showing of the film at about 1–2 minute intervals:)

Schacht objects to being made to look at film as I ask him to move over; turns away, folds arms, gazes into gallery . . . (Film starts). Frank nods at authentication at introduction of film . . . Fritzsche (who had not seen any part of film before) already looks pale and sits aghast as it starts with scenes of prisoners burned alive in a barn . . . Keitel wipes brow, takes off headphones . . . Hess glares at screen, looking like a ghoul with sunken eyes over the footlamp . . . Keitel puts on headphone, glares at screen out of the corner of his eye . . . von Neurath has head bowed, doesn't look . . . Funk covers his eyes, looks as if he is in agony, shakes his head . . . Ribbontrop closes his eyes, looks away . . . Sauckel mops brow . . . Frank swallows hard, blinks eyes, trying to stifle tears . . . Fritzsche watches intensely with knitted brow, cramped at the end of his seat, evidently in agony . . . Goering keeps leaning on balustrade, not watching most of the time, looking droopy . . . Funk mumbles something under his breath . . . Streicher keeps watching, immobile except for an occasional squint . . . Funk now in tears, blows nose, wipes eyes, looks down . . . Frick shakes head at illustration of "violent death"—Frank mutters "Horrible!" . . . Rosenberg fidgets, peeks at screen, bows head, looks to see how others are reacting . . . Seyss-Inquart stoic throughout . . . Speer looks very sad, swallows hard . . . Defense attorneys are now muttering, "for God's sake—terrible." Raeder watches without budging . . . von Papen sits with hand over brow, looking down, has not looked at screen yet . . . Hess keeps looking bewildered . . . piles of dead are shown in a slave labor camp . . . von Schirach watching intently, gasps, whispers to Sauckel . . . Funk crying now . . . Goering looks sad, leaning on elbow . . . Doenitz has head bowed, no longer watching . . . Sauckel shudders at picture of Buchenwald crematorium oven . . . as human skin lampshade is shown, Streicher says, "I don't believe that." . . . Goering coughing . . . Attorneys gasping . . . Now Dachau . . . Schacht still not looking . . . Frank nods his head bitterly and says, "Horrible!" . . . Rosenberg still fidgeting, leans forward, looks around, leans back, hangs head . . . Fritzsche, pale, biting lips, really seems in agony . . . Doenitz has head buried in his hands . . . Keitel now hanging head . . . Ribbontrop looks up at screen as British officer starts to speak, saying he has already buried 17,000 corpses . . . Frank biting his nails . . . Frick shakes his head incredulously at speech of female doctor describing treatment and experiments on female prisoners at Belsen . . . As Kramer is shown, Funk says with choking voice, "The dirty swine!" . . . Ribbontrop sitting with pursed lips and blinking eyes, not looking at screen . . . Funk crying bitterly, claps hand over mouth as women's naked corpses are thrown into pit . . . Keitel and Ribbontrop look up at mention of tractor clearing corpses, see it, then hang their heads . . . Streicher shows signs of disturbance for first time . . . Film ends.[15]

Note: In this case, ellipses do not represent omitted information.

not have been hard to exterminate even greater numbers." In answer to my rather naïve questions as to how many people could be done away with in an hour, etc., he explained that one must figure it on a daily 24-hour basis, and it was possible to exterminate up to 10,000 in one 24-hour period. He explained that there were actually 6 extermination chambers. The 2 big ones could accommodate as many as 2,000 in each and the 4 smaller ones up to 1500, making a total capacity of 10,000 a day. I tried to figure out how this was done, but he corrected me. "No, you don't figure it right. The killing itself took the least time. You could dispose of 2,000 head in a half hour, but it was the burning that took all the time. The killing was easy; you didn't even need guards to drive them into the chambers; they just went in expecting to take showers and, instead of water, we turned on poison gas. The whole thing went very quickly." He related all of this in a quiet, apathetic, matter-of-fact tone of voice.[16]

There were four charges against the Nazis at Nuremberg: (1) Conspiracy to commit crimes alleged in other counts; (2) Crimes against peace; (3) War crimes; (4) Crimes against humanity. Not all of the defendants were indicted on all counts. Twelve Nazis were found guilty and sentenced to death by hanging. Two of these were never executed: Martin Bormann, who was tried in absentia but was never captured, and Goering, who managed to have poison smuggled to him and committed suicide the night before his execution. Three men were sentenced to life in prison, and four more to terms ranging from ten to twenty years in prison. Three of the accused were acquitted.

Three of the Nazi leaders expressed remorse and took responsibility for their actions.

GUSTAVE GILBERT: Von Schirach's face was grave and tense as he marched to his cell, head high. "Twenty," he said, as the guard unlocked the handcuffs. I told him his wife would be relieved to know that he had not gotten the death penalty, which she had feared. "Better a quick death than a slow one," he answered.[17]

ALBERT SPEER: I accepted the sentence. I waived the right to an appeal to the Four Powers. Any penalty weighed little compared to the misery we had brought upon the world. "For there are such things," I noted in my diary a few weeks later, "for which one is guilty even if one might offer excuses—simply because the scale of the crimes is so overwhelming that by comparison any human excuse pales to insignificance."

Today, a quarter of a century after these events, it is not only specific faults that burden my conscience, great as these may have been. My moral failure is not a matter of this item and that; it resides in my active association with the whole course of events.[18]

GUSTAVE GILBERT: [Dr. Hans] Frank smiled politely, but could not look at me. "Death by hanging," he said softly, nodding his head in acquiescence. "I deserved it and I expected it, as I've always told you. I am glad that I have had the chance to defend myself and to think things over in the last few months."[19]

World War II, the greatest human conflict in history, was over, but the world and the men and women who fought the war would never be the same. As Zion Park, Hugh Nibley's land of burning rocks, had metamorphosed into a world of steaming warm-springs and massive icicles, the world outside had also changed.

Salt Lake City, various dates, 1946

Tovarich,[a]

Emerging from the lost world of the Utah-Arizona boundary country I find another of your notes awaiting me at the Hurricane post-office. They had given up hope of ever seeing me again and were on the verge of burning it; I hope now that they have learned a simple lesson—Nibley *always* comes back. It is a terrible blow to learn, as I do by inference, that things I wrote you long ago in a black and somewhat hysterical mood, are being preserved. For what? How much do you want? I assure you the tension, suspicion, and sheer despair that filled the air of Heidelberg were at times simply unbearable. Everybody was flying off the handle, but I was particularly miserable because I knew the funda-mental excellence that lay beneath the rubble-heaps of folly and ruin, and that a vast and admirable intelligence was being dedicated to wanton destruction. Why must the Germans behave that way? I was

[a] *Tovarich:* Russian for "friend" or "comrade"

" Abenteuer:
Adventurer

walking behind an elderly couple in the woods one day as they discoursed on Hitler. He was nothing but an Abenteuer," they decided, a sordid opportunist—and they might have known it all along, fools that they had been, for couldn't anyone see that he had *dark* hair instead of blond! My adolescent thinking was all cast in the German mold, and that I do not regret; it is the Germans themselves who have not been true to their great tradition—you have no idea how sterile and immoral the Nazi mind was, or do you? They were tactless and incorrigible and played right into the hands of the real perennial war-makers—their bad manners were their undoing, but I knew all along that in the field of geopolitics and trouble-making they were strictly second-string. Stop me, my sweet, before I get too specific.

I have been moving around like mad. Going to be stuck in Salt Lake for the summer. I am an editor, no less. Also doing quite a bit of hack writing. But when the leaves begin to fall I shall repair to Provo, for Brother Brigham's celebrated academy has charms that make the blandishments of Claremont seem positively repulsive by comparison. . . .

The solitude of the desert did much to alter my weak and impressionable mentality. . . . Right now I am finishing up one of my pretentiously documented studies, and desperately fear that the final touches will require a flying visit to Berkeley, in which case I hope to have a glimpse of your rude but noble countenance in the not too utter future and experience the benign offices of that delicious counter-irritant whom the world knows as your devoted, if misled, wife. Try to carry on until then, with the assurance that old Nibs will back you up every time you try to go forward.

Love & kisses (free trial package),

Hugo

THE NEXT WAR

The defeated Führer and the disappointed professor agreed that the German people had fallen short of expectations. On one other point they agreed as well: Hugh Nibley and Adolf Hitler both expected the fall of the Reich to lead to the rise of the Soviet Empire, with military and cultural leadership passing to the Russians. But although Nibley talked the talk of Russian superiority and painted the picture of a future where Pushkin and Tchaikovsky were king, he walked a walk as American as Louis Armstrong. While Hitler dismissed America to the end, Hugh Nibley praised the Russians; but he also hinted at a third way that didn't depend on an ancient culture, but had more to do with his own Mormon faith. What he never acknowledged during the war was the possibility that what had actually won the war was neither the Teutonic culture of Goethe nor the Slavic one of Pushkin, but the American culture of Hugh Nibley and several million other misfits like him. He didn't seem to notice that the mantle of world leadership now lay on his own and his fellow Americans' shoulders. He went home to a long and prolific career lecturing and writing a huge body of work, none of which could ever have been produced under either the German or the Russian scholarly systems. Much of his writings are strong intellectual defenses of Mormonism, the "most American of religions." It's true that his scholarship draws heavily on intellectual traditions that seem exotic to most Americans, but that is the strength of the American intellectual tradition—it is an inclusive rather than an exclusive system. Anything that has value and can stand on its own merits can find a place in America. It was in World War II that America became the leader that it is today. It overcame its inferiority complex regarding the "old countries" most of its citizens had come from and

Hugh Nibley's dog tags, Screaming Eagle patch, and discharge papers

brought its own unique strength onto the international stage. In a similar way, it took World War II to make Hugh Nibley into a real American.

The bitterness between the American and British commanders didn't end with the war. It continued in the Battle of the Memoirs, which was in turn carried on by the generals' respective supporters in the Battle of the Biographies. Churchill wrote his "kind" history, which calls the Arnhem debacle a victory. Montgomery, who during the war had showed open contempt for what he saw as Eisenhower's gross incompetence, continued after the war to make the case that he could have and should have been the savior of the West if he had been given what he asked for and if Eisenhower had only followed his orders instead of the other way around. He was made Chief of the Imperial General Staff of the British armed forces and also Deputy Supreme Commander of NATO forces in Europe. In 1946 King George VI made him 1st Viscount Montgomery of Alamein. He continued to insult people, including Eisenhower after he became president.

Eisenhower, whose great genius was in the politics of keeping the coalition together and functioning, had always spoken respectfully of Monty in public and showed remarkable patience with him in private as well. In his memoirs he expressed his exasperation with the British commander, but still in civil terms. In private conversations and later in interviews, his real feelings came out. To his trusted aide, Walter Bedell Smith, he described Montgomery as "a psychopath" and an egomaniac who "never made a mistake in his life."[1] Another time he called him "just a little man, he's just as little inside as he is outside."[2]

Patton called Monty "a tired little fart."[3]

This schoolyard name-calling by mighty leaders might be just hot air except that it illustrates an important world change that took place during the war. It was during the Battle of Normandy that General Bradley took over command of the American 12th Army Group from Montgomery, and at that moment America became a full-fledged superpower and the British Empire gave its last gasp.

Eisenhower oversaw the occupation of Europe after the war, then returned to America where he became army chief of staff and devoted his energy to dismantling the giant war machine America had built during the war. He became President of the United States through the dark early years of the Cold War when the Soviet military appeared equal to or stronger than America's. Always more of a peace-seeking diplomat than a bloodthirsty warrior, he tried very hard to establish a trusting peace between America and the Soviet Union, and he was deeply disappointed that he left office with the animosity between the two countries still roiling. In his farewell address to the nation he warned them that since World War II, armed conflict had changed from an occasional unfortunate necessity to a growth industry.

Omar Bradley became army chief of staff when Eisenhower vacated that position, and Chairman of the Joint Chiefs when that position was created in 1947. Patton, the consummate warrior who had always been more comfortable in battle than in peaceful civilian life, was hit by a car and killed shortly after the war ended. Maxwell Taylor followed Eisenhower and Bradley into the offices of army chief of staff and Chairman of the Joint Chiefs. He was then made a special military adviser to Presidents Kennedy and Johnson, where he was one of the chief architects of the Vietnam (brushfire) war

EISENHOWER'S FAREWELL ADDRESS

DWIGHT D. EISENHOWER: Our military organization today bears little relation to that known by any of my predecessors in peace time, or indeed by the fighting men of World War II or Korea.

Until the latest of our world conflicts, the United States had no armaments industry. American makers of plowshares could, with time and as required, make swords as well. But now we can no longer risk emergency improvisation of national defense; we have been compelled to create a permanent armaments industry of vast proportions. Added to this, three and a half million men and women are directly engaged in the defense establishment. We annually spend on military security more than the net income of all United States corporations.

This conjunction of an immense military establishment and a large arms industry is new in the American experience. The total influence—economic, political, even spiritual—is felt in every city, every state house, every office of the Federal government. We recognize the imperative need for this development. Yet we must not fail to comprehend its grave implications. Our toil, resources and livelihood are all involved; so is the very structure of our society.

In the councils of government, we must guard against the acquisition of unwarranted influence, whether sought or unsought, by the military-industrial complex. The potential for the disastrous rise of misplaced power exists and will persist.

We must never let the weight of this combination endanger our liberties or democratic processes. We should take nothing for granted only an alert and knowledgeable citizenry can compel the proper meshing of the huge industrial and military machinery of defense with our peaceful methods and goals, so that security and liberty may prosper together.[4]

AMERICAN CONCENTRATION CAMPS

CARLTON MARTZ: General John L. DeWitt was responsible for the defense of the West Coast. Without any real evidence, he believed that people of Japanese ancestry, citizens and non-citizens alike, could not be trusted. He said that the lack of any sabotage on the West Coast only proved that they were waiting for the Japanese invasion to begin.

Working with others in the War Department, General DeWitt developed a plan to remove all the Issei and Nisei [Japanese Americans] from their homes in the Western states and lock them in prison camps. The Justice Department, FBI, and Army intelligence all concluded that such a drastic action was not necessary. President Franklin D. Roosevelt, however, accepted General DeWitt's recommendation.

On February 19, 1942, President Roosevelt issued Executive Order 9066. This gave General DeWitt authority to order the mass evacuation of Issei and Nisei from the West Coast and other military areas. This order affected about 120,000 citizens and non-citizens of Japanese origin. The stated purpose of removing this entire ethnic group was for "protection against espionage and against sabotage." Congress made it a crime to refuse to leave a military area when ordered to do so.[5]

Camp where Japanese-Americans were held during World War II

and served as ambassador to South Vietnam during that war.

The oddball gang of Camp Ritchie were by no means idle after the war. Lucien Goldschmidt went back to his rare book business, where he prospered and stayed in contact with Nibley for the rest of his life. George Allen returned to Philadelphia where, like Goldschmidt, he thrived in the rare book business and married an Indian princess. Max Oppenheimer returned to Los Angeles and became a leading expert in Spanish literature,

Paul Springer, left, and Hugh Nibley, 1947

but he didn't leave military Intelligence entirely behind. He helped set up the CIA and went back to work for that institution for several years. George Bailey served as a translator at the surrender negotiations in Reims and Berlin, then worked as an American liaison to the Red army after the war. He wrote the book Germans, *which became a huge international best-seller. During the eighties he was director of Radio Liberty, a sister organization to Radio Free Europe, broadcasting into Eastern Europe. He wrote several other books, including one that accurately predicted the fall of the Soviet empire.*

Paul Springer received bitter words about the German race from a disillusioned Hugh Nibley in Heidelberg, but he found out for himself that even safe stateside service could wound a young American's idealism.

PAUL SPRINGER: I look at what they did here in putting the Japanese in the concentration camps—there was an ironic feature about it. The man, the architect of that, was that great lover of racial tolerance and the universal brotherhood of man, Earl Warren. He's the one that went to Roosevelt and talked Roosevelt into giving the orders. And I was a court reporter on DeWitt's staff during relocation, so I was in the middle of it, and it was very disillusioning.

Springer had come some distance since he sang his racist ditty in 1941. He was now an officer in the Judge Advocate General Corps, and then practiced law in San Francisco, where he eventually became a probate judge. He stayed in close contact with Nibley by mail, though the tone of the letters got milder. They would also meet up from time to time at Zion Canyon. Goldschmidt also visited the canyons of the west with his wife and children, and Nibley introduced him to Springer. As a Mormon, Hugh Nibley believed the prophecy of Isaiah that when the day came that God would establish His city of Zion on earth, peace would prevail. A popular Mormon hymn goes, "How blessed the day when the lamb and the lion / Shall lie down together without any ire, / And Ephraim be crowned with his blessing in Zion, / As Jesus descends with his chariot of fire!"[6] Nibley had evidence of the possibility of such miracles because in the earthly Zion Park of burning red rocks, the Prussian Junker Springer and the Jewish Goldschmidt became fast friends and remained so until their deaths.

Herta Pauly became a professor of philosophy, and Anahid Iskian continued to work for Goldschmidt. Neither of Nibley's old flames ever married.

And what Hugh Nibley had once called the "plush-bottom generation" would come to be known as "the greatest generation." At the time it didn't seem like such a great generation to belong to, and Hugh Nibley was not alone in his discouragement.

HUGH B. BROWN: I [was] asked to go to Brigham Young University as coordinator of some 2,000 LDS boys who had returned home from the service. Many of them were in a state of near apostasy because of what they had seen and heard in military service. They had difficulty in harmonizing the idea of God with what they had seen, especially those who had been in Germany and had seen the atrocious things that were done during the war.[7]

HUGH NIBLEY: I remember when I came to the BYU, in the first meeting we had with the Religion Department the session chief said, "Now don't talk about the 'last days.' Now we've conquered all evil and for at least 200 years we'll be able to enjoy perfect peace because we have nothing to fear because of those great men in Washington and London and Paris. Those great men will see us through." They actually believed that. But I was not impressed by those great men because I could remember watching Winston Churchill taking a leak by the side of the road while he flashed the V for victory, and I remembered moments in the 1920s when everything was just lovely, stock was shooting up, and everybody was getting rich, we thought the Dow Jones would just keep on rising till it took us right into a Millennium of peace and prosperity. But we were wrong.

When I first came to BYU Ernest Wilkinson, the president of the university, and I were very chummy. He wanted to know about my experiences in the war, and it was a lot of fun exchanging stories because he had been in World War I. But then something I said came out and made it clear I wasn't an officer and from then on he was ice cold. He wouldn't speak another word to me because I hadn't been an officer. This was the attitude of Ernest Wilkinson. When Colonel Jesse Stay came to join the administration President Wilkinson announced proudly at an assembly that Colonel Stay was there and everyone who had been an officer was invited to come up and shake his hand. But anyone who had not been an officer was not invited—only officers were to come to the stand to shake Colonel Stay's hand.

Phyllis Draper

DWIGHT D. EISENHOWER: The sergeant *is* the Army.[8]

Before beginning work at BYU, Nibley had been interviewed by one of the Church leaders, John A. Widtsoe, who suggested it was about time he got himself married. His previous attempts at matrimony hadn't worked out very well, so he resolved to marry the first single woman he met in Provo. When he arrived there, he went first to the housing office to find himself a place to live. There was a clerk there, a young cellist, the daughter of a Swedish immigrant widow, who three years earlier had spent the summer at a music camp with Hugh Nibley's brother and sister. Phyllis Draper had just turned twenty. Hugh

Nibley married her a few weeks later. They had eight children.

Like most World War II veterans, Hugh Nibley didn't talk a lot about his experiences in the war. When he did it was always in little snippets, never whole stories, never enough to get a sense of what really went on. He didn't keep war mementos except his Screaming Eagle patch, his dog tags, and the briefcase taken from the German major Harmon killed. The patch and dog tags he never showed to anyone; they stayed hidden in his drawer. The briefcase he put to good use for some twenty-five years until it finally wore out.

He said the war for him was a private war, one he fought alone, even as a part of a huge military machine. His profession was the same—he taught and wrote his

Hugh and Phyllis Nibley with Paul Nibley, 1947

own way, as though in his own private school. He taught at BYU for more than half a century and became the Mormon Church's strongest intellectual defender against anti-Mormons who attacked it from the outside. At the same time, he often aimed sharp criticism at the Mormons themselves for what he saw as their failure to live up to the ideals they claimed to follow. He seemed to go out of his way to make people uncomfortable, especially anyone who appeared complacent and believed that mankind was in a position to run its own affairs. He gained a reputation as a man full of paradoxes.

BYU PROFESSOR TRUMAN MADSEN: There have been some things said about Brigham Young University by others, but none of them are as painfully critical as what Nibley occasionally says. And the same is true about certain aspects of the Church, institutionally speaking. He really is its gadfly critic. . . . Is he a cynic and a pessimist with all kinds of negative things to say? Yes. Is he an optimist, an idealist with great hope for the future? Yes. Some say you can't get those together. He does.

Most of the controversy he stirred was about religion. In one case—perhaps the biggest public controversy he caused at BYU—it was about war. As he had in Germany in 1929, Nibley threw away discretion and started crying repentance from the Doctrine and Covenants. This time it was during the Vietnam conflict. What set it off was a documentary film shown on campus called No Substitute for Victory.

The Daily Universe (an official publication of Brigham Young University), March 26, 1971

Editor:

Recently the doctrine has been propagated hereabouts that there is No Substitute for Victory—military victory. May I call attention to a very strong statement on the subject in the D.C. [sic] 98:16–17: "Therefore, renounce war and proclaim peace, and seek diligently to turn the hearts of the children to their fathers, and the hearts of the fathers to the children; and again, the hearts of the Jews to the prophets, and the prophets unto the Jews; lest I come and smite the whole earth with a curse, and all flesh be consumed before me."

"Renounce" is a strong word; we are not to try to win peace by war, or merely to call a truce, but to renounce war itself, to disclaim it as a policy while proclaiming (that means not just announcing, but preaching) peace without reservation. . . .

If we persist in reversing the words of the Savior, "Who takes up the sword shall perish by the sword,"*a* to read perversely, "Who does not take up the sword shall perish by the sword," we shall deserve what happens to us. This is not a protest; just a timely reminder, that we may remember when it happens that we have been warned and forewarned.

Hugh Nibley
Professor
Ancient Scriptures

a "Then said Jesus unto him, Put up again thy sword into his place: for all they that take the sword shall perish with the sword" (Matthew 26:52).

The next week saw a lot of letters on the subject of victory and the religious implications of war. Most but not all of the letters disagreed with Hugh Nibley. Some brief examples:

EPILOGUE: THE NEXT WAR

Editor:

. . . To arrive at the conclusion that taking up arms in the defense of liberty is inconsistent with true Christianity, one must first disregard the words of two prophets (see "Can War Be Justified?" by Pres. David O. McKay), the Old Testament, a considerable volume of scripture in the Book of Mormon, the message of the First Presidency[a] concerning our military obligation, and the New Testament account of Jesus, who used *physical force* in driving evil men from the temple. . . .

Editor:

Bro. Hugh Nibley recently expressed his views on war. I do believe we should realize that there are other views expressed by reknowned [sic] men of the church. consider the following views of Dr. John A. Widtsoe, late member of the Quorum of the Twelve:[b]

"A war can be called just, only when waged against sin and for the victory of the truth; when it battles for the preservation of the principles which make up the plan of salvation, then warfare is righteous. If it is waged to defeat the attempt to enslave men under tyrannical rule, it becomes a war against sin. Such a war should be supported by all who love right above wrong; by all who adhere to the right of free agency for which the heavenly battle was fought long ago. . . ."

Nibley's letter stirred so much controversy that the paper got tired of it.

The Daily Universe, April 2, 1971:

EDITOR'S NOTE: The Spring Break offers the *Universe* the opportunity to take a permanent breather from letters on Dr. Hugh Nibley's letter of March 26 and on the film "No Substitute for Victory." After today, no more letters on either subject will be published.

We appreciate the interest manifested.

So the public argument on Hugh Nibley's Vietnam letter ended. On one side were those horrified by war and ready to renounce it, on the other side were those who believe wars are necessary when we know in our hearts that we are in the right and defending

[a] *First Presidency:* The highest governing council of The Church of Jesus Christ of Latter-day Saints

[b] *Quorum of the Twelve:* The second highest governing body, after the First Presidency, of The Church of Jesus Christ of Latter-day Saints

freedom, especially from communism. But then there is the problem of definitions. Freedom. Right. Justice. Truth. Who defines what they mean?

ADOLF HITLER: If, with the help of his Marxist creed, the Jew is victorious over the other peoples of the world, his crown will be the funeral wreath of humanity and this planet will, as it did thousands of years ago, move through the ether devoid of men. . . .

Hence today I believe that I am acting in accordance with the will of the Almighty Creator: *by defending myself against the Jew, I am fighting for the work of the Lord.*[9]

My feeling as a Christian points me to my Lord and Savior as a fighter. It points me to the man who once in loneliness, surrounded only by a few followers, recognized these Jews for what they were and summoned men to fight against them and who, God's truth! was greatest not as a sufferer but as a fighter. In boundless love as a Christian and as a man I read through the passage which tells us how the Lord at last rose in His might and seized the scourge to drive out of the Temple the brood of vipers and adders. How terrific was his fight against the Jewish poison. Today, after two thousand years, with deepest emotion I recognize more profoundly than ever before the fact that it was for this that He had to shed his blood upon the Cross. As a Christian I have no duty to allow myself to be cheated, but I have the duty to be a fighter for truth and justice.[10]

Was there ever a war where men marched off to die as their leaders gave speeches about how their cause was unjust, against the will of God, and intended to destroy freedom?

HERMANN GOERING: Why, of course, the *people* don't want war. Why would some poor slob on a farm want to risk his life in a war when the best that he can get out of it is to come back to his farm in one piece. Naturally, the common people don't want war; neither in

Russia, nor in England, nor in America, nor for that matter in Germany. That is understood. But, after all, it is the *leaders* of the country who determine the policy and it is always a simple matter to drag the people along, whether it is a democracy, or a fascist dictatorship, or a Parliament, or a Communist dictatorship.

No Substitute for Victory, *video jacket, detail*

GUSTAVE GILBERT: There is one difference. In a democracy the people have some say in the matter through their elected representatives, and in the United States only Congress can declare war.

HERMANN GOERING: Voice or no voice, the people can always be brought to the bidding of the leaders. That is easy. All you have to do is tell them they are being attacked, and denounce the pacifists for lack of patriotism and exposing the country to danger. It works the same way in any country.[11]

Hugh Nibley's letter didn't stop No Substitute for Victory *from packing in full houses at BYU.*

JOHN WAYNE: Now all men of good will certainly want peace. But do we want peace at any price? Peace without freedom?
. . . [H]ere in America the commies are allowed to teach in our schools, parade through our streets and our capital, while those in high position choose to remain silent. . . .
To hell with world opinion! We must speak up and take a stand. Only then will this great nation of ours survive.[12]

There is another irony in the incident of the letter to the Universe. *The narrator of* No Substitute for Victory *was America's hero in classic war movies, John Wayne. Who would know about war and how to win it more than John Wayne? After all, we had seen him win countless battles against impossible odds. In one popular movie,* The Longest Day, *we'd seen him as an airborne trooper entering the French town of*

Ste.-Mère-Église on June 6, 1944, in the battle of Normandy, injured but with undaunted determination to lick the Nazis.

Of course, in a culture that worships celebrity, no one pointed out that John Wayne's expertise on war was all pretend. He was nowhere near Ste.-Mère-Église in June 1944. He made the movie two decades later and stayed in luxury hotels, ate gourmet food, and got paid large amounts of money to pretend to be an airborne trooper. There were stunt men on hand to do anything dangerous, and the blood came out of bottles from Max Factor. The other irony that no one ever pointed out in the debate about No Substitute for Victory *was that Hugh Nibley had actually been at Ste.-Mère-Église fighting the battle John Wayne pretended to fight, only he was living in a foxhole eating K-rations and watching real people really die.*

In this battle of words about Vietnam, Hugh Nibley never mentioned his own war experience. In all the debate he never played the personal experience card: I was there, he could have said. I went to war. I fought. I shot at people at the same time I hoped I wouldn't hit them. I saw the faces of the dead and dying. I heard the 88s explode around me as the jeep ploughed through the surf to Utah Beach. I dodged bullets among the headstones in Carentan. I heard the bullets popping through the glider I rode into Holland. I was there when

Ad in the BYU Daily Universe, *March 27, 1971*

the young medic swam the canal under fire. I was there when General Taylor sulked in his tent because Colonel Johnson refused to duck and died. I drove the jeep from Slijk-Evijk in the glow of artificial moonlight while the Germans fired big guns. I was there when Harmon put the gun to his head. I was there when Benoit and Herren went off to Bastogne to die in my place. I was there when a great country I loved dissolved into putrid ruins. I was there when the god of battles became the god of brothels. I saw the war. It's the saddest thing there is. I renounce war not because of what I have read, but because of what I lived.

He could have said all this. But he didn't. The scriptures, he thought, would carry more weight than his experiences. So the Normandy veteran quoted scripture while the movie star billed as the expert on war talked tough.

WILLIAM TECUMSEH SHERMAN: I confess, without shame, I am sick and tired of fighting—its glory is all moonshine; even success the most brilliant is over dead and mangled bodies, with the anguish and lamentations of distant families, appealing to me for sons, husbands and fathers. . . . It is only those who have never heard a shot, never heard the shriek and groans of the wounded and lacerated (friend or foe), that cry aloud for more blood, more vengeance, more desolation. . . .[13]

There is many a boy here today who looks on war as all glory, but, boys, it is all hell.[14]

I helped make a documentary film about Hugh Nibley in 1983 and 1984, and for the first time I began to hear larger pieces of his war stories. He refused to write his own memoirs, but he finally agreed to let me interview him, and in the late nineties he finally started to talk. In the summer of 2003 severe arthritis in his spine confined Hugh Nibley to his bed.

As he sat in that bed I read him the manuscript to this book. He didn't like to hear a lot of what he had written before the war. He was appalled at the arrogance and callousness of the young professor he had been at Claremont. He didn't want me to publish that chapter. Then my mother talked to him about it, and he agreed that it was an important part of the story. He finally gave his permission to have that part of himself exposed.

Hugh Nibley in Heidelberg with the only companions he kept through the whole war: the carbine and the book

EPILOGUE: THE NEXT WAR

A few months after he was confined to bed his twenty-fourth grandchild was born—my daughter—and I took two-week old Isabella Nibley to meet her grandfather for the first time at his bedside. He grinned, as he always does with babies, and with more energy than I had heard from him in many months he shouted, "That child is a Jew, you know!" Actually she is one-half Filipina, one-eighth Swedish, a dash of Scottish, and a pinch of Irish, English, and Welsh, and one thirty-second Jewish, but that was enough of a Jew to make Grandpa proud.

Hugh Nibley died February 24, 2005. When he did, he left an important part of this book unfinished. We had agreed that I would take his various writings, speeches, and notes on war and edit them into an essay that would be his personal statement on the subject. Because we never completed that essay, and because I won't put his name on one he hadn't read and approved, I'm left to finish this alone.

It's not an easy task, because he doesn't seem to make sense. The statement he made with his letter to the editor to renounce war seems to contradict the statement he made by the action of enlisting in the army and fighting. And he never retracted either statement. He always considered war folly, even the war in which he fought as a volunteer. He held soldiers in high esteem, but he had no admiration for the industry of war. He was never the stereotypic pacifist. He played war with me when I was a child, showing me the proper way to toss grenades and set an ambush. He bought me a surplus helmet for Christmas and was as excited as I was at the BB gun I got that was an exact replica of the .30-caliber carbine he had carried through Europe.

Was Hugh Nibley proud of what he did in the war? I know he was proud of how he waterproofed the jeep so it didn't stall going in to Utah Beach. He was proud of his association with the Screaming Eagles, though I don't think as a soldier he considered himself on a par with the paratroopers. He was proud of how he stole electricity from the German generators in Holland. He was proud of having guessed the Bulge attack was coming, though it did no good.

He was not proud of having destroyed Germany. I don't think that made him feel victorious.

His statements seem to contradict and make no sense, but then, what does make sense when it comes to war? An industry spending trillions of dollars to destroy human life—does that make sense?

Americans seem to be shocked when they hear ugly details of war. Perhaps it's

Hugh Nibley in Cairo, 1984

because so much of our experience of war comes from the sanitary and romantic version put out by Hollywood. We are especially shocked when we learn that Americans commit acts that don't fit our image of being the "good guys." But has there ever been a war in history that was not filled with atrocities by all sides? War is a time when good people do bad things. When loving mothers and fathers send their children out to slaughter beloved sons and daughters. Does this make sense?

DWIGHT D. EISENHOWER: I hate war as only a soldier who has lived it can, only as one who has seen its brutality, its futility, its stupidity.[15]

It made no sense to the butcher woman in Karhlsruhe when Hugh Nibley warned her of fire from heaven. It made no sense to the army brass when he warned them the Germans would be coming through the Ardennes. It made no sense to the freshman at BYU to renounce war.

Hugh Nibley was a man whose business was to study texts that are filled with contradictions and paradoxes that often make no sense.

"Renounce war and proclaim peace."

"Blessed are the meek: for they shall inherit the earth."[16]

"Love your enemies, bless them that curse you, do good to them that hate you, and pray for them which despitefully use you, and persecute you."[17]

"Take no thought for your life, what ye shall eat, or what ye shall drink; nor yet for your body, what ye shall put on."[18]

"God hath chosen the foolish things of the world to confound the wise; and God hath chosen the weak things of the world to confound the things which are mighty."[19]

"Whosoever shall seek to save his life shall lose it; and whosoever shall lose his life shall preserve it."[20]

The scriptural world where Hugh Nibley spent most of his time is filled with paradox and seeming nonsense. So what, in the end, did Hugh Nibley believe about war? The answer lies in another one of his paradoxical statements, that the war he fought was a "private war." Hugh Nibley was a religious man, but his religion was also a private one, a religion that was valid only in the first person: I believe. I worship. I repent. When religious verbs move into the second person—You believe; you worship; you repent—they lose much of their power. Religion in the third person—They believe! They worship! They repent!—can lead to bloody crusades in the name of the Prince of Peace because the first step in waging war is to define differences and establish an "us" and a "them" so we all know whom to hate. And nothing is more tyrannical than religious verbs in the imperative with the force of arms to back them up: Believe! Worship! Repent—or else! We're gonna have to slap that dirty little _____ (fill in the appropriate slur word).

I believe that what Hugh Nibley was saying is this: The spiritual danger of war is greater than the physical danger.

HUGH NIBLEY: I knew there would be more war after World War II. I knew what we had just been through wasn't going to end the war at all. You could see that very plainly. The next one might be worse; it might not be so bad—but it would certainly come. The end of World War II was just an activity setting up the next war; that's all it was doing. The thing that was most disturbing about World War II was that too many people enjoyed what was going on as long as they were not too closely involved. I mean those who weren't actually in jeopardy at all—it couldn't go on too long to suit a lot of them. Of course many people in business felt that it was great; but all down the line in the U.S. military, only 8 percent ever saw combat action in World War II, and a lot of the ones who didn't were actually enjoying it. Yes, people actually enjoy war. Can you deny for a minute that Reagan enjoyed invading Granada in 1983? He reveled in it! He enjoyed it! Or that certain men who get power enjoy being the big military man, strutting around on the world stage, rattling the sword? There's too much pleasure in that. So they will never resolve never to have another war.

Hugh Nibley admired the tough paratroopers he served with, but he had even more praise for the heroism of the Austrian farm boy who kept his oath and wouldn't crack under interrogation. He would rather have been the boy walking to his death singing "Der Lindenbaum" with a peaceful heart than one of the warriors who rampaged and raped their way to victory, then drank themselves into a stupor to forget what they had seen and done. To me his most eloquent statement on war and peace was in the way he died—slowly, confined to his bed, unable to walk or even go out in a wheelchair into the nature he loved. As the sharp line between this world and the next began to blur, the warring polarities of life and death began to resolve their differences; and bits of life began to slip away as death slowly embraced him. He lost the ability to write. His voice became weak. Finally he could barely read. He just sat and watched CNN. Another private battle. And still he was more an observer than a combatant. A couple of weeks before he died this is what he heard:

LIEUTENANT GENERAL JAMES MATHIS: "Actually it's quite fun to fight [Afghans], you know. It's a hell of a hoot," [Lieutenant General

James] Mattis said, prompting laughter from some military members in the audience. "It's fun to shoot some people. I'll be right up there with you. I like brawling.

"You go into Afghanistan, you got guys who slap women around for five years because they didn't wear a veil," Mattis said. "You know, guys like that ain't got no manhood left anyway. So it's a hell of a lot of fun to shoot them."[21]

Hugh Nibley never got over the feeling that his people hadn't learned much from the experience of World War II. He was saddened when America adopted preemptive warfare as a policy.

DWIGHT D. EISENHOWER: All of us have heard this term "preventative war" since the earliest days of Hitler. I recall that is about the first time I heard it. In this day and time . . . I don't believe there is such a thing; and, frankly, I wouldn't even listen to anyone seriously that came in and talked about such a thing.[22]

It was strange, having grown up without a television in the house, to see my father doing nothing but watching television. I couldn't imagine how a man who had always been so full of vitality and mental and physical activity could tolerate so much doing nothing. Many times during his last two years he asked me, "Why am I still here?" He was so thin and frail he looked like one of those pictures from Auschwitz. I know he was frustrated. I asked him once if I could get anything for him. He thought for quite a long time, then answered, "A pass to go anywhere." And yet in the two years that I watched his physical self fade away, often in great pain, always with lots of reasons to be bitter, I never heard one word of self-pity from him.

VIKTOR FRANKL: When a man finds that it is his destiny to suffer, he will have to accept his suffering as his task; his single and unique task. He will have to acknowledge the fact that even in suffering he is unique and alone in the universe. No one can relieve him of his suffering or suffer in his place. His unique opportunity lies in the way in which he bears his burden.[23]

Nibley returns to Carentan, 1984

Hugh Nibley bore his burden well. As he lost even the basic dignity of dealing with his own bodily functions and feeding himself, still he bore it with a nobility he inherited from the grandmother he loved so much.

VIKTOR FRANKL: In spite of all the enforced physical and mental primitiveness of the life in a concentration camp, it was possible for spiritual life to deepen. Sensitive people who were used to a rich intellectual life may have suffered much pain (they were often of a delicate constitution), but the damage to their inner selves was less. They were able to retreat from their terrible surroundings to a life of inner riches and spiritual freedom. Only in this way can one explain the apparent paradox that some prisoners of a less hardy make-up often seemed to survive camp life better than did those of a robust nature.[24]

Jewelry taken from concentration camp victims. Each ring represents a marriage and a family destroyed by Nazi hate.

Is it possible to gain more by bearing life's burden well than by living the good life? Is it possible for a prisoner in Auschwitz to be more free than his SS guard? Is a man whose spirit is free truly a prisoner—even in Dachau? Viktor Frankl claimed there were those in the concentration camps who found the meaning of their lives.

VIKTOR FRANKL: [A] young woman knew that she would die in the next few days. But when I talked to her she was cheerful in spite of this knowledge. "I am grateful that fate has hit me so hard," she told me. "In my former life I was spoiled and did not take spiritual accomplishments seriously." Pointing through the window of the hut, she said, "This tree here is the only friend I have in my loneliness." Through that window she could see just one branch of a chestnut tree, and on the branch were two blossoms. "I often talk to this tree," she said to me. I was startled and didn't quite know how to take her words. Was she delirious? Did she have occasional hallucinations? Anxiously I asked her if the tree replied. "Yes." What did it say to her? She answered, "It said to me, 'I am here—I am here—I am life, eternal life.'"[25]

In the closing arguments of the Nuremberg trial, one of the prosecutors read an eyewitness account of a mass execution by a Nazi death squad.

Hugh and Alex Nibley on Utah Beach, 1984

EPILOGUE: THE NEXT WAR

GUSTAVE GILBERT: Without screaming or weeping these people undressed, stood around in family groups, kissed each other, said farewells, and waited for a sign from another SS man, who stood near the pit, also with a whip in his hand. During the 15 minutes that I stood near I heard no complaint or plea for mercy. I watched a family of about 8 persons, a man and a woman both about 50 with their children of about 1, 8 and 10 and 2 grown-up daughters of about 20–24. An old woman with snow-white hair was holding the 1-year-old child in her arms and singing to it and tickling it. The child was cooing with delight. The couple were looking on with tears in their eyes. The father was holding the hand of a boy about 10 years old and speaking to him softly; the boy was fighting his tears. The father pointed to the sky, stroked his head and seemed to explain something to him. At that moment the SS man at the pit shouted something to his comrade. The latter counted off about 20 persons and instructed them to go behind the earth mound. Among them was the family which I have mentioned. I well remember a girl, slim and with black hair who, as she passed close to me, pointed to herself and said, "23." I walked around the mound and found myself confronted by a tremendous grave. People were closely wedged together and lying on top of each other so that only their heads were visible. Nearly all had blood running over their shoulders from their heads. Some of the people shot were still moving. Some were lifting their arms and turning their heads to show that they were still alive. The pit was already two-thirds full. I estimated that it already contained about 1,000 people. I looked for the man who did the shooting. He was an SS man, who sat on the edge of the narrow end of the pit, his feet dangling into the pit. He had a tommy gun on his knees and was smoking a cigarette. The people, completely naked, went down some steps which were cut in the clay wall of the pit and clambered over the heads of people lying there, to the place to which the SS man directed them. They lay down in front of the dead or injured people; some caressed those who were still alive and spoke to them in a low voice. Then I heard a series of shots. I looked into the pit and saw that the bodies were twitching or the heads lying motionless on top of the bodies which lay before them. Blood was running away from their necks.[26]

Here again the paradox: is it possible a picture so hideous and painful can be such a beautiful portrait of human love and dignity? As I read this I think of what Hugh Nibley said about war and the way he lived and I ask myself: given my choice, would I rather be the SS guard or a member of that loving family going to their death? Is it only in the face of death that we come to understand life? Is it possible to find peace in the battlefield? Is the man who sings the beautiful "Der Lindenbaum" in a state of war? Is it possible for a soldier to renounce war, even as he obeys his officers and shoots at the enemy?

Renounce war? Give no thought for what we will eat or wear? It makes no sense. But remember, his was a private war. His declaration was not political any more than was Jesus' Sermon on the Mount. The most important thing to him was not the political position on war, but a personal spiritual stance on what it all means. He hated war and volunteered to fight. The objective was not to take himself out of the war, but to take the war out of himself.

VIKTOR FRANKL: What was really needed [in the concentration camps] was a fundamental change in our attitude toward life. We had to learn ourselves and, furthermore, we had to teach the despairing men, that *it did not really matter what we expected from life, but rather what life expected from us.* We needed to stop asking about the meaning of life, and instead to think of ourselves as those who were being questioned by life—daily and hourly. Our answer must consist, not in talk and meditation, but in right action and in right conduct. Life ultimately means taking the responsibility to find the right answer to its problems and to fulfill the tasks which it constantly sets for each individual.[27]

HUGH NIBLEY: I remember the dream I had in the foxhole outside Carentan. The one where Dave Bernay woke me up and I felt so happy because it was just a dream and I hadn't actually committed the terrible crime I had dreamed about. There I was in the middle of a battle, and I was completely happy. It came to me very strongly: I shouldn't be *happy* in this circumstance! But it's not what happens to you that matters. It's not what becomes of you, it's what you become that's important.

NOTES

NOTES TO CHAPTER ONE: THE SEEDS OF WAR

1 Churchill, *Second World War, Illustrated and Abridged,* 7.

2 Hitler, *Mein Kampf,* 349–50.

3 Shirer, *Rise and Fall of the Third Reich,* 167, 168.

4 Hitler, *Mein Kampf,* 351.

5 Gilbert, *Nuremberg Diary,* 44.

6 Gilbert, *Nuremberg Diary,* 50.

7 Ford, "The international Jew, the world's foremost problem."

8 Hitler, *Mein Kampf,* 51–52.

9 Frankl, *Man's Search for Meaning,* 49–50.

10 Roosevelt, "Joint Address to Congress Leading to a Declaration of War against Japan, December 8, 1941."

11 Speer, *Inside the Third Reich,* 121.

12 Borkin, *The Crime and Punishment of I.G. Farben,* 88–89, 92–93.

NOTES TO CHAPTER TWO: YOU'RE IN THE ARMY NOW

1 Oppenheimer, *An Innocent Yank at Home Abroad,* 134–36.

2 Frankl, *Man's Search for Meaning,* 26–28.

3 Heller, *Catch-22,* 122.

NOTES TO CHAPTER THREE: THE HALL OF CROOKED MIRRORS

1 Bailey, *Germans*, 21.
2 Allen, *To Bastogne for the Christmas Holidays, 1944*, 4.
3 Oppenheimer, *An Innocent Yank at Home Abroad*, 151.
4 Bailey, *Germans*, 22.
5 Bailey, *Germans*, 23.
6 Bailey, *Germans*, 23–24.
7 Bailey, *Germans*, 25.
8 Bailey, *Germans*, 21.
9 Oppenheimer, *An Innocent Yank at Home Abroad*, 134.

NOTES TO CHAPTER FOUR: GIRDING THE LOINS

1 Kipling, "Tommy," in *Portable Kipling*, 613–15.
2 Oppenheimer, *An Innocent Yank at Home Abroad*, 165.
3 See Geick, *Lichfield, The U.S. Army on Trial*, for a detailed history of the trial and related history.
4 Oppenheimer, *An Innocent Yank at Home Abroad*, 158–59.
5 Oppenheimer, *An Innocent Yank at Home Abroad*, 159.
6 Thompson, in Sikorsky, "From British Cassandra to American Hero."
7 Oppenheimer, *An Innocent Yank at Home Abroad*, 156.
8 Oppenheimer, *An Innocent Yank at Home Abroad*, 178.
9 Ryan, *Longest Day*, 107.
10 Rapport and Northwood, *Rendezvous with Destiny*, 133.

NOTES TO CHAPTER FIVE: NORMANDY

1 Eisenhower, "Order of the Day, June 6, 1944."
2 Churchill, *Closing the Ring*, 556.
3 Ambrose, *Eisenhower*, 139, 140.
4 Churchill, *Closing the Ring*, 556–57.
5 Ryan, *Longest Day*, 66.
6 Ryan, *Longest Day*, 206, 207–9.
7 McCrae, "In Flanders Fields," in *In Flanders Fields and Other Poems*, 15.
8 Ambrose, *D-Day*, 199, 206–7.
9 Ambrose, *D-Day*, 238.
10 Grossman, *On Killing*, 3–4.
11 Grossman, *On Killing*, 205.

NOTES

12 Rapport and Norwood, *Rendezvous with Destiny,* 188–90.

13 Burgett, *Curahee!* 174–76.

14 Churchill, in *Wicked Wit of Winston Churchill,* 81.

15 Mueller, "Der Lindenbaum."

16 Frankl, *Man's Search for Meaning,* 38–39.

NOTES TO CHAPTER SIX: FALSE STARTS

1 Ambrose, *D-Day,* 577.

2 Ambrose, *Band of Brothers,* 63.

3 Eisenhower, *Crusade in Europe,* 292.

4 Hamilton, *Monty,* 469.

5 Ambrose, *Eisenhower,* 133.

6 Bradley, *Soldier's Story,* 416.

7 Ryan, *Bridge Too Far,* 508–9.

NOTES TO CHAPTER SEVEN: MARKET-GARDEN

1 Bowen, *Fighting with the Screaming Eagles,* 85–86.

2 Ryan, *Bridge Too Far,* 424, 425.

3 Bowen, *Fighting with the Screaming Eagles,* 114, 115.

4 Ryan, *Bridge Too Far,* 508.

5 Ryan, *Bridge Too Far,* 479.

6 Rapport and Northwood, *Rendezvous with Destiny,* 374.

7 Ryan, *Bridge Too Far,* 444.

8 Ryan, *Bridge Too Far,* 509.

9 Burgett, *Road to Arnhem,* 140–41.

10 Bowen, *Fighting with the Screaming Eagles,* 152.

11 Ambrose, *Victors,* 215–16.

12 Speer, *Inside the Third Reich,* 406.

13 Homer, *Iliad,* 90, 339.

14 "Tex," Co. G., 501st PIR, in Rapport and Northwood, *Rendezvous with Destiny,* 827–28.

15 Frankl, *Man's Search for Meaning,* 47.

16 Ryan, *Bridge Too Far,* 591.

17 Ambrose, *Eisenhower,* 165.

18 Churchill, *Second World War,* 240.

19 Bradley, *Soldier's Story,* 419.

20 Tennyson, in *Alfred Lord Tennyson: Selected Poems,* 289–90.

21 Montgomery, *Memoirs of Field-Marshal the Viscount Montgomery of Alamein,* 267.
22 Ryan, *Bridge Too Far,* 597.

NOTES TO CHAPTER EIGHT: THE ARDENNES

1 Churchill, *Second World War,* 244.
2 Grossman, *On Killing,* 115–16.
3 Allen, *To Bastogne for the Christmas Holidays, 1944,* 5.
4 Speer, *Inside the Third Reich,* 415.
5 Oppenheimer, *An Innocent Yank at Home Abroad,* 213.
6 Ambrose, *Citizen Solders,* 346.
7 Rossetti, "Dante at Verona," 56.
8 In Rapport and Northwood, *Rendezvous with Destiny,* 511.
9 Bradley, *Soldier's Story,* 472–73.
10 Hamilton, *Monty,* 498.
11 Bradley, *Soldier's Story,* 484–85.
12 Ambrose, *Eisenhower,* 180.
13 Bradley, *Soldier's Story,* 488, 489.
14 Bradley, *Soldier's Story,* 467, 469.
15 Shirer, *Rise and Fall of the Third Reich,* 1234, 1235, 1236.

NOTES TO CHAPTER NINE: ENDGAME

1 Speer, *Inside the Third Reich,* 420.
2 Shirer, *Rise and Fall of the Third Reich,* 1421.
3 Speer, *Inside the Third Reich,* 440.
4 Speer, *Inside the Third Reich,* 453.
5 Shirer, *Rise and Fall of the Third Reich,* 1225.
6 Speer, *Inside the Third Reich,* 435.
7 Ambrose, *Band of Brothers,* 252.
8 Stacey, in Bauer, *History of World War II,* 865.
9 Patton, *War As I Knew It,* 230–31.
10 Pyle, *Brave Men,* 115–16.
11 Speer, *Inside the Third Reich,* 472.
12 Grossman, *On Killing,* 81.
13 Borkin, *Crime and Punishment of I.G. Farben,* 124, 125.
14 Borkin, *Crime and Punishment of I.G. Farben,* 28, 29.
15 Speer, *Inside the Third Reich,* 435n.
16 Shirer, *Rise and Fall of the Third Reich,* 1471.

17   Shirer, *Rise and Fall of the Third Reich,* 1477–78.

18   Shirer, *Rise and Fall of the Third Reich,* 1478.

19   Ambrose, *Band of Brothers,* 289.

20   Frankl, *Man's Search for Meaning,* 108–9.

21   Cowling, in *Dachau, 29 April 1945,* 23–24.

22   Ambrose, *Band of Brothers,* 270.

23   Bradley, *Soldier's Story,* 540–41.

24   Gilbert, *Nuremberg Diary,* 340–41.

25   Ambrose, *Band of Brothers,* 290.

26   Gilbert, *Nuremberg Diary,* 309.

27   Dyer, *War,* 278–79.

28   RAF air crew, in Dyer, *War,* 279.

29   Koche, in Dyer, *War,* 279.

30   Hoelderlin, *Hyperion and Selected Poems,* 127–29.

NOTES TO CHAPTER TEN: BACK TO ZION

1   Ambrose, *D-Day,* 579.

 2   Anonymous veteran, in Ambrose, *Citizen Soldiers,* 485–86.

 3   In Gilbert, *Nuremberg Diary,* 166.

 4   Heller, *Catch-22,* 242.

 5   Gabriel, in Grossman, *On Killing,* 272.

 6   Anonymous, "With Wondering Awe," in *Hymns,* 1985, no. 210.

 7   Shirer, *Rise and Fall of the Third Reich,* 1481.

 8   In Gilbert, *Nuremberg Diary,* 89.

 9   In Gilbert, *Nuremberg Diary,* 27.

10   Gilbert, *Nuremberg Diary,* 370.

11   In Gilbert, *Nuremberg Diary,* 72, 73.

12   In Gilbert, *Nuremberg Diary,* 22–23.

13   Gilbert, *Nuremberg Diary,* 353.

14   Gilbert, *Nuremberg Diary,* 268–69.

15   Gilbert, *Nuremberg Diary,* 45–46.

16   Gilbert, *Nuremberg Diary,* 249–50.

17   Gilbert, *Nuremberg Diary,* 433.

18   Speer, *Inside the Third Reich,* 523.

19   Gilbert, *Nuremberg Diary,* 432.

NOTES TO EPILOGUE: THE NEXT WAR

1 Ryan, *Bridge Too Far*, 77.
2 Ambrose, *Eisenhower*, 167.
3 Irving, *War Between the Generals*, 362.
4 Eisenhower, "Farewell Address."
5 Martz, "Wartime and the Bill of Rights: The Korematsu Case."
6 Phelps, "The Spirit of God," in *Hymns*, no. 2.
7 Firmage, *Abundant Life*, 108.
8 Eisenhower, New York *Times*, 24 December 1972; emphasis in original.
9 Hitler, *Mein Kampf*, 65.
10 Hitler, in Baynes, *Speeches of Adolf Hitler, Vol. 1*, 19–20.
11 Gilbert, *Nuremberg Diary*, 278–79.
12 *No Substitute for Victory*, produced, written, and directed by Chuck Keen.
13 Sherman, in Hart, *Sherman*, 402.
14 Sherman, *Sherman*, 1115.
15 Eisenhower, "Speech at Canada Club, Ottawa, Canada, January 10, 1946."
16 Matthew 5:5.
17 Matthew 5:44.
18 Matthew 6:25.
19 1 Corinthians 1:27.
20 Luke 17:33.
21 Mathis, in "General: It's 'fun to shoot some people.'"
22 Eisenhower, Press Conference, 1953.
23 Frankl, *Man's Search for Meaning*, 99.
24 Frankl, *Man's Search for Meaning*, 55–56.
25 Frankl, *Man's Search for Meaning*, 90.
26 Gilbert, *Nuremberg Diary*, 425.
27 Frankl, *Man's Search for Meaning*, 98.

BIBLIOGRAPHY

Allen, George R. *To Bastogne for the Christmas Holidays 1944.* N.p.: N.p., 1994.

Ambrose, Stephen E. *Band of Brothers: E Company, 506th Regiment, 101st Airborne: From Normandy to Hitler's Eagle's Nest.* New York: Simon & Schuster, 1992.

———. *Citizen Soldiers: The U.S. Army from the Normandy Beaches to the Bulge to the Surrender of Germany, June 7, 1944–May 7, 1945.* New York: Simon & Schuster, 1997.

———. *D-Day, June 6, 1944: The Climactic Battle of World War II.* New York: Simon & Schuster, 1994.

———. *Eisenhower: Soldier and President.* New York: Simon & Schuster, 1990.

———. *The Victors: Eisenhower and His Boys: The Men of World War II.* New York: Simon & Schuster, 1998.

Anonymous. "With Wondering Awe." In *Hymns of The Church of Jesus Christ of Latter-day Saints.* Salt Lake City: The Church of Jesus Christ of Latter-day Saints, 1985.

Bailey, George. *Germans: Biography of an Obsession.* New York: Avon Books, 1972.

Bauer, Eddy. *The History of World War II.* Edited by Peter Young. New York: Barnes & Noble, Inc., 2000.

Borkin, Joseph. *The Crime and Punishment of I.G. Farben.* New York: Free Press, 1978.

Bowen, Robert M. *Fighting with the Screaming Eagles: With the 101st Airborne from Normandy to Bastogne.* London: Greenhill Books; Mechanicsburg, Pa.: Stackpole Books, 2001.

Bradley, Omar N. *A Soldier's Story.* New York: Modern Library, 1999.

Burgett, Donald R. *Currahee! A Screaming Eagle at Normandy.* New York: Dell Publishing, 1967.

————. *The Road to Arnhem: A Screaming Eagle in Holland.* New York: Dell Publishing, 2001.

Churchill, Winston S. *Closing the Ring.* Volume 5, *The Second World War.* Boston: Houghton Mifflin, 1951.

————. *The Second World War, Illustrated & Abridged.* Boston: Houghton Mifflin Company, 1959.

————. In *The Wicked Wit of Winston Churchill.* Compiled by Dominique Enright. London: Michael O'Mara Books, 2001.

Compact Edition of the Oxford English Dictionary. 2 vols. Oxford: Oxford University Press, 1971.

Cooper, Belton Y. *Death Traps: The Survival of an American Armored Division in World War II.* Navato, Calif.: Presidio Press, 1998.

Dachau, 29 April 1945: The Rainbow Liberation Memoirs. Edited by Sam Dann. Lubbock, Tex.: Texas Tech University Press, 1998.

The Daily Universe, 29 March 1971.

Dyer, Gwynne. *War: The Lethal Custom.* New York: Carroll and Graf, 2005.

Eisenhower, Dwight D. *Crusade in Europe.* New York: Doubleday and Company, 1948, 1997.

————. "Farewell Address." 17 January 1961. http://www.eisenhower.archives.gov/farewell.htm

————. New York *Times.* 24 December 1972.

————. "Order of the Day, June 6, 1944." http://www.eisenhower.archives.gov/ssa/htm

————. Press Conference, 1953. http://en.wikiquote.org/wiki/Dwight_D._Eisenhower

————. "Speech at Canada Club, Ottawa, Canada, January 10, 1946." http://www.eisenhowermemorial.org/speeches/19460110%20Speech%20at%20Canada%20Club%20Ottawa%20Canada.htm

Firmage, Edwin B., ed. *An Abundant Life: The Memoirs of Hugh B. Brown.* 2d ed. Salt Lake City: Signature Books, 1999.

Ford, Henry. "The international Jew, the world's foremost problem, being a reprint of a series of articles appearing in *The Dearborn Independent* from May 22 to October 2, 1920." Dearborn, Mich.: The Dearborn Publishing Co., 1920. http://www.jrbooksonline.com/Intl_Jew_full_version/ij02.htm

Frankl, Viktor. *Man's Search for Meaning.* Revised and updated. New York: Pocket Books, 1985.

Gieck, Jack. *Lichfield: The U.S. Army on Trial.* Akron, Ohio: University of Akron Press, 1997.

Gilbert, Gustave M., *Nuremberg Diary*. New York: Da Capo Press, 1995.

Grossman, Dave. *On Killing: The Psychological Cost of Learning to Kill in War and Society*. Boston: Little, Brown, and Company, 1995.

Hamilton, Nigel. *Monty: The Battles of Field Marshal Bernard Montgomery*. New York: Random House, 1994.

Heller, Joseph. *Catch-22*. New York: Simon & Schuster, 1996.

Hitler, Adolf. *Mein Kampf*. Translated by Ralph Manheim. Boston: Houghton Mifflin Company, 1999.

———. *The Speeches of Adolph Hitler, April 1922–August 1939, Volume 1*. Edited by Norman H. Baynes. New York: H. Fertig, 1969.

Hoelderlin, Friedrich. *Hyperion and Selected Poems*. Edited by Eric L. Santner. Translated by Willard R. Trask. Adapted by David Schwarz. New York: Continuum, 1990.

Homer. *The Iliad*. Translated by E.V. Rieu. New York: Penguin Books, 1950.

Imboden, John D. In "The Confederate Side at Bull Run: In the Thick of the Fight." In *The Century War Book*. New York: Arno Press, reprinted 1978.

Irving, David. *War Between the Generals*. New York: Congdon & Lattès, distributed by St. Martin's Press, 1981.

Kipling, Rudyard. "Tommy." In *The Portable Kipling*. Edited by Irving Howe. New York: Penguin Books, 1982.

Martz, Carlton. "Wartime and the Bill of Rights: The Korematsu Case." In *Bill of Rights in Action*. "Victims of War." Summer 2002 (18:3). www.crf-usa.org/bria/bria18_3.htm

Mathis, James. As quoted by reporter. In "General: It's 'fun to shoot some people.'" 4 February 2005. http://www.cnn.com/2005/US/02/03/general.shoot.index.html

McCrae, John. "In Flanders Fields." In *In Flanders Fields and Other Poems*. N.p.: G. P. Putnam's Sons, 1919.

Montgomery, Bernard Law. *The Memoirs of Field-Marshal the Viscount Montgomery of Alamein*. Cleveland: World Pub. Co., 1958.

Mueller, Wilhelm. "Der Lindenbaum." Translated by Dr. Th. Baker. New York: G. Schirmer, 1903.

No Substitute for Victory. Produced, written, and directed by Chuck Keen. Hollywood Video Gems, Inc., 1971.

Oppenheimer, Max, Jr. *An Innocent Yank at Home Abroad: Footnotes to History, 1922–1945*. Manhattan, Kans.: Sunflower University Press, 2000.

Patton, George S. *War As I Knew It*. New York: Bantam, 1980.

Phelps, William W. "The Spirit of God." In *Hymns of The Church of Jesus Christ of Latter-day Saints*. Salt Lake City: The Church of Jesus Christ of Latter-day Saints, 1985.

BIBLIOGRAPHY

Pyle, Ernie. *Brave Men.* Lincoln, Nebr.: University of Nebraska Press, 2001.

Rapport, Leonard, and Arthur Northwood Jr. *Rendezvous with Destiny: A History of the 101st Airborne Division.* Old Saybrook, Conn.: Konecky & Konecky, 1948.

Roosevelt, Franklin Delano. "Joint Address to Congress Leading to a Declaration of War against Japan, December 8, 1941." http://www.fdrlibrary.marist.edu/dec71941.html

Rossetti, Dante Gabriel. "Dante at Verona." In *Poems. A New Edition.* London: Strangeways and Walden, 1881. http://www.rossettiarchive.org/docs/1–1881.sige3.del.rad.html

Ryan, Cornelius. *A Bridge Too Far.* New York: Simon & Schuster, 1974.

———. *The Longest Day: June 6, 1944.* New York: Simon & Schuster, 1959.

Sherman, William T. *Sherman: Memoirs of General W. T. Sherman.* New York: Penguin Putnam Inc., 1990.

———. In B. H. Liddell Hart, *Sherman: Soldier, Realist, American.* Boston: Dodd, Mead and Co., 1929.

Shirer, William L. *The Rise and Fall of the Third Reich: A History of Nazi Germany.* New York: Fawcett Crest, 1950.

Speer, Albert. *Inside the Third Reich.* Translated by Richard and Clara Winston. New York: Galahad Books, 1970.

Taylor, James, and Warren Shaw. *The Penguin Dictionary of the Third Reich.* Rev. ed. New York: Penguin Books, 1997.

Tennyson, Alfred, Lord. "The Charge of the Light Brigade." In *Alfred Lord Tennyson: Selected Poems.* New York: Penguin Books, 1991.

Thompson, Walter Henry. In Jonathan Sikorsky, "From British Cassandra to American Hero: The Churchill Legend in the World War II American Media." Ph.D. dissertation, Arizona State University, 1997. Abridgement of first chapter located at www.winstonchurchill.org/i4a/pages/index.cfm?pageid=360

INDEX

Note: Page numbers in italics indicate photographs.

INDEX

Watts, Emily, x

Wayne, John, 327–28

Weather observer, military, Hugh Nibley's training as, 43, 51–53, 55–56

Weigner, 81; transferred out of 101st Airborne Division, 95; death of, 223–24

Weimar, Germany, German constitution created at, 4

"Werewolves," German, Allies search for, 265

Western Front, Soviet army calls for assistance from Allies on, 71

Whittington Barracks, Lichfield, England, *74;* Hugh Nibley's arrival at, 73

Widtsoe, John A., suggests that Hugh Nibley marry, 322

Wigman, Mary, 16

Wilkinson, Ernest, 322

Wilson, George, 189

Wire, used for Allied communications, 190n

"With Wondering Awe," 301

Word of Wisdom, definition of, 66

World War I: Treaty of Versailles ends, 4; weaponry from, *188;* decisive battle in, 240n

World War II: Hugh Nibley's oral history of, vii–viii; histories of, viii; Hugh Nibley's friendships during, viii; racism during, xi; Hugh Nibley's personal perspective on, xi–xii; goals of, 2; official beginning of, 14; Battle of Stalingrad as early turning point in, 54; turning points in, 71; compared with WWI, 120–21; attitudes of soldiers in, 121; bayonet charges in, 130–31; American and British troops in, 153; airborne operations in, 170n; profiteers in, 173; courage of slave laborers in, 189; eagerness of British to end, 207; Germany's surrender ends European, 261; destruction and death in Europe due to, 263; end of, 288; American aid to nations after, 291, 294; soldiers' adjustment after, 299–300

Yamamoto, Isoroku, on consequences of Pearl Harbor attack, 30

Young, Brigham, on accidental assignment to hell, 147

Zhukov, Georgi, 260n

Zilske, Sergeant, 194

Zion Canyon, *301;* Paul Springer and Hugh Nibley in, *34*

Zon, Netherlands: Waco gliders landing in, *170;* Hugh Nibley's landing in, 172; boy and soldiers in, *195*

Zupsich, Joe, 251